Dedicated to teachers who . . .

can't wait for the bell to ring to start each day and
are organized and ready, so students know what to do;

delight in a challenge and
have the expectation that every child is capable of success;

honor students with dignity and respect and
expect the same in return;

are patient with works-in-progress and
care about the outcome;

have a never-give-up attitude and
a whole briefcase full of instructional techniques;

want to be the difference in students' lives and
ARE the difference in theirs.

They Quietly Walked in and Got to Work

On the first day of school, I stood at my classroom door to welcome my students. I observed them as they quietly walked in the room, sat down, and began their opening assignment.

Meanwhile, I watched as another teacher's class was in total chaos. As the teacher tried to quiet them to begin class, I thought, 'What a waste of time!'

Later in the week, the other teacher came to me and commented that my students were 'always so good!'

I explained to the teacher that it is not the students who are good; it's the procedures that have proven themselves. Procedures help me manage my class so that I can be an effective teacher.

Oretha F. Ferguson ■ **Fort Smith, Arkansas**

Oretha is a co-author and 2010 Teacher-of-the-Year for her school district. She conducts technology workshops and is a master of classroom organization.

Everything Is in Place
Right at the Beginning of the School Year

My classroom management plan is shared with my students on the first day of school, and I refer to this plan consistently. The students know what to do in the classroom, as well as how I expect them to act and to treat one another. They know how things work in our classroom because of the management plan and the procedures that are in place right at the beginning of the school year.

I do not have any major behavior problems with my students. Most importantly, I always get high academic results from my students.

Sarah F. Jondahl ▪ **Brentwood, California**

Sarah is a co-author and her classroom management plan was the "Aha" moment for the Wongs as they visited her classroom when she was a first-year teacher. She is a 2014 Teacher-of-the-Year for her school.

Acknowledgments

This book would not be possible without the contributions from the hundreds of educators who willing share with the profession. Grateful acknowledgment is made to these people and institutions for the permission to include their pictures, classrooms, ideas, and work in this book.

Bill Acuff
Ed Aguiles
Judy Akins
Bernie Alidor
Dave Allen
Stacey Allred
Loreta Anderson
Catherine Bailey
Susan Bailey
Brie Barber
Robin Barlak
Debra Beebe
Marcie Belt
Shoshana Berkovic
Briget Betterton
Cristina Bianchi
Alicia Blankenship
Danielle Blonar
Holly Bonessi
Melissa Boone
Wanda Bradford
Brockton High School
Amanda Brooks
Janifer Brown
Monica Burns
Marco Campos
Patricia Candies
Laura Candler
Christine Chang
Kazim Cicek
Kimberly Clayton
Darrell Cluck
Grace Ann Coburn
Maureen Conley
Ayesa Contreras
Angela Coombs
Marie Coppolaro
Pamela Cruishank
Judith Darling
Jamie Davis
Marie DeNardo
Jessica Dillard
Shannon Dipple
Richard Dubé
Melissa Dunbar-Crisp
Jon Eaton
Liz Eaton
Peggy Ervin
Phyllis Fassio
John Faure
Beth Featherston
Oretha Ferguson
Sarina Fornabaio
Bethany Fryer
Cindy Gaerhardt
Christopher Gagliardi
Andrea Gehweiler

Steve Geiman
Cindy Gerhart
Blake Germaine
David Ginsburg
Grand Heights Early Childhood
    Center
Susan Green
Diana Greenhouse
Jeff Gulle
Thomas Guskey
Brandy Hackett
Allie Hahn
Phillip Hale
Stacey Hanson
Jim Heintz
Stacy Hennessee
Angela Hiracheta
Jenn Hopper
Tena Hubble
Becky Hughes
Elizabeth Janice
Hilton Jay
Laurie Jay
Jacqueline Johnson
Sarah Jondahl
Stephen Jones
Alex Kajitani
Laura Keelen
Candi Kempton
Rose Kerr
Mary Lacombe
Joanne Ladewig
Tiffany Landrum
Suzanne Laughrea
Shirley Lee
Nikki LeRose
Mark Lewis
Linda Lippman
Sally Lutz
Marist School
Kristy Mascarella
Jessica McLean
Tammy Meyer
Christy Mitchell
Crystal Moore
Kara Moore
Sue Moore
LaMoine Motz
Holland Myers
National Violent Intruder
    Preparedness Solutions
Margarita Navarro
Teri Norris
Kasey Oetting
Shannon Page
Janene Palumbo
Janelle Papazian

Shelly Pilie
Pam Powell
Lucy Quezada
Sarah Ragan
Mike Reed
Rhiannon Richards
Greg Risner
Robert Vela High School
Ashley Robertson
Kathryn Roe
Eryka Rogers
Karen Rogers
Jancsi Roney
Noah Roseman
Wanda Rougeau
Charles Russell
Maria Sacco
St. Joseph Academy
St. Rose Elementary School
Elmo Sanchez
Heather Sansom
Kim Schulte
Terri Schultz
Kim Scroggin
Edna Serna-Gonzalez
Chelonnda Seroyer
Dan Seufert
Virginia Sherman
Sisseton Middle School
Jeff Smith
Staten Island School of Civic
    Leadership
Stephanie Stoebe
Kevin Stoltzfus
Susan Szachowicz
Cathy Terrell
Ronda Thomas
Renee Tomita
Megan Toujouse
Carolyn Twohill
Merlyna Valentine
Kathy Vohland
Whitney Weigold
Jeanette Weinberg
Peter Wells
Marya Wesner
Karen Whitney
Nile Wilson
Kristen Wiss
Cindy Wong
Kaleena Wong
Beverly Woolery

Thank You!

THE Classroom Management Book

Harry K. Wong

Rosemary T. Wong

and

Sarah F. Jondahl

Oretha F. Ferguson

with contributions by

Stacey Allred

Robin Barlak

Laura Candler

Jeff Gulle

Karen Rogers

Chelonnda Seroyer

and a host of other very effective teachers

HARRY K. WONG PUBLICATIONS, INC.
www.HarryWong.com

This book is printed on environmentally friendly paper. Join us in making a choice to save the planet.

The Authors

They are all teachers and exemplary classroom managers.

Harry K. Wong	High School, California
Rosemary T. Wong	Elementary and Middle School, California
Sarah F. Jondahl	Elementary School, California
Oretha F. Ferguson	High School, Arkansas
Stacey L. Allred	Special Ed and College Instructor, Indiana
Robin Barlak	Special Education, Ohio
Laura Candler	Elementary School, North Carolina
Jeff Gulle	Middle School, Kentucky
Karen Rogers	High School, Kansas
Chelonnda Seroyer	High School, Alabama

At home, many students do not know what problem, what struggle is going to hit their family next. When at-risk students walk into my classroom and discover that there is a procedure, a 'how to' handbook of sorts for nearly any issue that could arise, they are at ease. For some of these students, this type of orderly and smoothly running classroom is the first experience at a life without chaos.

Stephanie Stoebe ■ Round Rock, Texas

ISBN: 978-0-9764233-9-3
Library of Congress Control Number: 2018907896

15 14 13 12 11 10 9 8 7 6 5 4 3 2 1

Printed in Canada by TC Transcontinental Printing

Graphics Partner: Mark Van Slyke, Zebra Graphics, San Francisco, California

Harry K. Wong Publications, Inc.
943 North Shoreline Boulevard
Mountain View, CA 94043-1932

T: 650-965-7896
F: 650-965-7890
I: www.HarryWong.com

Cover QR Code: Listen to a special message from Harry and Rosemary.

The Greatest Gift

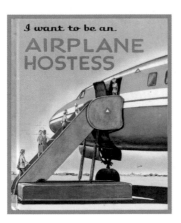

I read this book many times growing up in our very humble home in Kenner, Louisiana. I wanted to travel, see the world, and help people.

One day, my Riverdale High School principal, Mrs. Dorothy Donnelly, called me out of Sophomore Honors Biology to come to her office.

In the course of the conversation, she asked what I wanted to do with my life. I told her I wanted to be a stewardess.

She looked me straight in the eyes and said, "My dear, you can do better than that."

To this day, I can still see myself sitting in her office. I was wearing a little, purple, plaid skirt, green blouse, and matching plaid tie. Her words still echo in my head.

She was the very first adult in my life to ever share with me that I had potential.

This book sits in my home office as a reminder that I am living my dream—I travel the world and help people. Please understand, I am not putting down flight attendants. Every time I get on an airplane, and it is quite a bit, I want the most effective flight attendants there are because I am putting my life in their hands.

What I am sharing with you is that the greatest gift we can give children is belief in their power and ability as an individual, their importance without regard to their race, gender, background, or heritage, their dignity as a person with potential.

Right now, I invite each of you to rise to your potential and live your dream and be the teacher you were meant to be—a very effective teacher.

Rosemary T. Wong ▪ Mountain View, California

Getting Ready for the Most Important Career You Could Ever Have

Prerequisite Reading

THE Classroom Management Book is an extension of **THE First Days of School: How to Be an Effective Teacher**. Classroom management is one of three characteristics of an effective teacher.

To understand the research behind how classroom management relates to the development of an effective teacher requires prior reading of **THE First Days of School** with an emphasis on the information in the unit on Classroom Management.

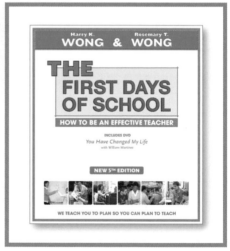

THE First Days of School is a must-read to help you fully understand the part that Classroom Management plays in your journey to become an effective teacher.

Making the Most of This Book

For more than twenty years, hundreds of thousands of teachers have successfully implemented the concepts in **THE First Days of School**, and they have shared their techniques with us. **THE Classroom Management Book** is a compilation of those ideas. It provides the details of what to do and how to do it, so you and your students can be successful.

The purpose of THE Classroom Management Book is to provide you with the skills to effectively manage a classroom that produces student learning and achievement.

It is not a "quick fix" for discipline problems in the classroom. It is for turning classroom chaos, lack of organization, and squandering of teaching time into student achievement.

THE Classroom Management Book has four parts:

- **PROLOGUE:** provides the background to the importance of classroom management

- **PREPARATION:** tells how to prepare for the first day or any day of the school year

- **PROCEDURES:** teaches in-depth, fifty procedures used to create a consistent learning environment

- **PLANS:** shows six plans used by practicing teachers for their first days of school

Spread throughout the book are **stories** of teachers, principals, parents, and administrators who have put the concept of a classroom management plan into consistent practice.

There are **forty QR (Quick Response) Codes** scattered on pages that lead you to additional information, PowerPoint presentations, rubrics, and ideas to help you develop a classroom management plan.

The **Contents** page lists all of the procedures taught in the book. Look through the list and find one or two procedures to use in your classroom. Teach and rehearse those procedures until they become mastery for your students. Continue to reinforce the procedures just taught and introduce two more. Repeat the process. You will notice a difference in your students and a difference in yourself using this technique.

The Complement to This Book

THE Classroom Management Book is the companion book for the eLearning course **THE Classroom Management Course**. The course is offered at www.EffectiveTeaching.com.

This online course was previously known as **Classroom Management with Harry and Rosemary Wong** and based on **THE First Days of School**. The course has been redesigned and aligned with **THE Classroom Management Book**. The outcome of the course remains the same—upon completion you will have created a binder with plans that will help you effectively manage a classroom to maximize learning.

> As a result of taking this online course, my teaching career has been saved.
>
> **Virginia Sherman ▪ Baltimore, Maryland**
>
> I thought that after teaching for eighteen years, I wouldn't find anything useful in the course, but boy was I wrong. I loved it and learned as much as a first-year teacher.
>
> **Edna Serna-Gonzalez ▪ Harlingen, Texas**
>
> I can't tell you how much the e-course served me. Procedures are in place, expectations are high, and the environment is safe, comfortable, and fun for the children. It is a learning classroom.
>
> **Stephen Jones ▪ Auckland, New Zealand**

Contents

PROCEDURES: For Students

PROCEDURES: For the Classroom

PROCEDURES: For Instruction

PROCEDURES: For Instruction *(continued)*

PROCEDURES: For the Special Needs Classroom

PROCEDURES: For Teachers

PLANS: For the First Days of School

EPILOGUE: A Call to Action

PROLOGUE
Classroom Management Defined

The Effective and Successful Teacher

The single greatest effect on student achievement is the effectiveness of the teacher.

Research on Effective Teachers

Effectiveness is achieved by employing effective practices. **Thomas Good** and **Jere Brophy** have spent more than thirty years observing classrooms and the techniques teachers use to produce achievement and learning. They observed teachers regardless of grade level, subjects taught, the diversity of the school population, or the structure of the school. Their book, *Looking in Classrooms*, spans several editions over thirty years and consistently concludes that effective teachers have the following three characteristics:

1. They are good classroom managers.
2. They can instruct for student learning.
3. They have positive expectations for student success.[1]

In 2008, thirty years after Good and Brophy's seminal research, **Robert Pianta** of the University of Virginia reported his observations of 1,000 schools. He said the same thing. There are three critical factors of effective teachers:

1. Organizational support
2. Instructional support
3. Emotional support[2]

In the same year, the **Mental Health Center at UCLA** reported the three barriers that prevent at-risk student learning:

1. Management component
2. Instructional component
3. Enabling component[3]

The words of the researchers may be slightly different, but they all consistently emphasize the same thing:

1. It is the teacher that makes the difference. **The more effective the teacher, the more effective the practices of the teacher, the more students will learn.**

2. **Classroom management is an essential element of student achievement.**

Three Characteristics of Effective Teachers

Decades of research have identified and defined the three characteristics of effective teachers. *THE First Days of School* was written to explain and implement these three characteristics:

1. **Classroom Management**
   The practices and procedures that a teacher uses to maintain an environment in which instruction and learning can occur.

2. **Lesson Mastery**
   How well a teacher provides instruction so students will comprehend and master a concept or skill to a level of proficiency as determined by the lesson objective and assessment.

3. **Positive Expectations**
   What the teacher believes will or will not happen and its influence on the achievement and success of students.

Classroom Management creates the foundation for an effective and successful classroom. It is invisible when performed at its best. It is apparent when it is missing from classrooms.

People Create Results

The quality of a school cannot exceed the quality of its teachers. Effective teachers and principals create effective schools. Programs and fads do not create effectiveness. **People create effectiveness.**

When teachers are effective, student achievement will increase. **John Goodlad**, while at UCLA, reported looking at forty years of educational fads, programs, and innovations and did not find a single one that increased student achievement. His findings bear repeating:

The only factor that increased student achievement was the effectiveness of a teacher.

An effective teacher is key for student success.

I See Results

Having procedures and following them each and every day, while being as consistent as humanly possible, really makes my class run smoothly and my job a lot easier.

This is why I love teaching—I see RESULTS. My students are learning.

Pam Powell ▪ Beaumont, California

[1] Good, Thomas and Jere Brophy. (2007). *Looking in Classrooms.* Needham, Mass.: Allyn & Bacon, pp. 313–314.

[2] Pianta, Robert. (2008). *Classroom Assessment Scoring Guide* (CLASS). "Neither Art nor Accident." Harvard Education Letter.

[3] National Center for Mental Health, UCLA. (2008). *Framework for Systematic Transformation of Student and Learning Supports.*

 1 •))

Read how effectiveness relates to The Four Stages of Teaching.

QR Codes

 There are forty QR Codes scattered throughout *THE Classroom Management Book*. The codes will take you to our website, www.EffectiveTeaching.com, and the information stored there.

A QR Code, Quick Response Code, has information coded in a pattern. This is a sample of what to look for throughout the book. When you see the code, scan it to access the additional information mentioned in the code. Much of this material, such as videos, PowerPoint presentations, or downloadable templates, is not possible to present on a printed page.

Access the information in the QR Code in two ways:

1. Install a QR Code scanner onto a mobile device. The scanner is free in any App store. Download the scanner compatible with your device. Once the scanner is in place, scan the code in the book and be taken directly to the information.

2. Go to *THE Classroom Management Book* page on our website, www.EffectiveTeaching.com. Click the "QR Codes" tab to be taken to active links for each code.

On page 300 is a list of all QR Codes referenced in the book.

Get It Right from the Start

Two weeks after school began, we received an email from **Amanda Bivens** of Dyersburg, Tennessee. She wrote again at the end of her first year of teaching and at the end of her second year of teaching. In her fifth year, she wrote that her colleagues voted her Teacher-of-the-Year.

I was about to begin as a terrified, brand new teacher and had no idea how to start school when the Wongs came to my school district to present at a preschool inservice.

When they showed a PowerPoint presentation used by a teacher to explain his classroom management plan (page 46), I was so enthralled that I immediately began to write mine in my head. I went home to work on my plan and finished it at midnight.

The next day—eight hours later—my first day of school went like clockwork. **The day went absolutely flawlessly. It was an awesome day.**

At the end of her first year of teaching, Amanda writes:

My first year ended, and I am so thankful for that first day when I had my students practice our classroom procedures (pages 60–207).

I never had to waste time repeating what they should be doing or reprimanding them for bad behavior.

It allowed me to be everything I wanted to be as a teacher and create an environment where students could just learn. I simply taught and enjoyed my students.

At the end of her second year of teaching, Amanda writes:

I just completed my second year of teaching and what a fantastic year I had.

For the second year in a row, I had students leaving my classroom in joyful tears—and these are fifth graders.

My state test scores came back, and my class had the highest test scores in the school.

I am only saying this to encourage teachers to **get it right the first day** and then enjoy the rest of the school year.

How to get it right the first and every day is the entire purpose of *THE Classroom Management Book*.

Definition of Classroom Management

Classroom management consists of
the practices and procedures a teacher uses to maintain
the environment in which instruction and learning can take place.

The Definition

The research definition of classroom management goes back more than forty years. All the major authors on classroom management, such as **Carolyn Evertson**, *Classroom Management for Elementary Teachers* and *Classroom Management for Middle and High School Teachers*, and **Robert Marzano**, *Classroom Management That Works*, quote the original research as we do in **THE First Days of School**:

> "Classroom management constitutes the provisions and procedures necessary to establish and maintain an environment in which instruction and learning can occur."
>
> Daniel L. Duke, editor of "Classroom Management." (Among the 1978 Yearbooks of the National Society for the Study of Education)

Kounin's Research

The original research on classroom management can be traced to the work of **Jacob Kounin** in 1970 when he observed forty-nine first- and second-grade classrooms. From his research, Kounin summarized that **good classroom management is based on the behavior of teachers—what the teachers do—not the behavior of students.**

Kounin concluded that it is the teacher's behavior that produces high student engagement, reduces student misbehavior, and maximizes instructional time.

 2))))

Read how to implement Kounin's six behaviors of good classroom managers.

Sanford's Research

Julie P. Sanford, University of Texas, in 1984 observed and noted the difference between effective classroom managers and ineffective classroom managers. **Effective classroom managers had classroom procedures.** The students took their seats immediately upon entering the room and began by copying the objectives and assignments for the day from the chalkboard, while the teacher quietly handled administrative chores.

Effective teachers had procedures that governed students with regard to talking, participation in oral lessons and discussion, getting out of their seats, checking or turning in work, what to do when work was finished early, and ending the class.

At the beginning of the school year, the effective classroom managers clearly explained their classroom organizational procedures and expectations and then followed their presentations with review and reminders of procedures and expectations in subsequent weeks. In all classes, the teachers gave clear, simple directions and were noted as excellent in structuring transitions.

Students were kept apprised of time left for an activity and were forewarned of upcoming transitions. Teachers brought one activity to an end before beginning another. They also told students what materials would be needed for an activity and had students get materials ready before beginning the lesson. When students were assigned to work in pairs or groups, procedures governed how students were to work with each other.

These teachers' manner in conducting class was task-oriented, businesslike, and congenial.

In contrast, Sanford described the classrooms of the ineffective classroom managers as having no procedures. There were no procedures established for beginning and ending the period, student talk during group work, getting help from the teacher, or what to do when work was finished.

These teachers had difficulty conducting transitions from one activity to another. They often did not bring one activity to an end before giving directions for another. They gave directions without getting students' attention and they seldom forewarned the class or helped students structure their time.

In essence, Sanford described these teachers as having no evidence of management with procedures.

Plan to Be Effective

Effective teachers have long known how to manage classrooms. **Good classroom management does not just happen; effective teachers *plan* good classroom management.**

If you are not managing your classroom, then your students are managing it for you.

The effective teacher knows that student achievement will only occur when the students' work environment is organized and structured, so their potential can be nurtured. Their self-confidence must be grown and self-discipline be instilled. Under the guidance of an effective teacher, learning takes place.

The purpose of effective classroom management is to ensure that student engagement leads to a productive working atmosphere.

A PRODUCTIVE LEARNING ENVIRONMENT

Well-Managed Classroom → Student Engagement → Productive Learning Environment

In a well-managed classroom, a variety of activities can occur simultaneously. The students are working and tuned in to the teacher; they are cooperative and respectful of each other; they exhibit self-discipline; they remain on task. All materials are ready and organized; the furniture is arranged for productive work; a calm and positive climate prevails.

In a well-managed classroom, students can work in multi-areas or on multiple tasks because they know what to do.

Procedures Form the Plan

The basis of classroom management lies in the procedures that form a management plan to produce the successful achievement of learning goals.

Procedures are the tasks students must do to increase their chances for learning and achieving. Procedures are the foundation upon which successful teaching takes place. Procedures set up students for achievement. Having procedures simplifies the students' task of succeeding in school and creating a positive learning environment.

A routine is a procedure that students do repeatedly without any prompting or supervision.

Watch the students in a well-managed classroom. They are responsible because they know the procedures and routines that structure the class and keep it organized. They are working; they are producing; they are learning and achieving.

And *you* can go home each day with a smile on your face!

The First Five Minutes

Effective teachers start class with respect, care, and procedures. Their students are taught to follow procedures automatically so that class starts immediately and efficiently. Little instructional time is wasted when starting class becomes a routine.

The bell has rung, and the students are still walking into the room. They wander around chatting, or texting on their cell phones, or brushing their hair, and perhaps exchanging playful punches—which can escalate into an argument, and maybe even a fight. At which point, the teacher says, "The bell has rung. Would you all please sit down?" No action.

"The bell has rung to start class. Sit down, please." No action.

"What's the matter with this class? The bell has rung! Sit down, right now!" Some action. The students sit down.

Why? Not because they respect the teacher, but because the students have the teacher trained. They know not to sit down until the teacher yells. <u>That's</u> the signal to sit down. And this is repeated, day after day, period after period, always ending with the same result: frustration and anger.

The teacher then takes attendance and everyone sits around for another two to three minutes, waiting for the task to finish. After five minutes have been wasted, class starts. Finally.

If five minutes are wasted per classroom period, this translates to thirty minutes for a six-period school day. Multiplying that by a 180-day school year equates to one month of school learning wasted each year in many school systems. Multiply that by twelve years of

schooling, and one full year of instruction is completely lost during a student's lifetime at school.

And that's a conservative estimate. **Shirley Hord**, from the Southwest Educational Development Laboratory in Texas, discovered that three to seventeen minutes are wasted at the beginning of each class period each school year. That is, from the time the first student enters the classroom until instruction actually begins, wasted time can range from 9 percent to 32 percent of total class time, which is up to one-third of school time lost. No one would tolerate wasting even a fraction of this time waiting in line at a supermarket or theater. At school, wasted time should be totally unacceptable.

It's all in how you start. Effective teachers use procedures so that class starts immediately and efficiently.

1. The teacher greets students at the door.
2. Students go through their start of class routine.
3. They sit in their assigned seats.
4. They look at the agenda and begin the opening assignment.

Meanwhile, the teacher is taking attendance or doing whatever housekeeping tasks are needed. At the end of five minutes, instruction begins.

Access the QR Code on page 290 to see how teachers plan their first five minutes and well into the first two weeks of school.

■ Difference Between Classroom Management and Discipline ■

Classroom management is NOT discipline;
they are not synonymous terms.

The Difference

The most misused word in education is "classroom management." Many educators incorrectly associate classroom management with discipline. Certainly, behavioral events frequently occur in class, particularly in classrooms where there is no management plan in place.

Classroom management is all about effective teacher instruction (what the teacher does) and effective student learning (what the students do).

There is a vast difference between classroom *management* and classroom *discipline*. Discipline is behavior management. **Fred Jones**, in his book *Tools for Teaching*, calls it discipline management.

> When you have a discipline problem,
> you manage the behavior;
> you do not manage the classroom.

Not the Same

Discipline is behavior management and is discussed in one chapter in **THE First Days of School**.

Classroom management is organization and is discussed in two chapters in **THE First Days of School**.

Classroom management is
NOT about **DISCIPLINE**.

Classroom management is
about **ORGANIZATION** and **CONSISTENCY**.

DISCIPLINE

- Discipline is all about how **students behave**.
- **Rules** are used to *control* how students behave.
- **Discipline plans have rules.**

CLASSROOM MANAGEMENT

- Management deals with how students do their **work**.
- **Procedures** are used to ensure students are productive and successful.
- **Classroom management plans have procedures.**

These differences may account for why some teachers have problems in their classrooms. More than 80 percent of behavior problems in the classroom have nothing to do with discipline. They are related to classrooms that lack procedures and routines. Teachers who *react* to behavior problems often spend more time trying to find ways to handle the behavior than they spend teaching. Conversely, the effective teacher has proactively created a classroom management plan that prevents these problems from occurring in the first place.

Classroom Management Is Planned

The number one problem in the classroom is not discipline.

> Most problems in the classroom are
> procedure related; they are not discipline problems.

It is much easier—and far more effective—to monitor and correct procedures than to institute tighter discipline.

Rules

- Rules are used to control people.
- Although rules are necessary, they create an adversarial relationship.
- When rules are broken, there are adverse consequences.
- Ideally, rules and policies are meant to be guidelines—not dictums set in stone.

DISCIPLINE
is concerned with how students *BEHAVE*.

PROCEDURES
are concerned with how things *ARE DONE*.

DISCIPLINE HAS penalties and rewards.

PROCEDURES HAVE NO penalties or rewards.

When students do something because no procedures have been taught, they are erroneously accused of being "discipline problems" in the classroom. In fact, students can only be responsible for their behavior when they know what procedures they are accountable for. **Thus, effective teachers who have smooth-running classrooms have a classroom management plan in place and teach procedures that become routines for students to follow.**

Discipline, although necessary, does not lead to learning. It only temporarily stops deviant

Ineffective *vs.* Effective Teachers

Ineffective teachers discipline their students to control their every action.

Effective teachers teach their students how to be responsible for appropriate procedures.

**Major Differences Between
Discipline and Classroom Management**

Discipline	Classroom Management
Is reactive	Is proactive
Is problem-driven	Is productivity-driven
Has negative consequences as punishments	Has rewards as increased learning time
Promotes compliance	Promotes responsibility
Stops deviant behavior	Produces predictable behavior

behavior. In most cases, getting students to behave entails nothing more than coercing students to comply. Although most teachers do not want to coerce students, they do so because they don't have a classroom management plan. When students are coerced, they are deprived of the opportunity to grow and become more responsible. **Procedures teach students responsible skills that serve them well in school and throughout life.**

Procedures organize the classroom, so the myriad of activities that take place can function smoothly in a stress-free manner. Students perform better when they know what the teacher expects them to do.

Nile Wilson of Landisville, Pennsylvania, uses a handbook with procedures so that each player functions as part of a team.

 3))

Access Nile Wilson's Orchestra Handbook and learn how she plans for student success.

Sports teams have managers. Apartment buildings have managers. Stores have managers. Their responsibilities are all the same:

1. Run an organization smoothly so that the people and components function as one collaborative unit.
2. Produce a result—win games, provide a service, or produce a profit.

Managing a classroom is no different.

1. Run and organize the students so that the classroom functions as one collaborative unit.
2. Produce a result from the students in the form of improved learning and develop skills and habits that contribute to a productive life.

Creating a well-managed classroom with established procedures is the priority of a teacher with each new group of students. **Good classroom management does not just happen; teachers must plan good classroom management.**

An Ounce of Prevention

Benjamin Franklin reportedly coined the phrase, **"An ounce of prevention is worth a pound of cure."** This means it is better to have a plan to *avoid* problems, rather than trying to fix them once they occur.

"Intervention" is an overused term in education. When a teacher steps in or intervenes to solve a problem, it is called an intervention. Intervention is akin to doing damage control and fighting constant brush fires.

A classroom management plan with a series of procedures that will prevent crises will stop the constant intervention needed to fix problems after they happen.

With a solid plan, you have an ounce of *prevention*, rather than a pound of intervention!

The Worst Four-Letter Word

Designers, architects, buyers, musicians, artists, writers, and chefs circle the globe looking for ideas. They find **inspiration from anywhere** and in everyone and are smitten by the intellectual perspective they experience.

The signature quality of effective teachers is they have an unquenchable curiosity and an admiration for what other teachers do, no matter the grade level, subject matter, or what country the teacher lives in. They intuitively practice forward-thinking problem-solving. **Effective teachers are "Aha" people.** They are able to stitch together ideas from a myriad of resources from around the world.

Your attitude and perception will affect what happens in your classroom. It is the old adage, is the glass "half-full or half-empty?" It is the difference between positive and negative thinking or the hopeful optimist who believes that learning can happen versus the failed attitude of the pessimist. With a classroom management plan in place, anything **CAN** happen in your classroom.

Effective teachers are "CAN" people, not "CAN'T" people. The worst four-letter word in the English language is "CAN'T."

C – I **COMPLETELY**   **A** – **ADMIT**   **N** – that I am **NOT**   **T** – **TRYING***

*courtesy of Melissa Dunbar

The Key to Success Is Consistency

The reason many students fail is that
they do not know what to do.

Classroom Management Creates Consistency

Effective teachers produce results from a classroom that is predictable, reliable, and consistent. Stores that are profitable, people who provide good service, and a team that wins all have consistency. They are dependable and you know what to expect.

You may have your favorite hair stylist or sales person. Or, you like a certain toothpaste or cereal. Why? They are predictable and dependable. They are consistent. You know the results you come to expect.

Students are the same, especially the really young ones or those who are at-risk. They want a teacher who is dependable, predictable, and reliable. **The effective teacher is a model of consistency.**

Students need to feel that someone is looking out for and is responsible for their environment, someone who not only sets limits, but maintains them. **School must be a safe and protected environment, where a student can come and learn without fear.**

The most effective teachers make everyone comfortable, yet have total control of the classroom. Teachers achieve this when they have planned for how the classroom should be managed for student learning and achievement. The purpose of *THE Classroom Management Book* is to help you acquire the knowledge you need to develop your plan.

Procedures Create Consistency

In an effective classroom, there is no yelling or screaming to get students to behave and do things. The students understand how the classroom is organized. The teacher has a consistent demeanor that the students appreciate.

Consistency in a classroom is created when there is repetition of actions and tasks—procedures. Consistency allows students to know beforehand what to expect and how to perform the classroom procedures. Without the constancy of procedures, class time is wasted getting tasks done. From walking into the classroom to exiting the classroom, the more all tasks are defined with procedures, the more time you will have to devote to teaching and learning.

Students accept procedures. Just let them know what the procedure is.

It is important that your students understand that classroom procedures are for their benefit. Following procedures eliminates confusion, provides predictability, and enables students to focus on class work—without distractions. **With procedures, students know exactly what they are getting and what will be happening.** Effective teachers spend the first weeks together as a class teaching students to be in control of their own actions in a predictable classroom environment.

Stacy Hennessee teaches in North Carolina and shared his students' reaction after he implemented procedures. **"They had never seen me smile so much. Before long, they *expected* a smile."**

The most important quality that must be established in the first weeks of class is CONSISTENCY.

Students thrive in a safe classroom environment where there are predictable procedures.

Special Needs Students Thrive on Consistency

Robin Barlak* is a former preschool, special education teacher in Parma, Ohio. Parents, classroom assistants, and students all know the structure of the classroom, so the students can focus on learning.

"I teach a variety of students with disabilities such as Down syndrome, speech and language delays, autism, severe behavior issues, and large and fine motor delays. In the mornings, the classroom assistants escort the students into the classroom. The students take off their coats and place them in their lockers. They then choose an activity center to go to like role-play, carpet, or media table.

Students are called to go to the bathroom one at a time. After the bathroom break, students are called in threes to the art table to complete an art project. The rest of the students are free to go from center to center.

Later in the day, we have daily circle time. Each student has an assigned sitting spot on the carpet. Depending on each student's needs, some students will sit in a cube chair, a Rifton chair, or a wiggle cushion. The class first sings the "Hello, so glad you are here" song, followed by the "Calendar Song," and then the "It's so good to see you!" song.

Classroom procedures are taught in the first days of school and constantly practiced. Within a special education classroom, there are many students with individual needs. There are also numerous support staff coming and going to meet the needs of the students. Physical therapists, speech therapists, occupational therapists, educational assistants, nurses, and sign language interpreters all need to know the classroom procedures. This allows them to better support the goals and objectives of each student.

Students with special needs thrive on the consistent structure and routine. Daily procedures and routines incorporate developmentally-appropriate practices to meet the individual needs of these students. Daily procedures and routines also give students security and predictability, so they can focus on learning."

*With great sadness, we share that Robin has passed away. Her love for the profession and her dedication to her students are evident in the legacy she leaves behind.

The Need for a Trusting Environment

People learn from those they trust.

The Surety of Consistency

Students must trust you before they will trust what you plan to teach. You would only ride in a car of someone you trust, allow yourself to be operated on by a doctor you trust, or purchase an item from a store that you trust. These products or services are dependable and reliable in their outcomes. There are no surprises, and you expect the same result each time. There is consistency. As a parent, you would trust your child to the care of an effective teacher.

Students want to come to a school where there are no surprises. They trust the learning environment that has been established. They know what to expect, and it happens each day. Trust comes from the surety of consistency.

In the early 1980s, **Douglas Brooks** observed the concept of trust when he recorded a series of teachers on their first day of school. Reviewing the videos, he found that those teachers, who began the first day of school with a fun activity or immediately on the subject matter, spent the rest of the school year chasing after the students. In contrast, those teachers who spent some time explaining how the classroom was organized so the students knew what to do to succeed, had an enjoyable and successful classroom experience every day. **The students trusted a classroom where they knew what was going to happen.**

The Value of Listening

There are many ethnicities, such as Native Americans, Native Alaskans, Asians, and some Latinos, in which wait-time is part of their culture. They defer to others to speak, including adults and parents. They do not respond well in a classroom with a frenetic teacher who is doing all of the talking.

Listening is a most effective, persuasive strategy. Nothing builds a connection and establishes trust like being heard.

Happiness Is Consistency

*The more consistent I am,
the happier my class is.*

The better they perform, the happier I am.

Shannon Dipple ▪ Dayton, Ohio

Consistency Builds Trust

One of the most important principles you can model for your students is to be consistent and predictable.

Many students come from homes where chaos and unpredictability are the norm. Students who may feel isolated and outcast, long to be on the same page as their peers. These students long for stability, direction, and purpose to their lives. Students will TRUST those teachers who provide classrooms that are safe, consistent, and nurturing, so they can learn, grow, and achieve success.

The easiest way to earn the trust of your students is to help them be successful. Research shows that providing such an environment for students will increase their achievement.

How you communicate your classroom management plan to your students also communicates your competence as a teacher. A classroom management plan conveys that you are caring and competent. The students can trust that their best interest is at the heart of all of your decisions.

Teaching is the responsibility you were hired to undertake. Learning is the reason your students come to school. The consistency you establish in the classroom will be in direct relationship to the amount of trust the students feel and the amount of learning that takes place in your classroom.

THE Classroom Management Book will help you meet and exceed your purpose in becoming an effective teacher.

Every Student Made Progress. Every. Single. One.

Sarah Ragan says, "I would be lost without procedures. None of what I teach would make a difference."

In **Sarah's** first year, because she was a Title I teacher, the school term started late for her. She watched the other first-year teachers with interest—she wanted to learn from what they did. Unfortunately, every single one of them struggled on their first day.

"Without fail, they engaged their students—not in learning, but in never-ending battles over pencils, hallway misbehavior, noise levels, and so on. I decided that would not be me. I had read **THE First Days of School** in college. That evening, I went home and wrote my **First Day of School Script**."

When the term started, Sarah explained the purpose of the procedures, walked students through their responsibilities, and made sure every single class member understood they would achieve success by working together.

From that day forward, there was never any doubt about what Sarah's students should be doing. **With procedures, the class was never lost.**

No Behavior Problems

Sarah proudly shares, "There is zero downtime. My students understand I expect them to work hard, but also to enjoy the learning experience. I've actually been assigned some of the more difficult students in school. I have no behavior problems. These students ask to come to my class. They don't know why they want to come, but I do.

"**My class is well-managed. Everything is organized, and I am well-prepared. They trust my class.**"

PREPARATION
Before the First Day of School

Prepare Before School Begins

Classroom Management begins
before the first day of school.

Plan and Then Plan Some More

Being prepared is essential—no matter the endeavor. Sports teams have preseason training camps, actors have production rehearsals, and schools have emergency drills. **The effective teacher plans, and then plans some more.**

Over-planning is a good thing! The effective teacher shares the classroom plan with students, so they comprehend their role in the classroom management plan and can become responsible for carrying out the plan. Students will come to understand the important role they play in classroom management, too.

Have a Plan

Have a plan, not only for the day, but for the week and the month and the year, and ten years from now.

Anticipate. Plan. Anticipate every situation that could arise.

Plan for every situation that could arise. Don't think second by second about what needs to be done. Have a plan. Follow the plan, and you'll be surprised how successful you can be.

Most people don't plan. That's why it is easy to beat most folks.

Coach Paul "Bear" Bryant ▪ University of Alabama

If you've ever painted a wall, you know that the preparation work takes longer than the actual painting. Poor preparation results in a poor paint job that has to be redone. **Invest time to prepare so that before the bell rings for a new school year, your students are following procedures as they begin their journey for a successful year ahead.**

Create a classroom environment with a **Culture of Consistency**, so everyone is on the same page. Consistency streamlines the classroom and allows for maximum use of instructional time.

A football coach goes into a game with a game plan. The game plan is drawn up from the collection of plays that are found in a play book. A coach does not wait for problems to occur and then thumbs through the play book hoping to find a play that "might" work.

When to Prepare

Preparation for a successful school year takes place before the first day of school. A long list of tasks needs to be defined in your mind. Stress and uncertainty can be lessened if you are organized and ready. Lack of planning will result in the following:

1. Wasteful use of time each day of the school year
2. Teacher frustration and fatigue in the first weeks
3. Indecision about what to teach during the first days of school
4. Chaos and confusion in the minds of the students

Imagine walking into a doctor's office and sitting in a waiting room where the magazines are strewn about and on the floor. The bulb is burned out in the old lamp. The phone is ringing incessantly. The music from above repeats the same song over and over . . . and over again. The receptionist is idly chatting on a cell phone, oblivious to anything or anyone in the room. You don't even receive a nod of welcome.

More than likely, this would be the last time you would set foot in that doctor's office—because you have a choice.

Most students do not have a choice. They are assigned to a classroom, and they trek from room to room, hoping you will be ready for them.

The saying, "First impressions are lasting impressions," rings true. **The first day of school is the most important day of the school year—not a day to wing it.** Show students you are ready for learning to take place and that you expect them to be ready to learn the moment they enter the classroom.

What to Have Ready for the Start of School

Your readiness before the first day of school is an excellent predictor of your effectiveness for the rest of the school year.

1. **Develop a Classroom Management Plan.**

The effective teacher develops a classroom management plan and has it in place before school begins. The plan outlines classroom procedures and ensures the class runs smoothly.

Procedures describe how things are to be done in the classroom. Procedures need to be taught, rehearsed, and reinforced until they become routines. (See page 47.) These are some of the procedures to include in your classroom management plan:

- How to enter the classroom (Procedure 1)
- What to do when the bell rings (Procedure 3)
- What to do with homework (Procedure 9)
- What to do when a pencil breaks (Procedure 17)
- What students do when they finish work early (Procedure 22)
- How to get the students' attention (Procedure 13)
- Where to find make-up work (Procedure 8)
- How to collect papers (Procedure 19)
- What to do with personal technology (Procedure 50)
- How to exit the classroom (Procedure 5)

Before school begins, devise a way to distribute and share your plan on the first day of school.

That's the Teacher I Hire

When I interview prospective new teachers, I ask, 'Tell me your classroom management plan.'

Ninety-nine percent tell me their discipline plan.

One percent tell me about procedures. That's the one I hire.

Kathy Vohland ▪ Oak Harbor, Washington

2. **Develop a Classroom Discipline Plan.**

While a well-managed classroom will minimize your discipline problems, effective teachers are proactive and plan to prevent behavioral problems from occurring in the classroom. A discipline plan includes these parts:

- Classroom rules for students to follow:

  Classroom rules keep student behavior in check. Rules are short, simple, and easy for students to remember. Post classroom rules prominently so that everyone can see them. Classroom rules carry positive and negative consequences.

- Rewards that students can work toward:

  A positive consequence is a reward. Class and individual rewards motivate students to work hard and focus on doing their best.

- Penalties for breaking classroom rules:

  A negative consequence is a penalty. Penalties must be clear and simple. They also need to be easy for the teacher to enforce consistently.

Give each student a copy of the classroom discipline plan. Instruct students to keep this information where they can refer to it easily.

Read the chapter in **THE First Days of School** that shows how to create a classroom discipline plan.

3. **Set Positive Expectations for All Students.**

Research shows that teachers who establish positive expectations for all students and provide the necessary support to achieve these expectations have high rates of academic success in the classroom.

Teachers who expect very little of their students get very little in return from their students. These are the teachers who are consistently frustrated with their students.

Conversely, teachers who set positive expectations for their students are rarely disappointed in their students. With clear objectives, students

will meet their teachers' expectations. Outline your expectations for students and include these expectations in a document and post them for students to see. Outline what students can expect from you.

What students can expect from the teacher:

- Offer quality instruction.
- Provide extra help.
- Create a positive learning environment.
- Give credit for practice.
- Give fair grades as evaluation of learning.
- Show respect.
- Enforce fairness.
- Give your best effort each day.

RESPONSIBILITIES   MR. HEINTZ

MY RESPONSIBILITIES AS YOUR TEACHER

1. To treat you with respect and care as an individual
2. To provide you an orderly classroom environment
3. To provide the necessary discipline
4. To provide the appropriate motivation
5. To teach you the required content

YOUR RESPONSIBILITIES AS MY STUDENTS

1. To treat me with respect and care as an individual
2. To attend classes regularly
3. To be cooperative and not disruptive
4. To study and do your work (<u>SUCCESS = EFFORT</u>)
5. To learn and <u>master</u> the required content

Jim Heintz, a high school teacher in Arizona, posts what the students can expect from him as well as what he expects from his students.

What the teacher expects from students:

- Be punctual.
- Come to class ready to work and learn.
- Bring all necessary books and supplies.
- Complete all assignments neatly.
- Follow established classroom procedures.
- Follow the posted rules.

- Keep a positive attitude.
- Listen and pay attention.
- Give your best effort each day.

Teachers' expectations of students greatly influence students' achievement in class and, ultimately, achievement throughout their lives.

4. **Plan to Welcome Students to Class.**

If a class roster is available before school begins, prepare and send a letter to each student and a separate letter to their parents. Let students and their parents know that preparations have been made for a successful year.

In the letter to students, list the items they need to bring to class on the first day of school. Also, explain what students can expect to learn on the first day and during the first week of school.

In the letter to parents, explain you've been preparing for the school year all summer long. Give parents this information:

- An overview of the year
- Your planning period
- Your contact information
- The school's contact information
- The class website address

Tell parents about the exciting school year ahead and invite them to attend Open House.

Plan to welcome students to the classroom on the first day of school.

- Write your name, room number, and subject taught on the board.
- Stand at the door and greet students with a warm smile.
- Check students' schedules to ensure they are in the right classroom.
- Introduce yourself and assure students they are in the right place.

Karen Rogers, a high school teacher in Kansas, has a plan ready before the start of the first day of school.

Darrell Cluck of Monroe, Louisiana, greets his students on the first day and every day of the school year.

5. **Prepare a First-Day Script.**

Plan what to do and say on the first day of school. Know exactly what to tell students the moment class begins. A script includes these parts:

- Your name and how it is pronounced
- How students are to address you
- Your professional experience
- How you have worked throughout summer to prepare for the school year

 4))

See what Karen Rogers uses to remind herself what it takes to start the school year successfully.

- How the classroom has been organized
- The classroom procedures that will allow everyone to be successful

6. Prepare a First-Day Packet.

Provide an information packet for the students to bring to the adults at home to review. The information will benefit the adults who are unable to attend Open House. Include this information in the packet:

- Introductory cover letter
- The classroom rules and consequences
- The homework policy
- A class contact list
- A supply list
- Acknowledgment receipt for return with signature

Keep these signature pages for future reference and parent-teacher conference discussions.

7. Prepare Lesson Plans.

Prepare lesson plans for the first ten days of school. These lessons will differ dramatically from the lessons planned for the remainder of the school year. **Your focus during the first two weeks of school is to teach procedures and get them established as routines in the classroom, so the rest of the year can be devoted to instruction. Of course there will be some instruction of curriculum material, but the emphasis is to get procedures learned and in place.**

Prepare extra activities to keep students learning during class time. Every moment is important in the classroom.

Your first ten days plan includes these parts:

- Introducing and discussing the classroom management plan
- Teaching, rehearsing, and reinforcing classroom procedures
- Content related lessons and activities

8. Prepare an Agenda.

The agenda is the plan for the day—the outline for what will be happening during your time with the students. An agenda consistently shows what the class will be learning during their time with you. **The basic parts of an agenda are the schedule, opening assignment, and lesson objective.** (See Procedure 2.) Many teachers also include the date, homework assignment, and important announcements or reminders.

Have a designated location in the room where the agenda will be consistently posted each day so that students can easily find it and refer to it.

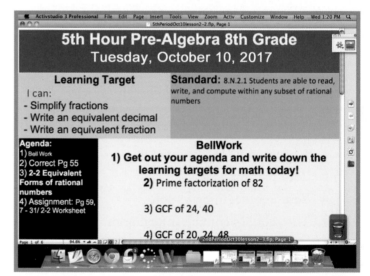

Every classroom at Sisseton Middle School in South Dakota has an agenda posted before the students enter for the period.

9. Prepare an Opening Assignment.

Prepare a short and easy-to-complete opening assignment for the first day of school. Give this assignment to students as they enter the classroom or have the assignment posted as part of the agenda. The opening assignment will engage the students in learning the moment they enter the classroom. An opening assignment on the first day of school demonstrates the following to students:

- The teacher is well-organized and prepared for class.
- The students are expected to start work immediately upon entering the classroom.
- Every moment together is a learning opportunity.
- The expectation is set for an opening assignment the rest of the school year.

10. **Organize the Classroom.**

In preparation for school to begin, organize the classroom to ensure a productive learning environment.

- Arrange desks so that every student is facing the front of the room and can clearly see you. Leave adequate space for students to enter and exit the room and to walk through the classroom aisles with ease.
- Prepare bulletin boards for the first day of school. Prepare one bulletin board to display student work. Prepare another bulletin board to introduce curriculum themes with units and grade level standards. Bulletin boards can be motivational as well as instructional. Keep the boards colorful, but not so busy that they become a distraction.
- Post essential information in the classroom.
  - ☐ Procedures
  - ☐ Rules
  - ☐ Expectations
  - ☐ Emergency information
  - ☐ Fire exits
  - ☐ Bell schedules
- Assign seats on the first day of school.

Begin your first day of school with a detailed plan. Refer to the plan to keep track of the day's progress. **Be ready for your students, and they will be ready for you. Together, you and your students will have a successful school year.**

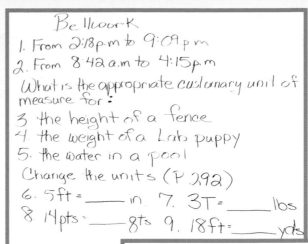

> Be llwork
> 1. From 2:18 p.m to 9:09 p.m
> 2. From 8:42 a.m to 4:15 p.m
> What is the appropriate customary unit of measure for:
> 3. the height of a fence
> 4. the weight of a Lab puppy
> 5. the water in a pool
> Change the units (P. 292)
> 6. 5ft = _____ in. 7. 3T = _____ lbs
> 8. 14 pts = _____ qts 9. 18ft = _____ yds

At Sisseton Middle School, opening assignments are called bellwork. Every classroom has the bellwork posted before the start of the class period.

Bellwork for Computer Classes

1. Find your chair.
2. Set your books aside.
3. Log in to your computer. (Remember this can take a while some days.)
4. Be prepared to work when the bell rings.
5. Sit quietly and listen for directions.

Time Wisely Spent

If I had eight hours to cut down a tree, I would spend five hours sharpening my axe.

Abraham Lincoln

 5 •))

Access more examples of first-day scripts and put together one before your first day of school.

A Complete First-Day Script Checklist

Sally Lutz is a tenth-grade, Intensive Reading, high school teacher in Florida. She uses a checklist format for her first day of school. As she completes each item, she checks it off the list.

✓ Cheerfully and enthusiastically greet students at the door, making eye contact with each. If names are known, greet students accordingly.

✓ Share personal information, expectations, and educational philosophy.

✓ Post a seating chart on the whiteboard for each class period. Instruct students to reference the chart as they enter the classroom.

✓ Place the journals at their desks (arranged in groups of four). Write prompts with explanations/directions on the whiteboard. This is where the weekly journal entry and the daily bellwork will be found throughout the school year.

✓ Take attendance quickly while students complete the opening assignment.

✓ Share with students that they are expected to be in their seats when the bell rings; otherwise, they will be marked tardy. Late passes are placed in a basket near the door and filed in student portfolios. After the third tardy they will be issued a referral and sent to the Dean's office, and detention will be served. Running through the door when the bell is ringing is not acceptable. The classroom is set up and conducted as a place of professional business. If the student is tardy or absent, a designated area and bin will house work that was missed.

✓ The first week's journal prompt will be copied as follows:

- Hi, Mrs. Lutz. My name is _____.
- My school schedule is _____.
- My interests and hobbies are _____.
- I did not do well on the FCAT because I _____.
- In this class I hope to learn _____.
- My address is _____.
- My home phone number is _____.
- I do/do not have my driver's license. (circle one)
- My favorite class is _____. Reasons _____.
- My least favorite class is _____. Reasons _____.

✓ On the outside of the journal, students write their first and last names/class periods. Journals are to be answered in complete sentences. Prompts are to be copied word for word from the board. Permanent markers will be provided with designations and instructions posted in the classroom explaining how to obtain and return them.

✓ Journals are kept in a specific location. How they are to be picked up and returned will be modeled. (Throwing them into the bin is not acceptable.)

✓ Show the bin for completed homework and in-class assignments.

✓ Share the bulletin board with classroom procedures (not rules), district dress code, class supplies, and syllabus. There will be a visual of each supply item on the ledge.

✓ Designate two bulletin boards for students. These will include photos, newspaper clippings of student accomplishments, or any newsworthy information about the students.

✓ The organization of the classroom and how it is run is explained and modeled. For example, in a designated closet, a numbered shelf is provided per class period for student supplies, materials, and the like.

✓ Distribute papers with syllabus, classroom procedures, and class supply list. Each informational paper will be on a different piece of brightly colored paper.

✓ Designate an area on the whiteboard for the date, assignments, and how to head a paper.

✓ Explain the word wall and its function.

✓ Point out bins where Hi-liters, rulers, dry-erase markers and erasers, glue, scissors, hole-punches, and sharpeners are stored. Explain how to properly obtain and replace the supplies.

✓ Identify one person from each group as the runner. This person will obtain necessary items needed for the day's work. Items will be listed on the board daily.

✓ If a pen or pencil is needed for the day's work, students may borrow supplies from Mrs. Lutz only if the student provides collateral.

✓ Share the I.O.N.U. System (I Observe No Unfriendliness). This system is based upon the book, *Likeability Factor*, by Tim Sanders.

✓ Review dismissal procedures. The bell does not necessarily dismiss students; Mrs. Lutz does. Students will not gather at the door; they will remain in their seats prior to dismissal.

✓ Prior to dismissal, make a quick sweep of the classroom for cleanliness. There should be no paper on the floor, all items should be properly returned to their rightful place, and desks should be in prearranged positions.

✓ Prepare a substitute folder. Inform students of your expectations if and when a substitute is needed—actually speaking to the class, giving out instructions for that day.

The Need for a Classroom Management Plan

A classroom management plan creates
a safe, positive, and consistent environment
where teaching and learning can take place.

A Sense of Purpose

A classroom management plan brings a sense of purpose to the classroom. The plan will help you create a culture of success, consistency, and academic excellence. You will connect with your students by being a pillar of stability for them.

Many students lead chaotic lives filled with unpredictability and insecurity. **Students want to know exactly what will be happening.** Students do not want surprises or disorganization. **The reason many students fail is that they do not know what to do.** Students want a safe, predictable, and nurturing environment. Students like well-managed classes because no one yells at them, they know what will be happening, they know how it will be happening, and learning takes place.

If you do not have a plan for your classroom, then the students will plan the classroom for you. Effective teachers spend the first two weeks teaching students to be in control of their own actions within a predictable classroom environment. Effective teachers have a classroom management plan, and they work their plan all year long.

Start with a Plan

The effective teacher starts the school year and every day with a classroom management plan. **The plan is created from the procedures, techniques, strategies, and solutions found in this book. Select from these to help you construct an effective classroom management plan.**

Bernie Alidor has his plan ready for the first day of school.

A classroom that is not well-organized quickly becomes chaotic and unsafe. It lacks a positive climate. Students figuratively check out of these classrooms. When students abandon the classroom emotionally, they start to create problems for themselves and others—the teacher included.

In a well-managed classroom, there is less stress for everyone. You rarely notice the hard work and preparation behind a well-managed classroom. The plan is invisible as the atmosphere is calm and work is purposeful. That is the classroom of an effective teacher and what this book will do for you.

Students Want and Accept Procedures

The classroom management plan of effective teachers is filled with procedures—a means of

Procedures maximize learning time for students.

accomplishing an action. Every time you want something done, there must be a procedure or a set of procedures to achieve it. For instance, there must be a procedure for taking roll, exchanging papers, registering students on the first day, taking turns speaking, and moving from task to task. If you don't have procedures in place, valuable time that should be spent learning will be wasted getting tasks done as there are no procedures in place to get the tasks done.

It is important that your students understand classroom procedures are for their benefit. Procedures

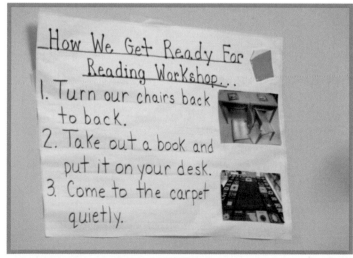

Students accept procedures. Just let them know what the procedure is.

eliminate confusion, provide predictability, and enable students to focus on class work—without distractions.

You cannot have responsible students if there are no procedures they can be responsible for.

Her Plan Made Her Legit

Kara Moore, a twenty-two-year-old, new teacher in Ohio, had a very successful first year as a teacher. On her first day, she said, "I was prepared. I had a plan and my students were going to know that I was LEGIT."

Then, one week before school began, her principal came to her and told her that she was going to teach a different subject, at a different grade level, in a different room, and on a different floor.

No problem. She succeeded because she had created a classroom management plan.

Students Secretly Crave Procedures

Christy Mitchell and **Grace Ann Coburn** had a classroom management class taught by **Greg Risner** at the University of North Alabama and succeeded as new teachers because they created a classroom management plan as part of their coursework. They were organized and ready for their first job offers.

Their plans, they say, consisted of **procedures, procedures, procedures!** They created a procedure for everything. They posted the procedures. They taught them. They demonstrated them. They practiced them. Once they did this, everything else fell into place. "Students knew what we expected from the beginning to the end. **The students secretly craved structure and management.**"

Many students come from very challenging home and life situations. Because their lives are disorganized and in chaos, they long for a classroom that is organized and structured. An organized plan will help students lay the foundation for wise use of classroom time. Learning will take place in an efficient and timely manner as you will have time to devote to what you were hired to do—help students make progress in their learning.

Blueprints are for contractors to build a home correctly. Agendas are used for meetings to help everyone stay on course. Maps are used for guidance to help you get from one point to another point safely.

Have your classroom management plan ready on the first day of school to ensure your class is on course for a successful school year.

Creating a Classroom Management Plan

Have a plan,
no matter the form.

Plan with Procedures

A Classroom Management Plan consists of a series of practices and procedures that a teacher uses to maintain an effective environment in which instruction and learning can occur. It's an operational manual for the classroom. It's a step-by-step guide for how to run a classroom.

A classroom management plan is a living document that changes as needed. Plans grow with need as situations present themselves in the classroom. Effective teachers are like fashion designers, graphic artists, and electronic engineers who are constantly tweaking their designs to attract new audiences and customers. With each new group of students, your classroom management plan will be tweaked to increase the chances for student success.

Research shows that sixteen percent of new teachers never make it beyond their first year of teaching and fifty percent will not make it beyond five years. **Yet, effective teachers keep teaching year after year because they never stop designing and tweaking their classroom management plans for both teacher and student success.**

Each day, plan your work and work your plan. Then, tweak your plan, as necessary each day, year after year.

The Questions to Ask

Visualize and ask yourself, "What is it that I want to design that will produce a positive learning environment?" Don't say, "What technology will I use?" "What program am I going to adopt?" "What educational philosophy or ideology will I install?"

Instead, ask:

1. **"What kind of classroom management plan will create a safe, organized, and productive environment, where I can teach and the students can learn?"**

2. **"What do I want the students to do, so I can teach and the students can learn?"**

The answers to those questions are the heart of your classroom management plan.

Classroom management is *not* about discipline. It is about how a classroom is organized, so the teacher can be an instructor, and the students can learn and achieve.

Classroom management plans vary from teacher to teacher; however, well-managed classrooms exist because effective teachers envision a type of classroom they want to create. They know the conditions that are necessary for a positive learning environment to emerge, and they implement a management plan to produce successful student learning.

The Start of a Middle School Plan

Cathy Terrell, a Spanish teacher at El Dorado Middle School in Kansas, says, "Before the first bell rings, my students are in their seats, quiet, and working. I have learned that the best way to start off a new school year is to have a detailed plan and script of exactly what will be said and done on that first day. My students love my class, and it is because of the procedures, guidelines, and activities that I have put into place to develop a more effective approach to teaching."

CATHY TERRELL'S FIRST DAY PLAN

At the door—before class:

- Greet each student at the door.
- Hand each student a welcome card with directions to a seat.
- Tell child to read and follow the instructions written on the board.
- Show students where their folders are located for each specific hour.
- Project opening assignment onto the screen with directions to locate the handout in their folder.

Begin class and welcome students:

- Go over PowerPoint presentation on classroom procedures.
- Have students guess characteristics about me based upon the graphics in slide.
- Ask students if any of them have some things in common with me.
- Talk about my love for teaching.
- Discuss classroom guidelines.
- Explain procedures for entering the classroom (which they used this morning as they entered) and refer to poster that reinforces entering procedure.
- Explain point system for bellwork and show stamp sheet example.
- Review schoolwide discipline plan and refer to poster that lists the rules.
- Take photos and explain that this will go on their "All About Me" paper, so that I can learn their names, faces, and a little about them.
- Explain dismissal procedure and then go through the procedure as the class prepares for dismissal.

Cathy's first day plan is just a portion of her classroom management plan. Being organized and ready and teaching the plan to her students gains her valuable instructional time throughout the year.

Teaching Others How to Plan

Diana Greenhouse of Joshua, Texas, started her first day of school in 2005 with a classroom management plan, and at the end of the year, she said, "What an incredible school year this has been.

When I look back at all I've accomplished in my first school year, it takes my breath away. My students learned, and I loved every minute of teaching. And it all started with having a plan."

At the beginning of her fourth year of teaching, she was asked to teach the classroom management workshop for all newly-hired teachers in the district. After five years in the classroom, Diana was appointed an assistant principal. She still teaches the classroom management workshop for the district. She shares with new teachers how they can be successful right from the start of their careers.

These are just some of the twenty-eight PowerPoint slides Diana uses in her classroom management workshop:

PREPARING FOR THE FIRST DAY OF SCHOOL

- Organize files, arrange, decorate
- Imagine royalty is coming!
- A place for everything
- Teach readiness by modeling readiness
- First Day Script

READINESS IS THE PRIMARY DETERMINANT OF TEACHER EFFECTIVENESS

CREATING YOUR FIRST DAY SCRIPT

- Students begin arriving at 7:20
- Activity on desk
- Name tents
- Student list on "clipboard"
- Ask your parents to confirm afterschool pick-up.....have a form ready for them to fill-in, such as:

HOW WILL YOUR STUDENT GET HOME?

NAME	STUDENT PICK-UP	PARENT DAYCARE	BUS#	BAND?

ESTABLISHING PROCEDURES

- The first 2-3 weeks of school are critical
- Introduce classroom procedures the first week
- State expectations
- Employ procedures that create consistency
- Create a PowerPoint presentation of your procedures
- Have students role-play procedures
- Rehearse as necessary

Effective teachers spend the first two weeks teaching students to be in control of their own actions in a consistent classroom environment

The First Days of School

IMPORTANT POINTS TO REMEMBER

- Prepare a First Day Script
- Welcome students, know their names, celebrate the First Day
- Establish procedures that create consistency
- State your expectations
- You are the greatest asset to your school!

6 •))

View all of the PowerPoint slides in Diana Greenhouse's presentation to beginning teachers.

Creating a well-managed classroom is the priority of a teacher the first two weeks of school. This is accomplished by establishing procedures for how to get things done in the classroom. These procedures over time are carried out automatically and become routines and thus establish a culture of consistency in how the classroom is run. It's like learning to ride a bicycle. Someone has to teach you how first, but once you know and are successful at it, you just hop on the bike and, without thinking about it, ride away.

Your students will respond to the consistency you have planned. Your procedures will become routines for your students. The procedures will become habits for your students and will be performed without even thinking about it. You don't even have to be in the classroom, and the students will all know what to do and carry out their routines—the benefit of having a classroom management plan.

Thanks for the Peace

Angela Hiracheta, from Taft, Texas, was miserable her first two years in the classroom. She was clueless as to what to do to turn around her situation. After learning about having a plan for success, she is now happier than ever and loving all of the time she has to teach.

 During my first and second year, I was completely clueless and going insane! I was SURE teaching was not for me, and I was surviving aimlessly and hopelessly. I didn't know how to put my teaching problems into words as I did not know what was wrong.

Then I learned about creating a classroom management plan with procedures, so there was no room for confusion WHATSOEVER.

I just ended my third year, and this is the first year I can honestly say I look forward to the next school year!! I've learned to organize myself and my classroom. This would not have been possible if I hadn't created and implemented my classroom management plan.

I used to look at the future of my teaching career with little confidence in my ability, but now I'm looking forward to improving my effectiveness even more.

I have much more time now, which I did not have before because I did not have any routines and structures. I even know my students more now by the mere fact that with routines in place, I can actually take the time not only to teach, but to get to know my students.

Thanks for the peace I've been waiting for in the teaching profession! I even have time to stay up late on weekends getting lost in a good book or movie—which was once a rare, rare luxury.

This is why I have a classroom management plan!

Presenting Your Classroom Management Plan

The first day of school is your most important day of the school year.
Share your plan with your students, so they know
what to expect during the school year.

Presenting Your Plan

Y ou have a plan that is filled with practices and procedures to create a successful year of learning for your students. Now, it's time to implement the plan. There are numerous ways to present your plan. **How you present your plan will determine your ability to teach for understanding and reinforcement.**

If your students are young, you may choose to talk them through your plan. For students who can read, many teachers distribute a hardcopy of their procedures, so the students can follow along during the explanation. Increasingly, teachers do all three of the following:

- Introduce the plan with a visual presentation.
- Provide a hardcopy of the plan for each student.
- Post procedure reminders in the classroom.

You will need to determine how best to present your classroom management plan to your students.

Practice presenting your plan to your students, so you can deliver it with the confidence that the plan will work. Know what you have written and how it will be explained. Be ready for questions of clarification and lack of understanding. The better prepared you are to present your plan, the more you will be perceived as knowing what you're doing, as opposed to making it up as you go along. Your degree of confidence will tell students that you have a plan for their success and you are ready to teach!

Procedures Taught Verbally

In some classes, such as PK-1 and certain special education environments, procedures are taught verbally.

Bernie Alidor teaches kindergarten in Pensacola, Florida. He uses a method he calls "modified modeling" to teach his students classroom procedures. Instead of just telling his students what the procedure is, Bernie first acts out an exaggerated skit of the wrong way to do the procedure.

For example, if a child needs to use the restroom, his procedure instructs students to raise two fingers. He begins to teach this procedure by jumping up and down, waving his hands, and yelling, "I got to use the restroom," or "I got to use the bathroom," repeatedly. The students typically laugh at his exaggerated acting.

Then he asks for a better way to ask permission to use the restroom. At least one student will always come up with the idea of raising a hand. Bernie simply modifies this with his desired two fingers signal.

These are the steps to Bernie's modified modeling:

- Act out the wrong procedure.
- Ask for class input on a better procedure.
- Model the correct procedure.
- Ask individual students to model it.
- Ask the whole class to model it.

Bernie continues going through the classroom procedures using this process for most of the day. Of course, it takes more than just one day of going over procedures for the students to master them all. He goes over each procedure every day, again and again, the first week of school. By the end of the week, most of the students know what to do, when to do it, and how to do each procedure. They also understand that by following the procedures, they will be prepared to have a good day and will be ready to learn.

Procedures Taped to a Desk

Alicia Blankenship of Katy, Texas, tapes some of her procedures on each student's desk. As the students enter the classroom for the first time, the procedures are there to guide them. Soon after the start of class, **Alicia teaches the procedures to her students**. These are reinforced until they become routines in the classroom, so her students will repeat the procedure **without any reminding or prompting**.

Some of Alicia's procedures include a HELP card inside an envelope pocket. If the student needs her help, the student removes the Help card, places it on the outside of the pocket, and continues to work. **The key is to keep students working.**

What Is Management?

Management is the act of managing, supervising, guiding, or caring of an organization, program, or project you have been entrusted with. A teacher is entrusted with managing a classroom as a learning environment, not disciplining a group of students into compliance.

For management to be effective, there needs to be some type of defined plan or system in place. This is often the downfall of teachers. They have no plan or system. As a result, their classrooms are haphazard and seem disorganized while students sit clueless in an ominous environment.

Management consists of three major actions:

1. Management **Creates** a plan. This classroom management plan becomes the road map for what work is going to be done.
2. Management **Implements** the plan. Teaching the procedures ensures that everyone knows what to do.
3. Management **Assesses** the plan. The results are noted to determine to what degree the plan is being achieved and if reteaching is necessary.

The effective classroom manager takes these three steps and sequences them into a continuing cycle: Create, Implement, and Assess. The results of the assessments become the continuing cycle of improvement that leads to further enhancement of how well the classroom is managed.

Without a plan, there can be no continuing cycle of improvement. Most classroom failings can be attributed to the failure to have a plan.

Hands are not wagging, accompanied by voices yelling for help. The students keep working. When the teacher comes to help, the Help card is placed back inside the envelope. Getting help remains a one-on-one interaction without any disruption of the class.

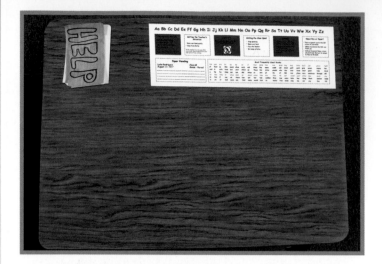

Teachers who must move from one room to another can choose to laminate their classroom management plan. Then, as the students enter the room, they pick one up and place it on their desk. When class is over, students return the laminated page to the designated location.

Procedures Placed on the Desk

Sue Moore of Hobart, Indiana, creates graphic reminders of classroom procedures. She places them in an acrylic stand on the student tables or around the classroom to serve as constant reminders of how the procedures are to be done.

Next to the Help card, Alicia lists several of the most important procedures for her classroom. They are posted on every classroom desk as a daily reminder to her students.

- Entering the classroom
- Getting the teacher's attention
- Movement in the classroom
- Getting the class quiet
- Dismissal
- Need a pen or pencil?

Underneath these procedures is an example of the heading for all papers. She maintains a list of correctly spelled words students will use in their writing.

Aa Bb Cc Dd Ee Ff Gg Hh Ii Jj Kk Ll Mm Nn Oo Pp Qq Rr Ss Tt Uu Vv Ww Xx Yy Zz

Entering the Classroom
- Come in without talking.
- Sit down quietly.
- Get out homework, if any.
- Do the bellwork.

We are sorry if you are not seated and working when the tardy bell rings.

Getting the Teacher's Attention
- Raise your hand quietly.
- Keep it up silently.

If the teacher has not come after one minute, place a help card on your desk and continue working.

Movement
Please remain seated until the teacher requests movement.

Getting the Class Quiet
- Stop speaking.
- Raise your hand.
- Face the Teacher.
- Be ready to listen.

Dismissal
- Stay in your seat until the teacher dismisses the class.
- Make sure the area around your desk is clean.
- Walk courteously out of the classroom.

Need Pen or Paper?
- Place a request card in the left corner of your desk.
- When you receive the item, say thank you.
- Before the end of class, return any materials that are to remain in class to the M.M.

Paper Heading

Lydia Rodriguez
August 23, 2017

Class #
Grade - Period

Most Frequently Used Words																	
the	you	are	be	by	we	an	if	then	make	two	way	been	long	may	little	back	just	great	right
of	that	as	this	word	when	each	will	them	like	more	could	call	down	part	work	give	name	where	too
and	it	with	have	but	your	which	up	these	him	write	people	who	day	over	know	most	good	help	mean
a	he	his	from	not	can	she	other	so	into	go	my	oil	did	new	place	very	sentence	through	old
to	was	they	or	what	said	do	about	some	time	see	than	its	get	sound	year	after	man	much	any
in	for	I	one	all	there	how	out	her	has	number	first	now	come	take	live	thing	think	before	same
is	on	at	had	were	use	their	many	would	look	no	water	find	made	only	me	our	say	line	tell

Sue creates the procedures with visuals and prints them for inserting in the stands. These are some of the procedures she has posted around the classroom:

Hand-Washing Procedures

1. Turn on the water.
2. Get **1** squirt of soap.
3. Wash and rinse hands.
4. Push button **2** times for paper towel.
5. Turn off water and put paper towel in garbage can.

Cafeteria Procedures

1. Use a quiet voice.
2. Keep your table area clean.
3. Stay in your seat.
4. Raise your hand if you need help.

Pencil Sharpener Procedures

1. Put pencil in sharpener.
2. Count to **5**.
3. Walk back to your table.

Morning Procedures

1. Walk in.
2. Follow lunch-count procedures.
3. Put folder in mailbox.
4. Say "Hi" to **2** friends.
5. Sit quietly at your table.
6. Begin your work job.

Pencil Trading Procedures

1. Put **1** dull pencil in white basket.
2. Get **1** sharp pencil from green basket.
3. Walk back to your table.

Procedures Posted on Paper

Jeanette Weinberg teaches in Yorktown, Virginia, and was named Teacher-of-the-Year after her second year of teaching. She has her individual procedures rolled

up on paper and stored in a cabinet until needed. After teaching the procedure, she brings out one of the rolled procedures to use when she needs to reteach or refresh the class on a procedure.

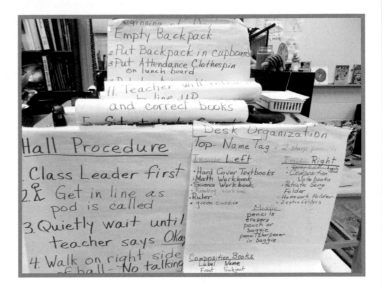

Procedures Posted on the Wall

Some teachers post important procedures on the wall or on a bulletin board to serve as a gentle, daily reminder to students. If needed, the teacher simply points to the procedure to remind the student what to do in the classroom.

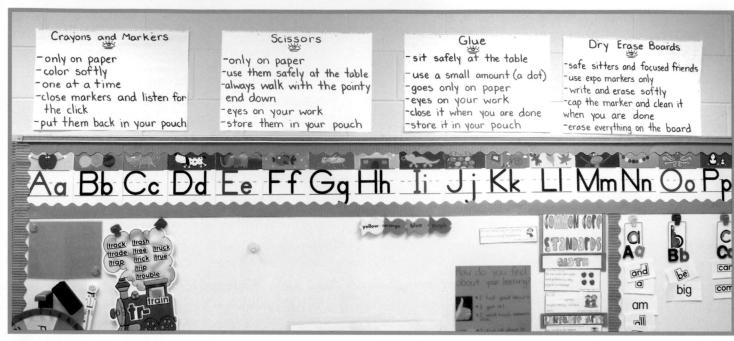

Kristen Wiss posts procedures to remind the students what to do each day in the classroom.

Procedures in Song

Alex Kajitani was one of four National Teacher-of-the-Year finalists in 2009. He credits his ability to help students achieve and learn to his classroom management effectiveness.

Alex is a very effective math teacher. He uses rap songs to teach math concepts. The "math raps" work well because they make math "cool" for students.

Alex Kajitani at the National Teacher-of-the-Year award ceremony in Washington, DC.

Because his students relate to the rap songs, he also teaches procedures with a rap song he wrote called, "The Routine Rhyme."

Each day the class practices "The Routine Rhyme." It takes only a few days for them to memorize it—just like the rap songs.

Alex says his "Routine Rhyme" has dramatically increased classroom time-on-task and productivity. Whenever a student is not following procedures, another student will rap the line from "Routine Rhyme," reminding the off-task student what to do. The rap song acts as a form of self-correction for the students and a time-saving classroom management tool for Alex.

Walking into class one day, he overheard one student say to another, "Man, we do the same thing in this class every day." With a smirk and a satisfied smile, Alex knew the class had the procedures down cold. Classroom procedures had become the routine for students.

Procedures in PowerPoint

Sarah Jondahl presents her classroom management plan using a PowerPoint presentation. Sarah teaches for understanding by modeling classroom procedures with the help of student volunteers during the presentation. This ensures that her students know what each procedure looks like and sounds like.

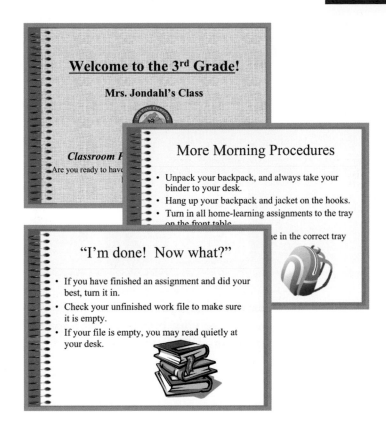

To reinforce her procedures, Sarah summarizes each classroom procedure as a text snippet she calls a "blurb." These blurbs are compiled in a packet and three-hole-punch format for students to keep in their binders. The first week of school, Sarah's students retrieve their blurb packets and read through selected procedures before attempting them in class.

LINING UP OUTSIDE

Whenever students are lined up outside before school, after recess, or after lunch, they are expected to be respectful. There will be no fooling around, pushing, or getting out of line. They must stand in a single file and wait to be invited into the classroom.

BELLWORK

Each morning, after students have put their attendance "stars" in the appropriate basket, they are to return to their desks to do silent bellwork. This will be done quietly and independently and will be corrected as a class and collected. During this time, the teacher will be taking care of attendance, notes from home, and other administrative tasks.

"The Routine Rhyme"

Aaaaaw, yeah, look at the time,
Time to get started with The Routine Rhyme.
Now I know what to do, each and every day,
It's Kajitani's class and we'll do it his way.

First bell rings, I calmly walk in;
My teacher at the door with a big ol' grin.

My pencil is sharp; my notebook is out;
I know the routine and that's what I'm all about.

Second bell rings, I'm in my seat on time,
Ready for the day and my IQ is gonna climb.

Get started on the warm up; homework on my desk,
Teacher marks it off, and he is impressed.
His hand goes up, and the room goes silent;
Nobody talks, yeah, don't even try it.

My pencil is sharp; my notebook is out;
I know the routine and that's what I'm all about.
Said my pencil is sharp; my notebook is out;
I know the routine and that's what I'm all about.

Warm up, homework, the notes are next;
Raise my hand to ask a question, if I get perplexed.
After the notes, it's activity time;
Yo, I never have to wonder with 'The Routine Rhyme.'

Two minutes left; time to clean up.
Trash on the floor; Yo, pick it up!
First bell rings, Kajitani says, 'Goodbye.'
When you know the routine, then the time sure flies!

'Cause my pencil is sharp; my notebook is out;
I know the routine and that's what I'm all about.
Yeah my pencil is sharp; my notebook is out;
I know the routine and that's what I'm all about.

See you tomorrow!

Alex Kajitani

7 •))

Rap along with Alex Kajitani's "The Routine Rhyme" and find the procedures in the song.

By reading the procedures, discussing them, and modeling the "Dos" and "Do Nots" of each procedure, Sarah's students thoroughly learn them. These steps increase the students' understanding of Sarah's expectations for how the classroom will operate during the school year.

Effective Teachers Adapt

These physical education teachers in Virginia are not in a traditional classroom. They don't have access to show a PowerPoint presentation, a bulletin board, a wall to post anything, and more than likely are not very good at rap music, but, they are creative and understand they need to get their procedures across to their students. So, they post procedures on a flip chart that sits on the gymnasium floor. When the students come to class, they are greeted with a welcome message, told to change into P.E. attire, and then to "Start Walking."

Effective teachers do not adopt someone else's plan or procedures and then mechanically use the plan. **Effective teachers are thinkers; they make their own success from what they adapt.**

Present your classroom management plan in a style and format that works for your classroom, for your students, for your unique set of circumstances.

 8 ◉))

Sarah's blurbs are an excellent compilation of the basic procedures taught in many classrooms.

I Cried Daily

I started in January. I replaced a teacher who never returned from winter break. I walked in, <u>NEVER</u> having stepped into a classroom—<u>NEVER</u> a student taught.

Chaos! No structure, procedures, or routines. The prior teacher allowed students to do whatever they wanted. They did yoga on Fridays, drank two-liter sodas, and munched candy and snacks.

My mother, who is a teacher, said that I must have a plan, and she told me how important it is to be prepared. On my first day, I went over my procedures, which I modeled and had them rehearse. The students stared at me like I was a fool!

I worked on these procedures every day until April, when I finally saw progress. In that time, the students tried everything. They even signed a petition to fire me and gave it to the principal. I never gave up, and I told them so, even though I cried daily after school.

Finally, at the end of the school year, some of the most resistant students thanked me and gave me big hugs. I would not still be teaching today had I not understood procedures.

Holly Bonessi ■ Tempe, Arizona

Creating a Plan in Powerpoint

The teacher is the presenter, not the PowerPoint slides

PowerPoint Helps to Communicate

PowerPoint is a software program commonly used by teachers as a visual aid to what is being taught. A PowerPoint file consists of a series of slides with text, pictures, videos, animations, or audio. The slides are shown as a presentation or slideshow with a video projector or some other display system. As the slides are advanced, information is revealed.

The purpose of a PowerPoint presentation is not to show slides. It is to reinforce what you are teaching. For this to happen, the slides must effectively help you communicate information or a task.

The presentation should be simple and support what you want the students to learn. **An effective slide supports what you are presenting.** The class will either read your slides or listen to you. They will not do both. A poorly designed slide with too many words and too complex a design will confuse the students, and they will not pay attention to you.

Slides that are filled with text tend to be read—by you. **Almost never read your slides word for word.** If your slides are too wordy, you become a drone and your students will tune you out. Your slides should enhance your words, while you should always be the main focus. **The slides are not the teacher; you are the teacher.**

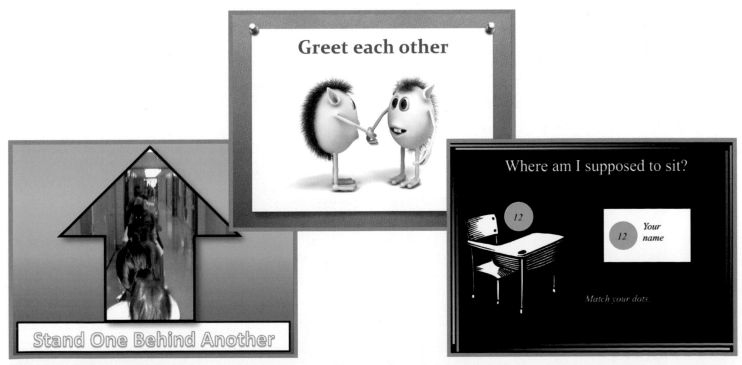

Slides with a picture and few words best communicate your message.

Reduce the Clutter

Remember when overhead transparencies were the rage? Teachers and speakers would put an entire 8½" x 11" page of typed words on the projector screen. Unfortunately, this same manner of communication got carried over to many PowerPoint presentations of today—slides crammed full of text with hardly any white space.

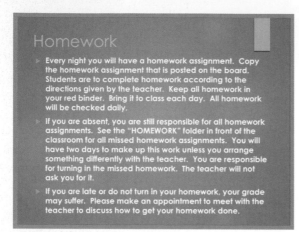

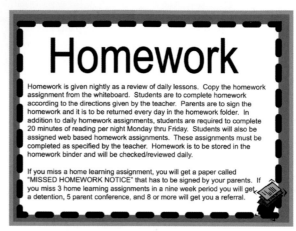

A cluttered slide with minimal white space overwhelms the audience and the message.

The current generation of students does not live in a text-based world. These students are surrounded by media consisting of colorful images and attention-getting sounds. Think visually when you create your PowerPoint presentation.

The screen is a visual medium. People look at a television screen and expect to see a picture. They do not expect to turn on the television to read. View the space on a PowerPoint slide as a visual medium, not as a text-driven page.

Resist cluttering a slide with too many words and distracting graphics.

1. Get to the point—immediately.
2. Highlight, by some means, what is important.
3. Keep it simple.

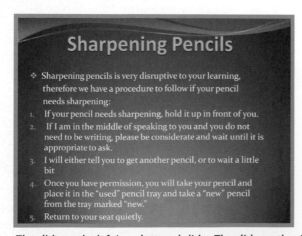

The slide on the left is a cluttered slide. The slide on the right is an enhanced slide that conveys the same message.

Point to the Beginning of the Sentence

When you gesture toward a PowerPoint slide, point to the beginning of a sentence. Bear in mind there are many English-language learners in our classrooms whose native tongues may be written from right to left.

A picture tells a thousand words and is often more effective than words in communicating an idea.

Characteristics of a Good Slide

A good PowerPoint slide has these qualities:

1. Words are kept to a minimum.
2. Pictures are used to help convey the message.
3. The combination of text and images is a visual enhancement of your verbal message.

Filling a slide with too many words detracts from its purpose as a visual aid. If you have long sentences on your slides, your students will tend to read ahead of you instead of listening to you. You will tend to read off your slides, turning your back to your audience. When this happens, you and your class are out of sync, and you rob yourself of an opportunity to connect with your students.

If your intention is to read to your students, do away with the slide presentation and give them a hardcopy of the information instead. When a slide contains too much information for an audience to follow easily, it is no longer a slide. It is a document. Print the document and give it to students instead of putting them through an incomprehensible presentation.

Number of Words to Use

Use as few words as possible. In fact, **a single word or phrase may suffice**.

Consider allowing the pictures on your slides to convey a visual narrative. The "Sit" slide, for instance, can be used very effectively by the teacher to convey a classroom procedure.

When creating slides, keep in mind that text font sizes must not be smaller than thirty points. Ideally, each slide contains fewer than three or four phrases or sentences. Resist the urge to overload your slides with bullet points—otherwise known as "death by bullets."

Death by PowerPoint

Committing any of these fatal errors when creating a PowerPoint presentation will cost you your audience:

1. Complex diagrams
2. Dense spreadsheets
3. Too many distracting animations
4. Long lists of bullets
5. Word-heavy slides
6. Reading every sentence

Be selective. Do not put too much information on each slide. Three or four bullets with a short phrase will suffice. In the slide, "Our Morning Routine," students will tend to read the procedure instead of listening to the teacher. The teacher is clueless as to whether students comprehend the procedure.

Our Morning Routine

- Enter the classroom quietly and find your seat (with your name tag).
- Immediately take out the homework materials from the night before, which are listed on the whiteboard, and have your homework out and ready to be checked.
- Quietly begin the morning bellwork. (Do this in your yellow spiral notebooks.)
- If you complete your bellwork, you may get your group book basket and silently read.
- During bellwork your group will be excused to put your backpacks in your cubbies and complete the attendance/lunch chart.

The same information can be shared in an easier-to-digest format. Each bullet corresponds to one step in a procedure. The teacher uses the information on the slide to support the teaching of the procedure.

Our Morning Routine

- Enter quietly.

- Take out homework materials.

- Begin bellwork.

- Complete the attendance/lunch chart.

Isolate the Text

Rather than crowd a slide with lengthy bullets or numbered points, consider using animation to reveal bullet points one at a time.

There are two schools of thought on the animation of bullet points. Some presenters say, "Reveal all the bullets at the same time—let your audience see the whole forest." These presenters like to refer to previous bullets to show relationships, just as the trees in a forest form a relationship.

Other presenters say, "Reveal the bullets one at a time, so the audience is focused on the point you are making."

Rick Altman, author of *Why Most PowerPoint Presentations SUCK*, favors showing all the bullets on a slide at once. **However, be very careful to limit the number of bullets used on a single slide—and keep sentences or phrases brief.**

Say It First

Remember, you are the teacher. You are the presenter. Show the slide after you introduce what you have to say first.

**Say it First.
Show it Next.**

This way, when the students see the slide, they will have heard you introduce the slide. Then, when the slide is shown, you can elaborate on the subject or rehearse the procedure.

Employ Actual Photos

PowerPoint is visual software, so you may opt to use only graphics in your presentations and allow your pictures to convey the message.

It is helpful to use photos to show students exactly what a procedure looks like, and tell them what it means.

"Backpacks and jackets are kept in a designated location in the classroom. Below each hook is a piece of tape with your name."

*The verbalization of this slide is,
"Put papers in the slot for your period."*

The best visual source for your presentations exists right in your own classroom. Take pictures of your classroom and insert them in your slides. Your students will enjoy recognizing their schoolmates and their classroom, and you project a sense of credibility when you can talk about your students and the success you have achieved together.

Background and Color

Design is not about decoration or ornamentation. It is about making communication as effectively as possible. This means ensuring that your message is clear and easy to understand—especially to the many English-language learners in our classrooms.

It is ineffective to overload a slide. Clutter is confusing. Allowing for whitespace gives the audience visual breathing room and helps provide contrast.

Two excellent background and color schemes are black on white, or white on black. The dramatic contrast between black and white helps the audience focus on the point you're making. Keep in mind, however, that colors set moods. Black is foreboding, while white is uplifting. Red is alarming, blue is tranquil, and green is neutral.

It's important to remember that it is not your slide's background or color that determines its effectiveness. Rather, it is how well and simply your slide communicates your message to your audience.

Using Digital Pictures in a PowerPoint Presentation

Use good lighting when taking your pictures. Avoid shadows on faces or on the main subject of the picture.

If the picture seems too dark or light, you may be able to improve it by selecting the picture and then clicking the "Brightness" and "Contrast" buttons on the Picture Toolbar.

If your photo is too big for the slide after inserting it into PowerPoint, resize it to fit the slide by dragging one of the <u>corner</u> handles. Do not resize it with the <u>side</u> handles; this will change the aspect ratio and distort the picture.

Use the "Crop" button to remove any unnecessary background. Once the picture is cropped, you can enlarge it and focus on your subject. It's OK to use the side handles when cropping, but be careful; this actually removes part of the photo—rather than resizing it.

Procedure 5:
Name and Number On Your Work

1) Name and Number are on the table.

2) Write your Name and Number on your work.

3) Start on your work.

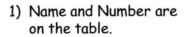

When preparing your slides, choose color schemes that appeal to the grade level you teach—young children like bright, exciting colors. You might also pick colors that reflect your personality or various themes. For instance, a physical education teacher used the school colors for his presentation to a high school class.

My Pet Peeve

"My pet peeve is the folks who put their logo on every slide," says **Nancy Duarte**, author of *Slide:ology*.

At conferences, some teachers put their names on every slide and even include a copyright symbol. It is egocentric to put your name on every slide. The students know who you are—or, we hope they do. Putting a name or a copyright symbol on every slide adds clutter. Put the information on the title slide and the ending slide if you feel the need to include it in your slideshow.

Don't Over-Animate

There is a feature in PowerPoint called **animation**. This allows the presenter to draw attention by moving words, revealing key ideas, and adding sound and video to the slideshow.

Don't over-animate. It's tempting to make slides that flutter like a bird or soar like a rocket. Every change to a presentation is a distraction. Autistic students and students with ADHD become agitated and hyper when there is too much animation on a slide.

It is all right to

- emphasize a word or phrase in a different color.
- add a picture or a video clip to a slide.
- isolate bullets—one to a slide—to enhance audience understanding.

Don't become the teacher who wants to show off your proficiency with PowerPoint. You know you are using animation inappropriately when the animation

Advancing Your Slideshow

 A wireless presenter is a remote unit that allows you to change slides from anywhere in the classroom. They are available in several brands through online retailers. The device allows you to walk around the room, engage the students, and change slides seamlessly.

Changing slides can be a distraction if you are not familiar with how to use a wireless presenter device.

- You constantly turn away from the audience to advance a slide. This causes students to switch their focus from the presentation to watching what you are doing.
- You search for the button or icon to move to the next slide.
- You disrupt the connection you've made with students to focus on the software program.

Professional speakers have a video monitor set up between them and the audience, so they can focus their attention on the audience. Position your computer screen similarly. Keep it between you and your class, or position it to the side where you can see it from the corner of your eye. Know your presentation and do not use your computer screen as a crutch. If you are not familiar with your presentation, take the time to rehearse it.

During presentations, advance your slides by clicking discreetly on the wireless presenter. Keep the wireless presenter in your hand so that you can operate the controls without looking at the device. Stay focused on your students, and they will stay focused on you.

- does not add value to the content or serve a purpose.
- distracts the students from your message.
- startles the students.

Putting Concepts into Practice

Stephanie Stoebe, 2012 Texas Teacher-of-the-Year, teaches in Round Rock, Texas, and uses a PowerPoint presentation to share her procedures with her students. As effective teachers do, she is constantly looking for ways to improve her skills, so she has a greater influence on her students. Stephanie reworked her PowerPoint presentation after some pointers from us. She says, "I am much happier with it. It is cleaner and simpler for the kids!"

These are some of her "Before" and "After" slides.

Creating effective PowerPoint presentations will help you add impact to your words.

Before

When I Need to Get Your Attention

- I Say: 1, 2, 3, eyes on me
- You Say: 1, 2, eyes on you
- I will always give this prompt from the center of the classroom.
- All attention will be on me because I have something important to say!

Entering the Classroom

- Greet me at the door! I am happy to see you today!
- Go to your seat and get your journal out from under your desk.
- Respond to the writing prompt on the board.
- When finished, you may read silently.

THERE ARE FAR BETTER THINGS AHEAD THAN ANY WE LEAVE BEHIND —C S Lewis

Working in Groups

- I like for us to work in groups! Together we are smarter.
- If I am with a small group and cannot be disturbed, I will have a red cup at my table. Please work independently.
- If I have a yellow cup at my table, that means you may ask a peer for assistance.
- If I have a green cup at my table, you may come ask me for assistance.

Got Supplies?

- There are two containers at the front of the class. One is for sharpened pencils, one for dull.
- If you need a pencil, or a sharper pencil, gain my attention by raising your hand and pointing to the pencil bin at the front of the class.
- I will give you a thumbs up to proceed.
- Switch out your dull pencil for a sharpened one.
- If you should find an extra pencil in the hallway or floor, please donate it!

After

When I Need to Get Your Attention

- I Say:
- 1, 2, 3, eyes on me

- You Say:
- 1, 2, eyes on you

Entering the Classroom

- Greet...
- Seat...
- Respond...
- Read!

THERE ARE FAR BETTER THINGS AHEAD THAN ANY WE LEAVE BEHIND —C S Lewis

Working in Groups

- Red = ask yourself
- Yellow = ask a peer
- Green = ask me

Got Pencil?

- No pencil?
- Dull pencil?
- Found a pencil?

9 •))

View another example of a PowerPoint presentation that has been shared with us.

Organizing the Slides in Your Presentation

There are five basic parts to include in your first day of school PowerPoint presentation. Prepare at least one slide for each of the parts.

1. Identify yourself and welcome students with positive expectations.
2. Provide general information about the class.
3. Explain what a procedure is.
4. Prepare one slide for each procedure.
5. End with a slide that expresses your positive expectations.

I. Identify yourself and welcome students with positive expectations.

Welcome to Mrs. Nelson's
3rd grade classroom
where you will
go on new Adventures
and make new Discoveries
every day.

2. Provide general information about the class.

3. Explain what a procedure is.

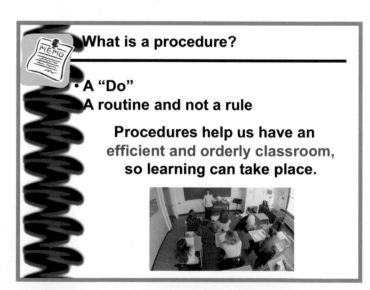

4. Prepare one slide for each procedure.

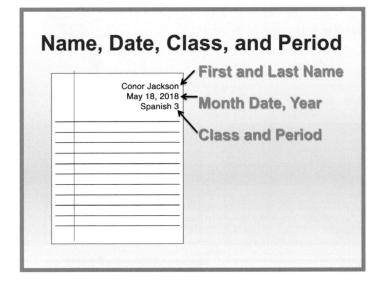

5. Conclude with a slide that expresses your positive expectations.

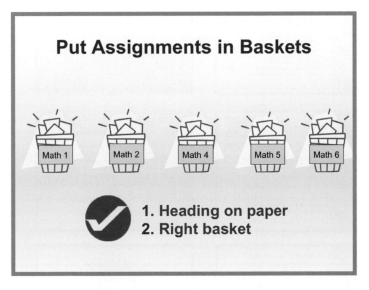

The PowerPoint Helped *ME*!

My PowerPoint set the tone with the students and let them know that I was very sincere and professional about the manner in which our classroom would run.

The PowerPoint helped ME to organize myself, *as I knew exactly what I needed to do to prepare for my first days of school. It kept me focused as I would go through each slide and make a check list of everything that I needed to do to implement my plan.*

Having my plan and procedures helped us all get off to a good and strong start with no surprises. Students actually love the structure of knowing exactly what to do when they walk through the door each morning.

Cathy Terrell ▪ El Dorado, Kansas

10 ◉))

See how Karen Rogers checks for understanding after she introduces her classroom management plan.

From Warrior to Effective Teacher

Kazim Cicek spent the first three years of his teaching career referring to himself as a warrior—students fought him, and he fought his students. He feared he would have to quit teaching.

Kazim says, "I had never heard the words 'classroom management' or the concept of 'procedures,'" during his training to become a teacher. Fortunately, just before the start of his fourth year of teaching, he saw a flyer advertising a seminar on "How to Be an Effective and Successful Teacher." It was free, so he figured, what did he have to lose; after all, he was losing the battle in the classroom.

During the seminar, Kazim had his Aha moment while he listened to us talk about classroom management.

Kazim went home and took four days to create a PowerPoint presentation of his classroom management plan. He based his plan on the examples he had seen at the seminar and was ready to present his plan on the first day of school.

His classroom management plan saved his teaching career. Today, Kazim is a happy and successful educator with more than ten years of teaching experience.

We've shown Kazim's classroom management plan to educators around the world. It is, arguably, the most copied PowerPoint presentation on Earth.

Several years later, at our urging, Kazim modified his original slides to reduce the number of words and added pictures of his students.

His before and after slides contain the same information. They were redesigned to take the students' focus off of the slide and put the students' attention on the teacher.

Before

After

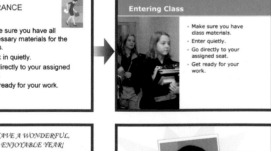

How to Teach a Procedure

There is a procedure for how to teach a procedure.

Procedures Must Be Practiced

An effective teacher has a classroom management plan filled with procedures and routines. **A well-managed, smooth-running class depends on the teacher's ability to teach procedures.** Procedures create an efficient and orderly classroom so that learning can take place.

The students of Nikki LeRose, a preservice teacher in Fort Wayne, Indiana, show how they feel about procedures.

Create a safe, orderly, and productive classroom with these steps:

1. Develop a set of procedures for every classroom activity.
2. Use the three-step method for teaching a procedure.
3. Practice the procedures until they become routines.

If it is so simple to teach students classroom procedures—as the examples and personal stories in this book will attest—why are some teachers still so frustrated in the classroom?

We often hear from teachers, "I tell my students what to do. I tell them over and over again, and my students just will not do what I ask them."

**The solution is simple:
Procedures must be rehearsed.**

To prepare for an emergency, for instance, it is not sufficient just to tell students what to do. The class needs to practice the procedure. That is why we have fire drills, lock down drills, and tornado drills.

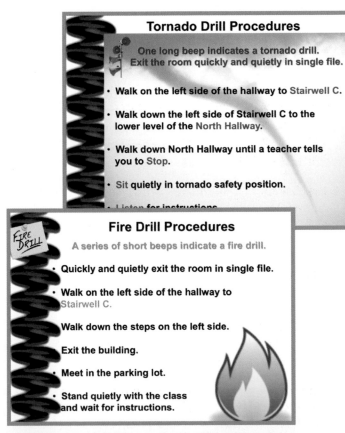

Tornado Drill Procedures

One long beep indicates a tornado drill. Exit the room quickly and quietly in single file.

- Walk on the left side of the hallway to Stairwell C.
- Walk down the left side of Stairwell C to the lower level of the North Hallway.
- Walk down North Hallway until a teacher tells you to Stop.
- Sit quietly in tornado safety position.
- Listen for instructions.

Fire Drill Procedures

A series of short beeps indicate a fire drill.

- Quickly and quietly exit the room in single file.
- Walk on the left side of the hallway to Stairwell C.
- Walk down the steps on the left side.
- Exit the building.
- Meet in the parking lot.
- Stand quietly with the class and wait for instructions.

Oretha Ferguson briefs her students with her PowerPoint presentation of emergency procedures before the students walk through the steps and practice them.

Telling a student what to do is insufficient. This is the same reason why some parents cannot get their children to do what they are told, no matter how often they repeat themselves. These parents do not realize what experienced coaches and music teachers know.

All procedures must be practiced.

Many entertainers dream of performing at Carnegie Hall. When students ask, "How do you get to Carnegie Hall?" the music teachers' mantra is always the same—"Practice, practice, practice." Telling students what to do repeatedly doesn't work.

Ask any coach or music teacher about their methods. Instead of telling their protégés what to do, the coach will run the plays and the music teacher will rehearse the songs over and over. After a game or concert, the coach and the music teacher immediately return to practicing.

Some coaches and music teachers have teams that play better and choruses that sing better than others. Some coaches and music teachers are able to work with average players and singers to produce award-winning teams and choirs. How do they do this? They practice, practice, practice . . . .

Similarly, some teachers have beautifully managed classrooms because they know how to teach and practice procedures. It is no surprise to learn that these teachers also inspire their students to achieve extraordinary results. **Classroom success lies in how you teach procedures.**

The Heart of *THE First Days of School*

Some say that the chapters on Classroom Management are the heart of *THE First Days of School*. These chapters have proved extremely helpful to teachers.

Much of *THE Classroom Management Book* has been written with these chapters in mind.

To fully understand the background to procedures and the process of teaching them, please read the unit on Classroom Management in *THE First Days of School*.

Difference

In theory, there is no difference between theory and practice. In practice, there is.

Yogi Berra ■ **Greatest catcher in baseball history**

The Three Steps to Teaching Classroom Procedures

Most teachers who fail at teaching procedures do so because they merely tell the procedure to the class. To teach something to someone, you model, explain, show examples, allow for discussion and questions, ask for a demonstration of an understanding of the teaching, and assess the demonstration for learning.

There is a procedure for teaching a procedure. All procedures can be implemented in three easy steps. Most importantly, teach the procedure step-by-step. **Teach, rehearse, and reinforce are the three steps used to teach every procedure shared in this book.**

TEACH

State, explain, model, and demonstrate the procedure.

REHEARSE

Students rehearse and practice the procedure under your supervision.

REINFORCE

Reteach, rehearse, practice, and reinforce the procedure until it becomes a habit—a routine.

How Effective Teachers Use the Three-Step Approach

TEACH — **Explain and model the procedure for the class.** Consider asking several students to role play the procedure. Show a video of a past class following the procedure. Some teachers create skits for selected procedures.

Students need to see what the procedure looks like or how it sounds. Some students need to experience how a procedure feels when it is being done correctly. Talk out loud while demonstrating and modeling the steps for each procedure.

Never assume your students know what you want them to do, or that they can "figure it out" on their own. Allow time for discussion, questions, and clarification.

REHEARSE — Break students into small groups to practice with each other. This is called guided practice. Then have them practice on their own. This is called independent practice. **As students practice the procedure, observe them in action.** This is how you determine if they can do it correctly.

Do not ask questions. To avoid embarrassment, some students will not respond to questions such as, "Is there anyone who does not know what to do?" or, "Are there any questions?"

If a procedure is not done correctly, there is no consequence. Remember, a procedure is not a rule. **You simply do what the good coaches and great music teachers do**—run the play or sing the song again. As an effective teacher, you rehearse the procedure again, and again.

Learning a procedure is similar to learning a skill, and some students need a great deal of practice to be able to use a skill accurately and automatically. There will be students who have problems with following directions: organizing, sequencing, listening, and focusing. For these students, keep them practicing until they are able to demonstrate they can do the procedure correctly.

The Facets of Practice

Perfect Practice Makes Perfect.
Sloppy Practice Makes Slop.
And, No Practice Makes Nothing.

REINFORCE — As you observe students practicing the procedures, keep an eye out for students who look lost or who are not following directions. Verbally coach these students and physically demonstrate what you would like them to do. Guide students with prompts and encouragement. Avoid showing frustration if some students cannot learn a procedure on the first try. Some students will need more coaching than others. Effective teachers are patient and understand the need to teach and reteach a procedure for reinforcement.

Acknowledge students that are following the steps of the procedure. **Encourage a student who follows a procedure by specifically affirming the action or deed, rather than by dispensing a generic word of affirmation.** Tell the student specifically what he or she did well. Say, "Marvin, I see you know where to put your book bag when you come to class," rather than "Good job, Marvin."

The Effective Teacher

Our DVD series, *The Effective Teacher*, shows how the three-step technique is used to teach the procedure for passing in papers. It can be seen in "Part 4: Procedures and Routines."

If Students Don't Follow Procedures

So, what if you teach a procedure and your students do not follow the procedure? What if your students blurt out their comments in class instead of waiting for their turn to speak?

The most common solution to this problem is

All procedures must be rehearsed.

Practice

What we do best or most perfectly is what we have most thoroughly learned by the longest practice.

Henry David Thoreau ■ American author, poet, and philosopher

Procedures

Plan for success
Rehearse and reinforce
Organize before students arrive
Costs nothing to do
Extra time gained for teaching and learning
Don't wait until next year; do it now
U make a difference in students' lives
Rehearse some more
Experience a class that hums with learning
Success is yours because procedures work!

This is where most teachers fail in establishing procedures in the classroom. They only tell students what to do, and they do not practice the remaining two steps (rehearse and reinforce) to teaching a procedure.

Then, if rehearsing and reinforcing do not result in the procedure, you have two choices:

1. Change the steps in the procedure and reteach.
2. Change the procedure to a rule.

By changing the procedure to a rule, you will need to create a consequence if the rule is not followed. Use this sparingly, if at all, as you will spend your time in confrontations and monitoring compliance, rather than being engaged in positive endeavors with your students.

Emphasize that the purpose of having classroom procedures is to ensure that everyone knows what to do. Students do not like surprises or being left in the dark. Having procedures creates a bright, safe, and consistent learning environment.

If you have a student who refuses to follow a procedure, do not escalate the situation by raising your voice. Be calm and patient.

Remind the student that a procedure is not a rule. There is no punishment if a procedure is not followed. Ask the student, "Do you have a part-time job? Tell me one thing you do at your job. Are there procedures in place to get the job done correctly?"

If the student does not have a part-time job, ask the student to tell you the procedure for opening a locker.

If lockers are not used at your school, ask the student, "Have you ever placed a phone call? What do you have to do in order to reach the person you are calling?"

Use the student's response to point out that procedures are not orders—they are steps used to accomplish a task.

Discipline is confrontational. **Procedures are non-confrontational and allow you to put your energy into creating opportunities for students to learn and achieve.**

 11 •))

Read this simple dialog to understand the words to use when teaching a procedure.

How to Praise

A very caring special education teacher with several autistic students could not figure out what was happening in her classroom. She thought she was delivering praise by telling the student, "Good job!" However, each time she praised a student, every student in class would chime in saying, "Good job, good job, good job." It took the teacher "forever" to calm down the class and get everyone back on task.

Do not issue generalized, complimentary praises that carry no specific personal meaning, such as "nice work," "great kid," or "good job." When students hear this, they have no idea who the teacher is referring to.

There is a more effective way to acknowledge that the student is on the right track. Throughout this book, you will see such phrases as "specific praise," "thank

and acknowledge what the student did," and "confirm the deed." (See *THE First Days of School* for more information on how to "Praise the Deed and Encourage the Student." This is the work of **Barbara Coloroso** and more recently of **Carol Dweck**.)

When you affirm a deed, the student knows that you are talking specifically about a task or action. You are affirming an accomplishment or encouraging appropriate behavior.

"Angela, you spelled all the words correctly. I know you can do it again." End with a smile, make eye contact with the student, and wait for confirmation. When you receive the student's confirmation say, "Thank you!" and, if appropriate, pat the student on the back or give a high-five.

"Class, thank you for walking behind each other and for not disturbing the other classrooms."

The Class Proceeded Without Me

Terri Schultz of Liberty Township, Ohio, experienced the dread that sends shivers up every teacher's spine—the substitute not showing up in the classroom as expected. Fortunately, Terri also experienced the joy every teacher dreams of—the class proceeded without any adult in the classroom.

" Procedures have worked for me and have made me look good with my students, their parents, my administrators, and peers. One night I was ill. I called for a sub and stayed home the next day. The next day, my students came to first period and there was no sub.

The students took out their daily work and began working. When most had finished, one student went to the front, used the "lesson key" and led the class through the answers. He then looked at the agenda for the schedule and had everyone take out their grammar homework. He used that key and went over the homework with them.

After twenty minutes into the period, they still didn't have a teacher. The self-appointed leader wrote out a pass for another student and sent him to the office to check on the teacher situation.

When the office was notified, there was concern and distress. The principal went to my classroom with the student. He told me when he entered the room, the students were seated and working on the current grammar lesson with the student leader working it on the overhead. The principal asked the student for the sub plans and started to leave the room.

The student leader then said, "Mr. Principal, could I have the plans back? **I haven't finished teaching yet.**"

Procedures and organization have empowered my students and me. Everyone knows what to do. I, also, have no referral problems since I've been using procedures.

How to Start the First Day and Every Day

Teacher greetings create a positive classroom climate
and can increase student engagement.

Greet Students Every Day

Your classroom management plan is ready. Your PowerPoint presentation has been created. Your seating assignments are done. You stand with eager anticipation, and a few butterflies, waiting for the school year to begin. You will have seven to seventeen seconds to make an impression on your students. What you do and how you do it will be the first thoughts your students will have of you.

Stand at the entrance of your classroom and greet each student. Put a smile on your face, extend your hand in greeting, and say, "Welcome, I'm so glad you're here!" Say it with sincerity. Say it with confidence. **Say it, each and every day of the school year.**

Your smile, your handshake, your warm greeting may be the only positive interaction a student has all day long. Let it come from you. **As you greet your students each day, you connect with them. You show that you care that they are in your classroom.**

Extending a greeting and being greeted is a life skill. You are greeted when you visit someone's home, arrive at a business, board an airplane, enter a place of worship, sign in at the doctor's office, or just see a friend. A greeting is the natural prelude for what is to come. It sets the stage for what will follow.

This sign in the entry at Robert Vela High School in Edinburg, Texas, greets the students.

The welcome students receive as they enter the school building and enter your classroom will set the tone of anticipation for the day and for the year.

In schools where students are greeted, discipline and bullying are diminished, and more importantly, students are on task and doing their classroom work.

This is the doorway of high school teacher Karen Rogers as she welcomes students to her classroom.

Greeter Leaders

At the **Staten Island School of Civic Leadership** in New York, when the K-2 students reach their classroom door, they find a teacher and a student waiting to greet them.

The students are greeted by a classmate and their teacher each day.

Loreta Anderson, one of the kindergarten teachers, explains that at the beginning of every school year, the primary teachers look for students who would like to be "Greeter Leaders" for the month. The teachers model the "greeter leader procedure" for the children. They teach the procedure with the teacher shaking hands with the greeter leaders and welcoming them to school. The children then demonstrate the procedure back to the teacher, so that they can check for understanding and tweaking during the first days of school.

Then, they guide two students to stand by the classroom door and offer their right hand to shake the hand of each classmate while saying, "Good Morning," as the classmates enter the classroom.

The student being greeted responds, "Good Morning," in return.

This routine is established early and continues throughout the school year with new "greeter leaders" rotating each month.

The Belief to Succeed

Brockton High School has 4,200 students and is the largest high school in Massachusetts and one of the largest in the nation. The campus has nine buildings and is the size of an aircraft carrier, yet the students feel comfortable at this high school because they are welcomed each morning.

The Research Behind Greeting Students

R. Allan Allday, University of Kentucky, did two studies based on the door greeter technique he read in **THE First Days of School**:

1. Effects of teacher greeting on student on-task behavior[1]

2. Effects of teacher greeting to increase speed to on-task engagement[2]

In both studies, observers clocked a select group of students over a period of time in a class period to see if they were on task or off task.

In the classroom where the teacher greeted the students at the door, there was an increase in student engagement from 45 percent to 72 percent. This was recorded when the students worked on the assignment and presented no discipline problems.

In the second study, **students got on task faster when they were greeted at the door**, in comparison to the control class that was not greeted.

Allan Allday says that in the classroom management class he teaches at the university, his primary focus is on changing teacher behavior, because teacher behavior (the hardest behavior to change in a classroom) impacts student behavior.

[1] *Journal of Applied Behavior Analysis*, 2007, 40, 317–320.

[2] *Journal of Applied Behavior Analysis*, 2011, 44, 393–396.

Susan Szachowicz, principal, and Charles Russell, teacher, stand ready to greet students as they enter the building to begin their day.

Susan Szachowicz, the principal, together with a teacher, greets the students each morning as they come through one of the four entrances to the school. She has been doing this every day for years and has watched the school, declared by the *Boston Globe* as one of the worst performing academic high schools with a 33 percent dropout rate, transform to a nationally-celebrated high school with a graduation rate of 97 percent.

At one time, Brockton had a culture that believed that every student had a right to fail, and fail they did. Today, there is a culture of consistency that says every student has a right to succeed. And, that message is delivered to the students each day they walk through the doors of the school and are greeted.

Welcome to Your Future

Darrell Cluck is a middle school teacher in Monroe, Louisiana, and he welcomes each of his students to his classroom by saying, "Welcome to our class. Welcome to your future." He also has student door greeters on a rotating basis stand with him to extend a greeting to their classmates. Discipline is not a problem in his classroom. His classroom is happy and friendly and filled with smiling students who know they are in a safe class where they can interact and learn together in an atmosphere of trust and respect.

Necessary to Each Other

When we seek connection, we restore the world to wholeness. Our seemingly separate lives become meaningful as we discover how truly necessary we are to each other.

Margaret Wheatley ▪ American writer and management consultant

Old Jewish Dictum

When you greet someone heartily with a warm smile and a friendly salutation,
all is well in that person's world,
if only for a fleeting moment.

The person feels a sense of validation,
that their existence in the universe has been acknowledged and recorded.

That they are known.

Darrell enthusiastically welcomes his students each day.

Every Classroom, Every Day

At **A. B. Combs** school in Raleigh, North Carolina, a student, along with the teacher, greet each student at the door. Once a week, a different student is selected to be the greeter, and they are all taught how to greet, how to shake hands, and how to respond. At A. B. Combs, there is a culture of consistency, as greeting each other is practiced in every classroom every day, year after year. A. B. Combs was once the lowest-performing school in the district. Today, it is known for academic excellence and personal leadership. And it begins with welcoming students every day in every classroom.

A greeting says, "I'm glad you're here."

Your Impact

There are students who must leave home without breakfast, who tolerate family discord, traverse past neighborhood gangs, endure bullying on the sidewalk or on the bus, and enter school through metal detectors. Are you the teacher who barely makes it to school

The Impact of Social Media

Social media has removed the physical element from making connections. With texting, tweeting, pinning, blogging, and liking, student interactions are with a screen and not with a body capable of empathy, comfort, care, and concern—for them.

The most important aspect of being an effective and successful teacher is with daily connections that show the students you can help them learn and succeed.

on time and scrambles to organize yourself and your lessons while the students are left staring and waiting and waiting for you to begin the class? Your frenzy has just set the tone for what is to follow.

Or, are you the teacher who is organized and ready with activities and lessons to engage the students in learning the moment they enter the classroom, who is a model of caring, calm, and stability as you welcome students into the class? Your constancy has just set the tone for what is to follow.

**You may be the first stable adult your students will have at this point in their journey.
You may be their beacon for a brighter tomorrow.**

 12 •))

Students want to know who you are and the answers to these seven questions.

Connect Every Day

While it's important to connect with students, you must do so in the context and confines of the classroom. Effective teachers do this by having at least one meaningful interaction with every student every class period. And they do it in the normal flow of teaching and learning.

David Ginsburg ▪ Academic Coach

It's in the Bag

Besides greeting students at the door on the first day of school, **Kim Scroggin** of Artesia, New Mexico, prepares a special welcome for each student's desk on the first day of school. Her organization and care alleviate the anxiety her young students feel. By the end of the day, the students know they are in the hands of a kind, supportive teacher.

Each desk is ready for the student's first day of school. The student's name and assigned number are written on the bus secured to the center of the desk. (This is the name and number the students will use as name and number go on all papers. With papers in numerical order, Kim can quickly see whose work is missing.)

The birthday cake die-cut is used to graph the birthdays for a math activity to teach graphing and to see who has birthdays and when.

The folder on each desk with the name and number is where all completed assignments are placed each day. (After the start of the school year, they will learn the procedure of putting papers in baskets by the teacher's desk.)

The "Guess Who" is a folded paper that will be used as a get-acquainted activity. (The students are to write three clues about themselves—hobbies, activities over the summer, sports, family, pets, movies, books—and then write their name under the paper. The papers are placed in a basket, each student picks and reads one to the class, and the rest of the students try to guess who it is.)

The yellow "Give Me Five" is the procedure for coming to attention. (See *THE First Days of School* for more information on this procedure.)

The Welcome Bag has 11 items that are symbolic of how they will be treated and how they are to treat each other. Along with the items is a sheet of paper that gives the meaning behind each item.

WELCOME TO YOUR NEW CLASSROOM!
THE ITEMS IN THIS BAG HAVE SPECIAL MEANINGS.
ENJOY!

The **cotton ball** reminds you that this room is full of kind words and warm feelings.

The **sticker** reminds you that we will all stick together and help each other this year.

The **rubber band** reminds you to hug someone.

The **penny** reminds you that you are valuable and special.

The **star** reminds you to shine and always try your best!

The **tissue** reminds you to help dry someone's tears.

The **toothpick** reminds you to pick out the good qualities in your classmates and in yourself.

The **bandage** reminds you to heal hurt feelings in your friends and in yourself.

The **gold thread** reminds you that friendship ties our hearts together.

The **eraser** reminds you that everyone makes mistakes and that is okay.

The **Life Saver** reminds you that you can come to me if you need someone to talk to.

WE ARE GOING TO HAVE A GREAT YEAR!

LOVE,
MRS. SCROGGIN

The items in the paper bag are taken out and discussed on the first day of school. A connection is forged with students as Kim lets them know they can count on her and each other.

PROCEDURES

PROCEDURES

The Start of Class Routine

By establishing a morning or class routine, students will assume ownership of their learning. Students who know what to do in the classroom produce results; results produce learning and achievement.

1. Remove jacket or coat. your locker.

2. Empty knapsack or bag.

3. Put runners or inside shoes on.

4. Walk into the classroom quietly.

5. Have 2 sharpened pencils and necessary books ready.

6. Hand in all completed homework.

THE **SOLUTION**

The beginning of class routine sets the tone and pace for the rest of the period or school day. Successfully completing a routine the first few moments of class time will determine how productive the day will be.

This procedure provides these opportunities:

1. Students given responsibilities from the moment they enter the classroom

2. Students waste little instructional time by following a consistent routine

3. Teacher's time freed to welcome students as they enter the classroom

THE **BACKGROUND**

A routine is a process or action that is done automatically with no prompting. A morning routine is what students do on their own to prepare for class to start. Start each class or day with a routine in place so that learning can begin the first minute of the school day. The bell does not begin the class. The teacher does not begin the class. The students begin the class on their own by doing their routine. This process becomes as automatic as looking behind before pulling out of a parking space.

Preparing for the start of class is just as important as preparing plans for the daily lesson. Students do not need down time at the beginning of class—students are ready to learn the moment they step into the classroom. The effective teacher has a deliberate plan for beginning each class or period. The teacher sets the pace for the day's learning and gets students working even before the bell rings.

THE **PROCEDURE STEPS**

Establish a morning or class routine. Routines lend structure to our daily lives. Use some examples to show how routines are a part of our lives. Musicians and athletes warm up before playing or working out. Warming up prevents injury, helps focus on the task ahead, and leads to a better performance.

Similarly, **effective teachers establish a routine to prepare students for the school day or class period**.

In an elementary classroom, this is a typical morning routine:

- Enter the classroom quietly.
- Remove coat or jacket and hang it up.
- Empty backpack or book bag.
- Get two sharpened pencils, textbooks, and materials ready.

- Hand in completed homework.
- Read the agenda for the day.
- Begin the bellwork assignment.

Nile Wilson has her students follow a start of class routine in her high school orchestra class.

OUR ORCHESTRA CLASS ROUTINE

- Quickly retrieve your instrument, music folder, and pencil.
- Be in your seat when the tardy bell rings.
- Follow the warm-up routine led by the warm-up monitor.
- Tune your instrument according to the guidelines.
- Participate in solfège exercises.
- Wait for further instructions from your director.

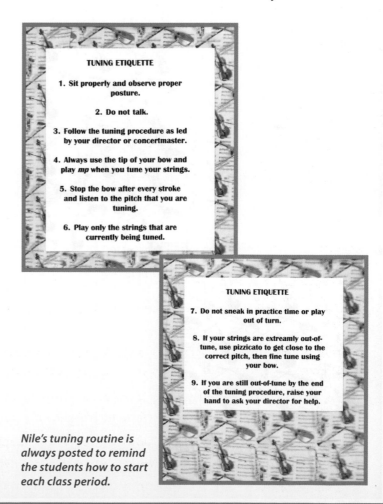

TUNING ETIQUETTE

1. Sit properly and observe proper posture.

2. Do not talk.

3. Follow the tuning procedure as led by your director or concertmaster.

4. Always use the tip of your bow and play *mp* when you tune your strings.

5. Stop the bow after every stroke and listen to the pitch that you are tuning.

6. Play only the strings that are currently being tuned.

TUNING ETIQUETTE

7. Do not sneak in practice time or play out of turn.

8. If your strings are extreamly out-of-tune, use pizzicato to get close to the correct pitch, then fine tune using your bow.

9. If you are still out-of-tune by the end of the tuning procedure, raise your hand to ask your director for help.

Nile's tuning routine is always posted to remind the students how to start each class period.

TEACH

Introduce students to the concept of the morning or class routine. Discuss why people stretch before starting a workout, musicians tune their instruments before playing, or chefs chop and prepare food before cooking. Teach students that every morning or class, they should follow the class routine to start work immediately.

If they forget what the routine is, a copy is posted. Show students where they will find the daily routine when entering the classroom.

The students in Ayesa Contreras' classroom in Cozumel, Mexico, go through seven items each morning in preparation for the start of learning.

REHEARSE

Model what the morning routine looks like and how it sounds. Have student volunteers model the morning routine and ask them to identify each step as they do it.

Have the entire class exit the classroom. Step-by-step, walk the class through the morning routine. Acknowledge students who are following the procedure correctly and redirect those students who are not.

REINFORCE

The next day, greet your students at the door and remind them about the morning routine so they can put it into practice. **It is helpful to have the morning routine posted <u>outside</u> the classroom door until it becomes a routine for the students.**

If the students fail to follow the morning routine, rehearse the steps with the class again so they will be successful the following day. Repeat the process until the routine is followed.

Teaching Independence

My greatest responsibility is to empower the students to become as independent as possible. Once the students are able to perform the 'getting started' routine on their own, that allows me to work individually with students who might need extra help with lessons from the previous day.

Renee Tomita ■ Oak Brook, Illinois

Morning Opening Procedure

I am a first-grade teacher in Central Islip, New York. As soon as my students enter my classroom they begin their morning opening procedures. The students empty their backpacks. Traveling folders are emptied of notes, lunch money, etc., and placed in a basket under the mailboxes. Notes are placed in my note basket.

Lunch money, snack money, or milk money is placed in the appropriate basket. If children have loose money they place it in an envelope, seal it, write their name on the envelope, and place it in the correct basket. All lunches and snacks are placed on the back counter.

Backpacks are placed in large plastic bins under the coat hooks. Coat hooks are marked with the children's names. **The children should not have to return to their backpacks until the end of the day if they have followed these procedures.**

Once they are unpacked, children pick up their morning work. This is usually a page with simple directions so the students can work independently. They are allowed to ask their tablemates for assistance and they can work together quietly on this work. If they complete the assignment they can quietly read a book while they are waiting for us to go over the morning work.

While the students are doing all of the above, I am taking attendance silently. I send the attendance down to the main office with the helper of the day. The helper also picks up the snack milk at this time.

The helper of the day picks an assistant for the day. The helper of the day does everything in my classroom for that day—runs errands, leads the line, does the calendar, reads the morning message, leads the phonics drill, and many other tasks for the day. **Helpers are chosen on a rotating basis, alphabetically by last name.** *This alleviates the time-consuming task of creating job charts and rotating jobs on a regular basis.*

Also during this time the principal comes over the intercom. The students stop what they are doing and stand and recite the Pledge of Allegiance. The school rules are also recited at this time. When we created our classroom rules, they were very similar to the school rules. The children are able to recite the school rules, which are reinforced on a daily basis.

I can't stress enough how important procedures and routines are. Many people do not believe that young children can follow procedures and routines. **My classroom is proof that it works.** *This is something I stress to parents and caregivers at Meet-the-Teacher Night. All of their children are capable of following procedures and routines in the classroom, as well as at home.*

Maureen Conley ■ Bohemia, New York

The Agenda

Posting an agenda allows students to know what to expect throughout the day. It prevents any surprises, which can easily distract different types of learners. It helps students and teachers to stay focused and on task and to transition smoothly to the next activity.

MR. GULLE
WEDNESDAY, FEBRUARY 28

DO NOW

On a piece of paper to be submitted . . .

1. Please identify 3 Ancient Roman Emperors that we have learned about so far.

2. For <u>each</u> emperor, describe the impact his actions had on the Roman Empire.

TODAY'S SCHEDULE

1. DO NOW assignment.

2. Discussion/Review of DO NOW assignment.

3. Republic/Empire Venn diagram (as a class)

4. Use material on U.S. government to compare to Rome.

TODAY'S OBJECTIVE

COMPARE and CONTRAST the governments of the Roman Republic, the Roman Empire, and the modern United States.

THE **SOLUTION**

You can get students on task the moment they enter the classroom. **Post an agenda that lets students know the sequence of events for the day.** It tells students what will happen, at what time it will happen, and why it will happen.

This procedure eliminates these problems:

1. Students wandering around the classroom because there is nothing to do

2. Students asking, "What are we doing today?"

3. Students transitioning poorly between activities

THE **BACKGROUND**

The most important detail for the teacher to establish at the start of school is CONSISTENCY. Students do not welcome surprises or embrace disorganization. Post a daily agenda where everyone can see it. Students will know exactly what will be happening throughout class—what they are to do, when they are to do it, and the purpose or focus of the lesson.

In the business world, employees start work without prompting from their supervisors. Employees are able to start work because they know what to do.

An agenda includes the day's schedule, an opening assignment, and a lesson objective so students are clear about what they are to learn, when they are to learn it, and why they are learning it. Students become responsible for starting the class or period when an agenda is posted.

1. An agenda enables students to be self-starters who are on task the moment they enter the classroom

2. An agenda empowers students with the keys to their own learning, so they don't ask, "What are we doing today?"

Your first priority when class begins is not to take attendance.

It is to get students to work.

There are three parts to an agenda. Each of these parts is important and will help maximize students' on-task time.

1. **Schedule**
2. **Opening assignment**
3. **Learning objective**

Students thrive in organized environments with routines and consistency. A daily agenda lists the day's subjects and activities in chronological order. Posting the daily agenda allows the teacher and students to refer to it throughout the day. This will help keep the teacher and students on task, while facilitating transitions from one activity to the next.

If there is no posted agenda, schedule or program, students will enter the classroom and wander around aimlessly until the teacher announces, "The bell has rung. It is time to sit down and be quiet." Students quickly learn that all the teacher wants them to do is to "sit down and be quiet." Soon the students will ask, "What are we doing today?"

When creating a daily agenda, you may choose not to include the start and end times for each subject or activity. Otherwise, students will watch the clock and continually remind you it is time to start the next activity. However, there are some instances when posting the times may be helpful. These include special classes or events students must attend at specific times, such as library time, school performances, and general assemblies.

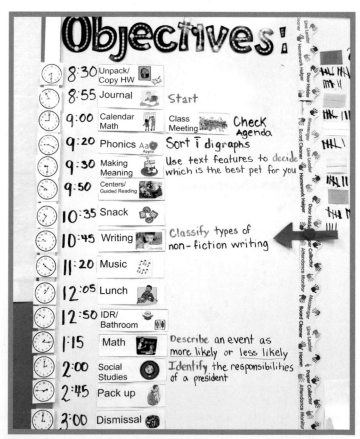

Journaling and silent reading are common opening activities used by teachers to engage the students in learning.

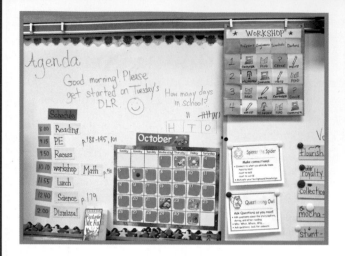

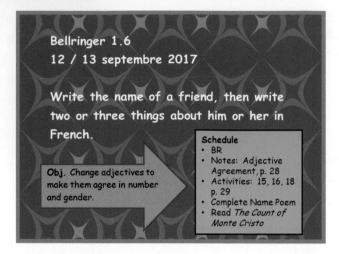

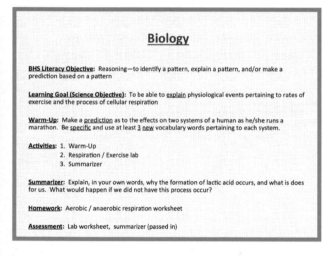

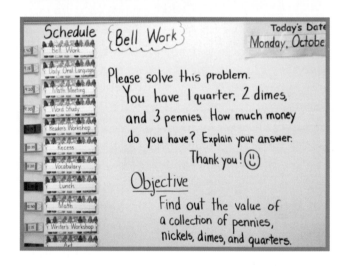

Biology

BHS Literacy Objective: Reasoning—to identify a pattern, explain a pattern, and/or make a prediction based on a pattern

Learning Goal (Science Objective): To be able to explain physiological events pertaining to rates of exercise and the process of cellular respiration

Warm-Up: Make a prediction as to the effects on two systems of a human as he/she runs a marathon. Be specific and use at least 3 new vocabulary words pertaining to each system.

Activities: 1. Warm-Up
2. Respiration / Exercise lab
3. Summarizer

Summarizer: Explain, in your own words, why the formation of lactic acid occurs, and what is does for us. What would happen if we did not have this process occur?

Homework: Aerobic / anaerobic respiration worksheet

Assessment: Lab worksheet, summarizer (passed in)

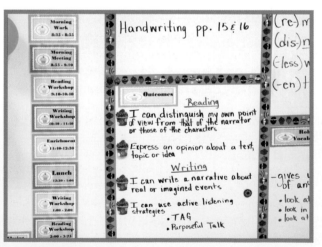

Today's Objective: To identify possible causes for the fish kill in Riverwood

Do Now:
1. Read the article on pages 4 – 5 in the textbook
2. Use the Post-it notes to mark words or phrases you don't understand

Today's Schedule:
1. Explain unknown words and confusing information in the article
2. Contrast facts vs. opinions in the article
3. Write a hypothesis about the cause of the fish kill

HW: A.2 Making Decisions: Uses of Water

These sample agendas are from different grade levels, but they all have three parts in common: 1) a schedule for the period or day, 2) an opening assignment for students to work on as soon as they enter the classroom, and 3) an objective for the day's lesson.

Modify your agenda with the date, period, class, or whatever else the students need for understanding what will be happening during their time with you.

Students can assist and be a part of the agenda routine. In elementary schools, at the end of the day the student with the classroom job of "board monitor" wipes the day's agenda off the board.

After the students leave, refer to the next day's lesson plans and post the next day's agenda.

In a high school classroom, the "white board technician" can replace the agenda on the existing white board template.

THE PROCEDURE STEPS

Post a daily agenda on the first day of school and each day thereafter. Designate a consistent classroom location for posting the agenda for the day or class period and post it consistently in the same location each day. Teach students to check the designated location for the agenda the minute they enter the classroom.

TEACH

Show the students samples of meeting agendas, graduation programs, theater playbills, or anything that illustrates a sequence of events. Use these samples to explain there will be a similar agenda posted in the classroom each day so students know what to expect.

Show the students how to read the agenda. Tell them to glance at the schedule first, look at what learning is going to take place with each objective, and then begin the opening assignment.

Tell students that the day's schedule and lesson objective will be explained in detail after the opening assignment is completed. **The students' first activity each day in the classroom will always be to complete the opening assignment.**

When it is time to explain the agenda, read each subject area or activity in the order that it will occur during the day. Highlight any special or unusual events so students know to expect something new.

I Would Know What to Expect

A staff meeting was held for a student who was being expelled because he had been in trouble all year. The principal turned to the student and asked, "What could we as teachers have done to make your year here a success? We feel we have failed because you have failed. What could we have done differently?"

The student looked at the teachers and said, "If you had all been like Mrs. Butler, I think I could have made it.

"I know everyone thinks she is strict, but I never got into trouble in her class. I knew exactly what to do from the minute I entered her room. She always starts with a daily quiz. There is a schedule, and she makes it very clear that we are to get right down to business—just like at my part-time job. **If all my classes were organized in the same way, I'd always have known what was expected.**"

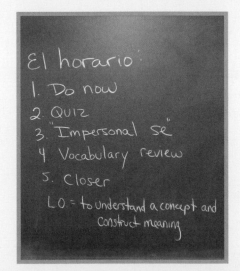

El horario:
1. Do now
2. Quiz
3. "Impersonal se"
4. Vocabulary review
5. Closer
LO = to understand a concept and construct meaning

REHEARSE

Assemble students at the door to practice entering the classroom. Instruct students to begin their start of class routine. In all probability, the routine will say to look for the agenda. Regardless, check the agenda and pay attention to the schedule, objective, and opening assignment.

Emphasize that the agenda will be posted before they enter the classroom and inform them that it will be in the same location each day. Remind students that there is no need to ask, "What are we doing next?" Students can simply refer to the agenda.

Ask students to look at the agenda and then to start on the opening assignment. Check that students are doing the opening assignment.

REINFORCE

Refer to the agenda and lesson objective during the period or throughout the day.

In the first week of school, draw students' attention to the agenda just before signaling a transition from one activity to the next. This reinforces that the classroom is being run on an agenda, and that there are no surprises in the classroom—only consistency and routines.

Point out that even if the teacher is absent, students will be able to explain to the substitute teacher what needs to be done. They do this by referring to the day's posted agenda.

Agendas Are a Part of Life

Why is an agenda posted in the classroom each day? If students ask this question, explain that agendas with schedules, opening assignments, and objectives play a crucial part in our daily lives— whether or not we are conscious of them.

Agendas: Meetings have agendas; sporting events have agendas.

Schedules: Airports have estimated flight arrival and departure times displayed on monitors; television programs are scheduled in regular time slots; movie theatres list the show times of movies; and doctors have scheduled appointments.

Opening Assignments: Employees start working the moment they arrive at their workplace; actors start working when the curtain goes up; and every musician plays when the conductor gives the downbeat.

Objective: In a court of law, the purpose of the case being tried is stated at the beginning of the trial; before boarding an airplane the flight's destination is always clearly stated.

There Is Only One Start to the Day and Year

In tennis, you are allowed two serves for each point. If your first serve is less than perfect, you are allowed one more serve to make it right.

In track and field, if you come out of the starting blocks before the race begins, a false-start alert is sounded and the runners return to their starting blocks to start all over again.

In teaching, however, you get only one shot at the first day of school. What you do on the first day of school will determine your success or failure for the rest of the school year. **Knowing how to structure a successful first day of school will set the stage for an effective classroom and a successful school year.**

Similarly, how students start the day or class period will determine how effective the remainder of the day will be. **Knowing how to structure a successful start to each day of the school year will set the tone for a productive work day—every day.**

The Freedom to Produce Results

The students in **Shannon Dipple's** classroom in Ohio know what to do from the moment they enter the classroom. These procedures have been taught, modeled, and practiced so that every morning, these procedures are completed *within the first two minutes.*

From the second students walk into the room, they have a morning routine to accomplish. They unpack their bags, turn in homework, sign up for lunch, turn in Teacher Mail, sharpen their pencils, and get straight to reading.

"From the moment students walk through the door, they know I expect results. More importantly, they know **what** results I want because I have left nothing to chance. They have been taught **how** to work towards my expectations," says Shannon.

A typical day could begin with a math bellwork assignment. Students who finish early can work on a challenge problem. There is no wasted time in Shannon's classroom.

Shannon has created procedures that **allow her classroom to run efficiently, free from chaos, and give her the freedom to produce results**.

This routine is consistent every single day.

"Every moment counts," says Shannon, **"so every moment is defined by a procedure."**

In addition to having time to produce results for her students, Shannon has time to host a website at www.k5chalkbox.com where she shares insights from her more than 20 years in the classroom.

THE **PROCEDURE**

An Opening Assignment

A sign of a well-managed classroom is when students enter and start work immediately—without prompting from the teacher. Posting a daily, opening assignment encourages students to fall into the routine of working, from the first minute of the school day.

THE **SOLUTION**

Posting an opening assignment for the start of class means students are on task from the first minute they enter the classroom. **An opening assignment gets students to work before the bell has rung.**

This procedure provides these opportunities:

1. Classroom time maximized
2. Students responsible for starting the learning for the day or class period
3. An atmosphere of learning established for the rest of the school day or class period

THE **BACKGROUND**

Every minute of the school day needs to be used effectively. Students are more productive if they have an assignment to work on as soon as they step into the classroom each day. This sets the tone for the class period or the day—the students are there to work and learn.

An opening assignment is short and manageable for students to work on independently—without requiring further explanation or assistance. These are some ideas for opening assignments:

- Completing a project that was started the day before
- Keyboard drills
- Handwriting practice
- A daily math review
- A daily oral language page
- A journal prompt
- A silent reading assignment
- A research activity

The opening assignment is not busy work. The task is a review of curriculum material, the application of a concept, an extension of a previous lesson, or a mind-engaging activity. Opening assignments are brief and generally take about five to ten minutes to complete.

The opening assignment is posted before the students enter the classroom and is posted in the same location every day. Finding the assignment is not a guessing game. Establish consistency by having the assignment waiting for the students and placing it in the same location each day.

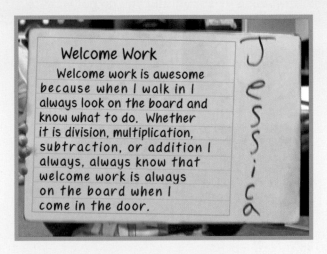

> **Welcome Work**
> Welcome work is awesome because when I walk in I always look on the board and know what to do. Whether it is division, multiplication, subtraction, or addition I always, always know that welcome work is always on the board when I come in the door.

Welcome Work Is Awesome

Jenn Hopper of Pollok, Texas, calls her opening assignment "Welcome Work." One day the Welcome Work assignment for the students was to tell the teacher what Welcome Work was.

Fourth-grade student, Jessica, says it is awesome because Welcome Work . . .

1. is always posted on the board, and
2. she always knows what to do.

Students will recognize and accept consistency when it is part of the classroom culture.

Opening assignments are commonly referred to as bellwork, bell work, or Bellwork. Choose a term that works best for you and your students.

- Bellwork
- Bell work
- Bell Activity
- Bell Ringer
- Prime Time
- Get Going Activity
- DOL (Daily Oral Language)
- Morning Work
- Warm Ups
- Do Now
- Opener
- Mind Matters
- Sponge Activity
- Write Now

Opening assignments are not graded. Grading generates anxiety—something you do not want to create for your students at the start of the day.

A daily opening assignment is posted for students to work on the moment they enter the classroom.

Classroom time lost is never regained. Imagine spending the first five minutes of class taking attendance, collecting homework, answering questions, and just settling in for the school day. Over the course of a year in a self-contained classroom, three days of instructional time are lost—forever.

Apply this same concept to a junior or high school setting with five periods per day. Over the course of a year, one month of instructional time is lost—never to be regained.

Every second counts in the school day. Engaging the students in learning the moment they enter your classroom maximizes the time you have to teach.

THE PROCEDURE STEPS

Each day, before the students enter the classroom, post the opening assignment in the same location. Students will know where to look for it so they can begin their day. Teach the procedure for the opening assignments on the first day of school.

The Most Dramatic Effect on My Teaching

Perhaps the most significant practice with the most dramatic effect on my teaching was the 'bellwork.' It impacted my classes in many positive ways. I never had problems with students coming late or coming into the class in a disruptive manner.

I had the role of Learning Leader at my school and shared how effective my daily procedures had created consistency in my classroom. Many of the teachers on my science team implemented daily bellwork and some of the other procedures that I used.

After seventeen years teaching and now four years as Assistant Principal at my current school, I have seen 'bellwork' in senior high science classrooms expand into many schools across the system.

Mark Lewis ▪ Centennial High School, Calgary, Alberta

TEACH

As students enter the classroom, tell them where they can find their first opening assignment. Have students locate their seats and start to work immediately on the assignment.

Tell students that the opening assignment is done independently and that all of the directions needed to complete the assignment are posted with the assignment.

Once students have had a few minutes to work on their opening assignment, explain that a new assignment will be posted at the same location each time they come to class.

Depending on directions, students will either turn in the completed assignment or keep it at their desks to review as a class.

REHEARSE

As students work on their first opening assignment, praise them for following the procedure correctly.

On the second day of school, as students enter the classroom, remind them beforehand to find the opening assignment as soon as they are seated and to start work immediately.

Commend students who are following the correct procedure, while observing and redirecting other students if necessary.

REINFORCE

Observe and comment on how students are working on their opening assignments. Thank the class each day for following the procedure.

If a student is struggling to follow the procedure, work individually with the student. Walk the student through the steps of how to begin the opening assignment procedure. Ask the student the next day if your help is needed to follow the procedure or is the student able to follow the procedure independently. Keep working with the student until independence is achieved.

Bellwork at the End of the Day

When one third of your class departs thirty minutes before the rest of the class at the end of the day, how do you capitalize on that lost time?

Elizabeth Janice of Temperance, Michigan, does the opening assignment at the end of the day, instead of at the start of the day.

She says, "I use bellwork in reverse order. The students who stay with me at the end of the day start on their opening assignment for the next morning. The children who leave early take their bellwork assignments home to prepare for the next day in class.

"Without this procedure, I would be cheating my students out of thirty minutes of learning time each day."

Bellwork Reduces Behavior Problems

As a Behavioral ESE teacher, I try to keep every day as routine as possible to ensure my students with the stability and predictability they require.

I begin each day by standing at my classroom door to greet each of my students. I welcome them into the classroom, and remind them their "Bellwork" is on their desk. By already having their bellwork on their desk, it sets the momentum for the day. While my students are busy working on their bellwork, I have the opportunity to conference with any student who is having difficulties at home or with school.

I have found keeping my students engaged on a defined task, from the time they enter the classroom, reduces behavior problems and overall produces a more productive day.

Blake Germaine ■ Sebring, Florida

Bellringer Times Three

Richard Dubé teaches 7th and 8th grades in Chattanooga, Tennessee. His Bellringer consists of three, short activities to engage the students in learning every day. The three activities are a quote, a warm-up exercise, and a puzzle.

The students in **Richard Dubé's** class begin each class period with three activities. In less than ten minutes his students have worked on literacy, reviewed curriculum content, and revved up their brains for the day. The activities are completed in this order:

1. Quote

Upon arrival, students turn to an open spot in their notebooks (left-hand page for student-created material) and write about the daily quote posted on the board. These requirements for completing these tasks are taught in the few weeks of school, until they become routines for the students.

- Must be three to five complete sentences
- Cannot be IDK (I don't know) or IDU (I don't understand) statements
- Can be, "I think this quote means that . . ."
- Can be, "I agree with this quote because . . ."
- Can be, "I disagree with this quote because . . ."
- Can be, "I am uncertain regarding this quote because . . ."
- Can be, "I think this is a metaphor for . . ."
- Can be, "I am not sure I understand but I think it means that . . ."
- Can be, "I think this relates to this class because . . ."

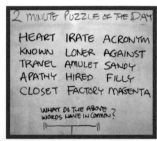

Measurement Warm Up
3/23

1. What is the base SI unit for distance?
2. What is the base SI unit for mass?
3. What is the base SI unit for density?
4. Density refers to the relationship between an object's _____ and its _____.
5. Fresh water has a density of _____ gram / cubic centimeter.

2. Warm-Up Exercise

After finishing the quote response, students move to the Warm-Up exercise showing on the screen.

Answers are checked as part of class discussion and students self-correct their answers. Students keep the Warm-Up exercises in their binders, filed in the appropriate section.

3. Two-Minute Puzzle of the Day

The final activity in the opening assignment sequence is a two-minute puzzle. These are logic, word, number, or visual puzzles. The solution is given as part of class discussion. Students keep the puzzle filed in their binders.

While completing the Bellringer tasks, student voices are quiet, "inside voices" with a respectful tone.

 13))))

Richard shares some of the favorite quotes he has used as part of his Bellringer activity.

4 THE **PROCEDURE**

Taking Attendance

Students of any age can be responsible for completing a task, provided the task is taught to them. Teaching students the task of counting themselves present for learning gives you time to greet students at the door without reducing instructional time.

THE **SOLUTION**

Instructional time is not used for any administrative tasks at the start of the day. **Taking attendance, lunch count, and checking homework can be accomplished as the students prepare for learning.** Non-verbal methods are more efficient than the traditional roll call and allow learning to begin without delay.

This procedure resolves issues and promotes these opportunities:

1. Streamlines the process of taking the attendance and other opening tasks
2. Allows the teacher to maximize learning time
3. Cultivates responsibility in students

THE **BACKGROUND**

The typical scenario of a classroom, where the teacher calls out each student's name and waits for a response, is a familiar one—and a misuse of instructional time. The school day is a busy one, with a myriad of routine administrative tasks. When teachers streamline the administrative tasks, they can focus on the most important goal—teaching. Reach that goal by establishing a procedure to give students the responsibility of being a part of taking their own attendance.

The methods to take attendance are many. Often, other information is gathered as part of the attendance procedure. The goal of this procedure is to streamline all administrative tasks so no instructional time is used. Modify it to fit your classroom situation, so you and your students can benefit from a task that takes care of itself in a short amount of time.

THE **PROCEDURE STEPS**

This is the procedure **Sarah Jondahl** uses in her classroom to take attendance and to get a lunch count. Young students thrive when given an important responsibility.

To help students learn to take their own attendance and lunch count, make a name card for each student. Write the child's name on a card with VELCRO® attached to the back. Mount the VELCRO®-backed name cards on a fabric-covered bulletin board, or on the students' cubbies.

Prepare two baskets, one labeled Home Lunch, and the second labeled School Lunch—or any variation that fits your situation.

Place the baskets on a counter, desk, or bookshelf. These baskets will stay in this location each day of the school year.

On the first day of school, take attendance and lunch count in the traditional way and teach the new procedure, so students can assume this responsibility the next time they enter the classroom.

Include in the classroom job roster the task of reposting the VELCRO® name cards to the board at the end of the day.

Once students learn this procedure, the teacher's time is clear to greet the children in the morning, answer questions, check for notes from home, complete the attendance count, and so on.

TEACH

1. After taking attendance and lunch counts in the traditional way, tell the class this is the last time you will be doing that job. From now on, it will be their responsibility. Explain the importance of accurate daily attendance and lunch counts.

2. Point out the location where all the students' name cards are posted. Show how the name cards can easily be removed by pulling on the VELCRO® backs.

3. Show students where the two lunch baskets are kept in the classroom.

4. Tell the class that this procedure is their first responsibility when they enter the classroom in the morning. Upon entering the classroom, they must

   - remove their name card;
   - place their name card in the correct lunch basket;
   - go to their desks; and
   - start the opening assignment.

5. Explain that once everyone is seated, the students whose name cards are left on the VELCRO® board will be marked absent for the day. Then show how the lunch count will be taken by counting the number of cards in the School Lunch basket.

6. Tell students they are to handle only their own cards and not their friend's card. Explain that it is OK to remind friends if they forget to check in when entering the classroom. But, friends must be responsible for moving their own name card to the appropriate basket.

7. Assign a student the task of reposting the VELCRO® name cards to the board at the end of the day.

Check-In Station

Provide each student with a pattern, such as a sport's ball, animal, fruit, or star. Allow the students to personalize the pattern. Laminate the pattern, punch a hole in the top, and hang it on a bulletin board with a push pin.

Divide the bulletin board into sections for lunch options. As part of the opening routine, when the students enter the classroom, they are to take their pattern and move it to the proper section. **At a glance, you can take the attendance and complete a quick lunch count.**

REHEARSE

Select a few students to demonstrate this procedure. Line them up outside the classroom door and have them walk in as if they are just arriving to class. Ask them to find their appropriate name cards, remove them, and place them in the correct lunch basket.

Remind them, as they continue on to their seats, that they are to begin their opening assignment.

Once they are seated, demonstrate how you will take roll and lunch counts for the day.

Compliment students who do this procedure correctly by telling them what they did to follow the procedure as instructed.

Rotate the practice group of students until everyone has had a chance to remove their name card from the board and place it in the appropriate basket.

REINFORCE

Remind students at the end of the school day what the procedure is for entering the classroom each morning.

The next morning, as you greet students entering the classroom, remind groups of students about their name cards.

Do not threaten punishment or give a consequence for forgetting this procedure. If you see a name card still posted and see the student is in class, quietly walk up to the student and say, "What's the procedure for taking attendance and lunch count?" Watch as the student goes up and moves the name card to the appropriate basket. As the rest of the class works on their opening assignment, affirm with a silent thumbs-up or a wink of the eye that the task was completed correctly.

The Benefit of Assigned Seating

When desks are assigned to students and there is consistency in who occupies that seat, taking attendance can be done at a glance.

An empty seat equates to a name. Three empty seats says that three students are absent—the three students who sit in those seats consistently each day.

A laminated seating chart for each group of students makes the attendance taking task easy as marks are made on the chart and can be later transferred to a permanent record keeping system.

Connecting and Checking Homework

Christopher Gagliardi teaches mathematics at **Brockton High School** in Massachusetts. Each class period begins in the same way, every day:

1. There is an opening assignment posted on the screen.
2. Students put their homework in the upper right corner of their desk.
3. Chris walks around the room and checks off the homework, simultaneously taking attendance and making a connecting comment to each student.

Chris has accomplished three tasks all in a few minutes at the beginning of class. While students are at work, he has taken attendance, checked for homework, and connected personally with each student.

No Need to Scramble for Lunch

Carolyn Twohill, a former principal at **Hendricks Elementary School** in Tucson, Arizona, started a procedure where students put their lunches in a class basket when they come to school. **Peter Wells,** the next principal, carried on the culture of consistency that had been built.

Two students from each class are assigned on a weekly basis to be lunch monitors. Just before lunch time, these two students take the basket to a designated location in the hallway. Their baskets join others in the hallway.

When the bell rings for lunch, there is no mad scramble in class to find and fight for "My Lunch."

The students go to the class basket and take out their lunch. There is a teacher watching the procedure, which takes but a few minutes.

At the end of lunch time, lunch boxes are returned to the class basket, and the class monitors return the basket to the classroom.

130 Students and No Time Wasted

With 130 students entering the classroom for marching band instruction, **Becky Hughes** of Wichita, Kansas, is standing at the door greeting each of them. Her students are responsible for taking their own attendance and getting ready for rehearsal to begin the class.

Becky has an Attendance Board with the name of each student on a musical note. As students enter the classroom, they go directly to the Attendance Board and remove their name (and only their name) and place it in the appropriate envelope next to the board. From there, they get their instruments and music out of their lockers and get ready for rehearsal to begin.

I'm Here – Now What Do I Do?

- in the hall
  BEFORE you come into the Band Room

- and put it in the appropriate folder

- for the order for the day

- to start rehearsal at 7:50

Once the bell rings indicating it's time for class to begin, Becky quickly goes over any announcements and begins warm ups while her Senior Drum Major takes down any names that are still on the Attendance Board. The student scans the room to see if those students are indeed absent, forgot to take their name down, or arrived late.

Names are then placed in envelopes marked absent, forgot, or tardy, and the envelopes are placed on Becky's desk.

A student returns all musical notes to the Attendance Board at the end of the day.

Dismissing the Class

Implementing a two-minute dismissal procedure ensures the classroom is clean, orderly, and ready for the next group of students. The procedure also prevents students from disregarding the teacher and rushing out the door the moment the bell rings. A dismissal procedure sends students out of class in a positive state of mind.

> STOP! LOOK!
> Before you go home,
> check these items:
> 1. Is my desk clean?
> 2. Is my desk area clean?
> 3. Do I have my homework?

THE **SOLUTION**

The bell does not dismiss the class. The teacher dismisses the class. **When a procedure is in place for dismissing the class, learning time is maximized, the classroom is in order, and students exit the classroom with a teacher-led cue.**

This procedure solves these issues:

1. Learning time lost while students wait to exit
2. Students gathering at the exit waiting for dismissal
3. The classroom left in disarray

THE **BACKGROUND**

In secondary classrooms, more than 100 students come in and out daily, and they all use the same materials. Activity areas, classroom supplies, and furniture must be kept orderly. Allowing a minute or two of clean-up time at the end of class, followed by a simple dismissal procedure, leaves the classroom in order for the next group of students.

In elementary classrooms, leaving the room in disarray will set a precedent that someone else will be responsible for cleaning up after them. Bringing closure to the end of the day and preparing for a new day are all a part of a dismissal procedure.

Without a dismissal procedure the following scenarios can occur.

SCENARIO 1

Everyone is working away, time slips by, and suddenly the bell rings. Students start scrambling. The teacher is caught off guard.

Before the teacher has a chance to say anything, one student is out the door and others follow. The teacher weakly dismisses the rest of the class. They grab their things and exit in a hurry, leaving the teacher with a big mess and only a few minutes to prepare for the next group of students.

SCENARIO 2

The teacher has completed instruction, students have cleaned up, but there is still a minute or two left in class.

Although students know they are to be seated, one or two stand up. Then, they start inching slowly toward the door. If they are not stopped at this point, they will eventually huddle around the door, poke each other, and creep into the hallway. A mad dash ensues at the sound of the bell.

SCENARIO 3

The end of the day is near. The teacher just keeps on teaching until the bell rings, trying to eke out every second of learning for the students.

When the bell rings, the students scurry to pack up and exit quickly to catch their ride for the journey home. The classroom is a sea of scattered chairs—some on desks, others on the floor, crumbled paper on the floor, and books that should have gone home for study left on desks. Back at the teacher's desk is a reminder for students that should have gone home with them. The students exited the classroom without the reminder and without the books needed for homework. The teacher is left to ready the class for the next morning.

THE **PROCEDURE STEPS**

Introduce this procedure on the first day of school, so students will follow the procedure upon exiting at the end of class.

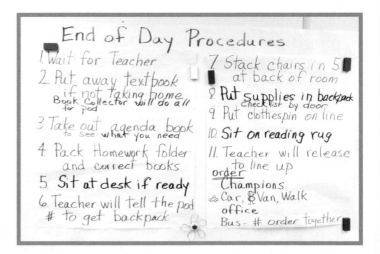

TEACH

Introduce students to your dismissal procedure. A simple dismissal procedure could be like this:

1. Make sure your area is neat.
2. Stay seated until there is a signal to exit.
3. Push in your chair as you leave.

Tell the students what the procedure will be at the end of class.

We have procedures in this classroom. Most teachers in this school have procedures. Teachers may have the same procedures for getting something done, but we may do them a little differently.

There is our class's dismissal procedure. The bell does not dismiss the class. I or whoever is the teacher will dismiss the class.

Two minutes before the end of the period, I will let you know that it is time to put away your materials, clean up, and get ready to leave.

When the bell rings, please do a final check that you have all of your personal belongings, your homework assignment, and any materials you need to complete your homework. Please pick up any garbage or papers near your desk.

There will only be a brief delay until I say, 'Have a nice day.'

When I say 'Have a nice day,' you are dismissed.

Please take your belongings, put your chair on top of your desk, and exit the classroom.

Thank you.

REHEARSE

Tell students that they are going to rehearse the final two minutes of the class period. This is the time to prepare for dismissal. Display the steps for students to see as they prepare for dismissal. Go through each step, one at a time, and have the students do it before moving on the next step. As students go through each step, check for understanding and correct if needed.

- Desk is neat and orderly.
- Work areas are clean and free of loose papers and litter.
- Homework is noted.
- Books and belongings are gathered at your seat ready for removal from the classroom.
- Exit the classroom when I say, "Have a nice day."
- Place your chair on top of your desk as you leave.

Announce there are two minutes of time remaining. Tell students to begin cleaning their desks and follow the steps leading up to leaving the classroom.

Walk around the classroom and make verbal observations:

- *This table is clean!*
- *This row is free from litter and is ready to go!*
- *Thank you for remembering to copy your homework.*
- *Whose jacket is this hanging on the hook?*

Correct and instruct as you move around the classroom, making sure that the classroom is clean, all belongings are gathered, and the room is ready for the next day or class.

Rehearse the procedure before the end of the period or day, so the students can be successful with the procedure on the first day of school.

Once the class is in tip-top shape and students are at their seats with their belongings, ask students, "When the bell rings, what do you do?" Walk students through the dismissal procedure steps. Let them exit the classroom as if they were being dismissed.

Invite the students back into the classroom and let them know how well they carried out the dismissal procedure. Rehearse the procedure, again, if necessary.

At the end of class, give students the two-minute notice. Remind them of what they need to do.

When the bell rings, impatient students may still leave before you have given the signal. Be ready to intercede.

- Gently but firmly stop the students from leaving.
- Say, "Please return to your seats and wait for me to dismiss the class. I want to see you follow the dismissal procedure perfectly. Thank you."
- Stay calm, smile, and be assertive—even when faced with loud sighs and eye-rolling expressions.

The Ease of the Path

The longer I follow the right path,
the easier it becomes.

An Effective Teacher

REINFORCE

Remind students that the point of the dismissal procedure is to maintain a safe and organized environment that prevents crowding around the door while waiting for the end of class. This procedure also ensures students will not exit the classroom in a hurry, leaving a mess behind for others to clean up.

As students are waiting for your verbal cue to dismiss them, invite them to look around the classroom and note how clean and orderly it is. Tell them you would like to it look like this every day when they leave. Thank them for following the procedure every day.

The best results are achieved when the teacher calmly and consistently follows and reinforces the class dismissal procedure all year long.

Daily Closing Message

Consider using a Daily Closing Message to bring closure to the class prior to dismissal. The message is a review of what has been done and learned during the class period. See Procedure 24 for the Daily Closing Message procedure.

A Safe Dismissal or a Tragic One?

Effective schools have constancy in how classes are dismissed, and there is constancy in how the school is dismissed. **Dismissal can be one of the most hectic, frustrating parts of the day.** With a school dismissal procedure, students leave in a safe, orderly manner allowing the teachers and the students to end their day in relative peace.

At **Grand Heights Early Childhood Center** in Artesia, New Mexico, **it takes only ten minutes for 400 kindergarten students to either be picked up or be placed on a bus after school.**

1. Each classroom teacher buddies up with the neighbor teacher. Both teachers are responsible for each other's classes.

2. Bus students have their bus number written on a piece of wide masking tape wrapped around one of their backpack straps.

3. When the dismissal bell rings, students move into the classroom from which they will be taken to either the parent pick-up area or the bus area.

4. Pick-up students are escorted to the gym/cafeteria.

5. Bus students are taken to the bus area and form a line behind their bus number painted on the ground.

6. Buddy teachers ensure students are lined up in the appropriate line by checking the number on the masking tape.

7. As the buses arrive, students are directed to the appropriate exit gate to board their bus.

This procedure takes the staff working in cooperation to make it run smoothly, but it is a quick, safe dismissal bringing a calm conclusion to the day.

As principal of an elementary school in Sayreville, New Jersey, **Ed Aguiles** restructures the first day of school to allow each teacher more time at the beginning of the day to present and teach their classroom management plan.

Then at the end of the day, the students are dismissed thirty minutes early, and they gather in the gymnasium or cafeteria where he and the vice-principal teach, rehearse, and reinforce the school dismissal procedure.

1. During the first two days of school, classes are dismissed thirty minutes early so that the schoolwide dismissal procedure can be practiced by all students and faculty.

2. Students are placed into three dismissal categories and released according to their groups.
   - Bus
   - Parent pick-up (walkers)
   - Before and after school care (BASC)

3. Parents or guardians send a note to school on each day they change the dismissal category of their student.

4. Lists are compiled each day, placing the student in the appropriate dismissal category.

5. Bus students receive a bus tag with their name and bus number at the beginning of the school year.

6. Upon daily dismissal, walkers are dismissed first. They proceed to the front office, where adults sign out their children from the office staff.

7. BASC students walk to the cafeteria where the three staff members who run the program check off each student from their attendance list.

8. Bus students walk to the cafeteria and stand at their bus line number, which is posted on the cafeteria wall. Teachers are assigned to each bus number to take roll.

9. As buses arrive into their assigned area in the parking lot, teachers with walkie-talkies communicate this to teachers in the cafeteria area.

10. As bus numbers are called out in the cafeteria, the two teachers assigned to each bus number escort their students to the bus pickup area.

11. Once all dismissal procedures have been completed for the day, all student dismissal lists are turned in to the front office.

12. Lists are reviewed to ensure all students are accounted for. If not, administration takes appropriate action to locate these students.

It takes ten minutes to dismiss 1,000 students and get them home safely.

Tiffany, a fifth-grader in Detroit, Michigan, died on May 21, 2010. Tiffany was heading home when she boarded the school bus, took her seat, and then leaned out of the window to wave to a friend. As the bus pulled away, Tiffany's head struck a tree, and she died in the arms of her younger brother.

Tiffany's death was totally inexcusable. There were no procedures in place to safely transport the students home. The school, in response to her death, cut down the tree. It wasn't until a year later that schoolwide procedures were put in place, so students could get home safely.

Collecting Notes and Forms

Having a designated spot for everything limits clutter and helps to keep the classroom organized. A simple procedure prevents important correspondence from being misplaced and helps the teacher become more efficient with paperwork from home.

THE **SOLUTION**

Keep a basket or box labeled "Notes from Home" on your desk. Instruct students to put all notes, forms, and messages from home in the basket. **Incorporate collecting these items along with taking attendance and lunch count, so it is accomplished in the first few minutes of a day or period.**

This procedure resolves these problems:

1. Losing important notes from home
2. Not responding to an urgent note in a timely manner

THE **BACKGROUND**

The key to a neat and organized classroom is having a designated spot for everything. A box, basket, or bin labeled "Notes from Home," reminds students this is the only area where important correspondence should be placed. The busy teacher can tell at a glance if there are key notes from parents that must be read immediately. **The box is not for school academic work.** Items such as homework, reports, tests, and projects are collected separately.

THE **PROCEDURE STEPS**

Create a box, basket, or bin with a sign that reads, "Notes from Home," "All Forms Here," "Special Notes," or whatever you choose it to be. Make a list of items that go in the basket and attach the list where students can easily refer to it. You'll need to choose the items that belong in the basket.

- Absence excuse
- Permission slip
- Fundraiser form
- Lunch money
- Written note from a parent or guardian

TEACH

1. Show students the "Notes from Home" box on your desk.
2. Explain that this is where they turn in all correspondence from home.
3. Run through your list of permissible items with the students, and show them where they can find this list if they need to refer to it.
4. Instruct students to place items in the Notes from Home box the first time they enter the classroom.

5. Tell them that homework, projects, and reports are not to be placed in this box. The basket is for notes and forms, not school work.

REHEARSE

Distribute cards with appropriate words on it for items that go in the box and those that don't go in the box. For instance, include cards that read, "Book Orders," "Note from Mom," "Book Report," "Homework," "Field Trip Form," etc.

Ask students to line up as if entering the classroom. Tell them to put the appropriate cards into the Notes from Home box. Instruct the students to hold on to those cards that do not go into the box.

Go through each card in the Notes from Home box and ask for confirmation of whether the card does or does not belong in the box. Use the same process for the cards students did not place in the box. Does it or doesn't it belong in the box? Explain why the cards fit or do not fit the criteria.

Redistribute the cards and go through the process again until all cards have been sorted correctly.

The day before a form is due, remind students that all correspondence from home should go into the Notes from Home basket as they enter the classroom the next day.

The next day, remind students as you greet them at the door to place the form in the box.

REINFORCE

The first time a student has a note from a parent and places it in the basket, thank the student for following the correct procedure.

Share with the students that you just received a note from home and explain how easy it is for you to spot the note in the basket. Explain how it allows you to quickly respond to their parents' concerns. Repeat this reinforcement as many times as needed to establish the procedure as a routine.

Collecting Papers at Tables

Margarita Navarro of Boca Raton, Florida, teaches art classes where the students sit at tables of four. She has student helpers collect all work. The student helper is the one sitting at the north corner of each table. After collecting the work at the table, the helper walks it to a collection box.

Using this system, Margarita has cut the number of students roaming around the classroom. She has also observed that it takes less time to collect papers. The student helpers feel important as part of the plan to streamline processes in the classroom, giving Margarita more time to teach and the students more time to be engaged in their projects.

Clean Up the Classroom Clutter

Eryka Rogers teaches in Oak Brook, Illinois, and believes taking time "up front" will pay back as the year progresses, and the students will be able to use time successfully with no wasted time. Organizing the classroom is key to using time meaningfully for student growth.

Visit **Eryka's** classroom, and you will see how organized she is. The organization spills over to her students as they organize themselves each day for learning.

Jessica Dillard of Valdosta, Georgia, has her own system to organize classroom and student materials. To prevent clutter during class time, Jessica places cloth bags over the back of each chair for the students to place their books and materials.

She has her classroom materials organized, so she can find them, and the students can find them, too.

Sarina Fornabaio teaches science in Brooklyn, New York. After a challenging start in her first months of teaching, she installed a management system that included organizing her classroom. She says teaching is now so much fun for her students and for herself!

Keep your desk free of clutter by storing papers in files to be acted upon later. Label four files:

1. Grade
2. Distribute
3. Copy
4. File

During the day, place papers in the proper file so that at the end of the day, you won't have a pile of papers to fumble through as you look for what you need. Your desktop stays free of papers.

Once everything is organized, devoting just ten minutes at the end of each day to putting things away will keep it that way the rest of the school year.

At the end of the school year, look at the boxes, the files, and the containers that you did not touch during the year. Ask yourself, "What's the worst possible thing that would happen if I don't have this?" If you can live with the results, toss it. Bring closure to the school year, and toss the clutter as you start to collect for the next school year.

THE **PROCEDURE**

Classroom Tardiness

Late students know what to do to report their tardiness and where to look for the daily schedule and opening assignment to get into the flow of the day—without asking for your help. You and the class will continue on task with the daily schedule and without distraction.

THE **SOLUTION**

When a student arrives late to school, it is disruptive to the entire class. **With a procedure in place, students know to quietly enter the classroom and get on task without distracting others.**

This procedure resolves these issues:

1. A tardy student disrupting class
2. Documenting the number of "tardies" for each student
3. Getting the tardy student on task

THE **BACKGROUND**

Students are easily distracted and will often look up from their work when the classroom door opens. When a student is tardy, there is no need to stop the flow of the lesson, brief the student about the class work, and try to get everyone back on task.

With a consistent morning schedule and a posted bellwork assignment, tardy students can easily get into the flow of the day without disturbing others.

In **Chelonnda Seroyer's** high school classroom, if students are tardy to class, they must place their excuse in the tardy slip basket on her desk, have a seat, and immediately begin working on the opening assignment for the day.

Class is never stopped for a student who is tardy. This eliminates any discussion about why they are late, where they were, who made them late, or why it wasn't "really" their fault. Her students know that if they were in another teacher's classroom, they must bring Chelonnda a slip from that teacher.

Many schools mandate that teachers track and document how often a student is tardy. Excessive tardiness affects a student negatively and needs to be discussed with parents. Because schools have varying tardy policies, it is important to

- find out the school's definition of tardiness,
- share the school's policy with students, and
- share the school's policy with students' families.

For instance, if the student enters the classroom eight minutes after the bell rings—instead of going to the office—is the student considered tardy? How should the teacher mark the student's attendance? How long after the start of class is the student considered tardy?

Many schools have the tardy student check in at the office first. The student then brings a tardy slip to class. This tardy slip lets the teacher know that the attendance has been changed in the office. It also provides the teacher with documentation that can be filed and brought out for parent-teacher discussions if necessary.

THE **PROCEDURE STEPS**

Establish a place for students to put tardy slips when they enter the classroom. Put the box, folder, or basket near the door, so students can deposit the slip before taking their seats.

TEACH

1. Tell the students the school's policy for when they arrive late. If they are expected to report to the office first, or come directly to your class, let them know this.

2. Tell students that when they are tardy, they should enter the class quietly.

3. If the student has a tardy slip from the office, designate a place for students to put the slip of paper. There is no need for the student to wave it to get your attention or otherwise disrupt the class.

4. Instruct the tardy students to go directly to their tables or desks, check the agenda posted in the classroom, and get to work.

REHEARSE

Model the correct procedure for what students should do when they are late. Ask a few students to pretend they are late, and then show the class the correct procedure. Acknowledge and affirm students for doing the correct procedure and rehearse it with more students as necessary.

REINFORCE

Remind students that they should not disrupt the class when they are late—you may be in the middle of teaching, or their classmates will be busy working. It is important that they quickly and quietly submit their tardy slip, go to their seat, and start working.

Acknowledge students with a positive non-verbal gesture when they follow the procedure during the school year.

The teacher keeps on teaching, and the class stays on task when a tardy student arrives.

Little Wasted Time

Think about your school.

Imagine . . .

The students walk into a class,
sit down, and immediately get to work.

No one tells them what to do;
they know where to find the assignment.

They go to their next class,
sit down, and get to work.

On to the next class.
The next class. And the next.

When this becomes the prevailing culture of the school, grade level after grade level, year after year, students know what to do no matter the time they enter the classroom. Consistency allows you to keep teaching, and the student becomes responsible for catching up with the instruction. But, that's easy because the student knows where to look for the information needed to quickly get on task.

Wanda Bradford, a principal in Bakersfield, California, has helped her teachers establish this consistency with a poem. She reports, "We start each day with a structured opening. Each teacher has a daily opening, and the students start the day on task."

*Each day begins with learning
when students come to class.
And without a lot of chatting,
they start the day on task.*

*With assignments clearly posted
students need not be told,
to quiet down and get to work
while the teacher takes the roll.*

*If daily routines are followed
less wasted time is spent.
Classes will run smoothly
with great class management.*

*Research has been proven
achievement gains will rise,
when effective teachers start the day
with time that's maximized.*

Schoolwide Tardy Policy and Procedure

Implementing a schoolwide procedure—a culture of consistency—for tardiness, makes it easy for all staff members to consistently enforce the policy. Students understand that a schoolwide policy means all teachers will treat tardiness in the same way.

Many times, a school tardy procedure is simply a set of guidelines listed in the student handbook. Enforcement of the policy is left up to individual teachers. This produces inconsistent results.

A schoolwide policy for treating tardiness reinforces a sense of fairness among students, but all teachers must follow it consistently.

The schoolwide tardy policy at a large suburban high school in the Midwest begins with a "one-minute bell" and gives the students a warning.

On the last tone of the "start class bell," students must have crossed the plane of the classroom door. If they have not done so, they are tardy, and they must get a pass at one of the designated tardy table stations. Tardy students who do not have a tardy pass are not admitted to class.

At the tardy table stations, teachers on supervision duty write passes for students. They record tardy data using a spreadsheet on a laptop. This information is immediately uploaded into the school's attendance-tracking system. This allows the teacher to see how many tardies the student has accumulated.

Only one person enters data, but anyone who views it can see how many tardies a student has for the purpose of writing passes.

The supervisory teacher writes a tardy pass for the student. Upon receiving a third tardy in a single quarter, the student will be notified of the following consequences:

- The fourth and fifth tardies will result in an hour of detention per tardy.
- The sixth and seventh tardies will result in a two-hour detention per tardy.
- After the seventh tardy, the student will be issued an office referral.

Students must serve detentions by the end of the next available detention date. Students who fail to serve detention in a timely manner will be referred to a school administrator.

Teachers are not permitted to excuse a student to another class. The student will be considered tardy regardless of the excuse given. This ensures all teachers' instructional time is respected.

Students will be recorded as absent if they arrive ten minutes or later after the "start class bell" has rung.

Staff members must work together for a schoolwide procedure to work. When staff members are consistent and supportive of each other, students become much more receptive to procedures.

The procedure for recording and giving consequences for tardiness is well-defined. There is no ambiguity about the procedure and no reason for a student to debate with the teacher about the procedure.

With a schoolwide policy in place, students make the extra effort to be on time for class, and classroom instructional time is not spent on administrative tasks.

Absent Folder

An Absent Folder provides students with a consistent system for getting back on track with learning. Students will know what work was missed, where it can be found, where it has to go once completed, and when it has to be returned.

THE **SOLUTION**

An Absent Folder is used to collect, in one place, all the work a student misses while absent. The student knows where to go to get the work they missed while they were away from the classroom. Another alternative is to provide absent students access to missed work through the Internet.

This procedure resolves these problems:

1. Collecting assignments for absent students
2. Finding missed work from absent students
3. Separating missed work from new work
4. Returning missed work from absent students

THE **BACKGROUND**

Going back to a previous day to locate an absent student's work is not an effective use of your time. An Absent Folder procedure assigns the absent student's seat partner the responsibility of collecting an extra copy of all work passed out and placing it in the Absent Folder. When the absent student returns, there will be no confusion as to where the student can locate the missed assignments.

Students can also use the Internet for daily access to missed work. They can access the assignments any time and any place. Listing the assignments in one place saves the time involved with repeating the same directions for multiple absences.

Posting assignments on the Internet gives students access to the work any time.

THE **PROCEDURE STEPS**

Because a student's absence is unpredictable, it's important to establish a procedure for handling missed assignments from Day One. Keep a basket in the front of the classroom with a few special, brightly-colored pocket folders. Label the folders with the classroom number, your name, and the words "Absent Folder." Use these special folders to store assignments for absent students.

TEACH

1. Explain to students that when their seat partner is absent, the partner who is present retrieves an Absent Folder from the basket and places it on their partner's desk. Throughout the day, as assignments are handed out, it is the partner's responsibility to collect an extra copy and put it inside the Absent Folder. The Absent Folder will contain a copy of every piece of work that was handed out on the days the student was absent.

2. Ask students to keep the papers in the folder in order, laying each assignment under the last page in the folder.

3. Tell students that the Absent Folder must stay on their partner's desk until the partner returns to school or a family member picks it up. When students return to school, they know they will find all missed work in a special folder on their desks.

4. Tell students that only missed work belongs in the folder. Any new work on the day the student returns to class does not go in the folder. The folder is only for work handed out when they are absent. This keeps new work separate from missed work.

5. Assign a due date for all missed work inside the Absent Folder. When all of the work is completed, ask students to return it to you in the same Absent Folder. You will know that anything inside the folder is work from a previous day, apart from current work that the rest of the class turns in.

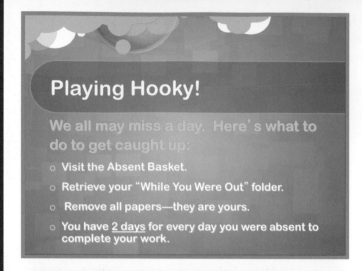

Playing Hooky!

We all may miss a day. Here's what to do to get caught up:

- Visit the Absent Basket.
- Retrieve your "While You Were Out" folder.
- Remove all papers—they are yours.
- You have 2 days for every day you were absent to complete your work.

Procedures when you are absent

- When you return from being absent, you will find a folder on your desk with all of your make up work.

- You will have the number of days you were absent to make up your work.

- Return your work in the absent folder.

Absent?

- ✓ **Check class website**
- ✓ **Call homework hotline**
- ✓ **Get folder when back**

- → **Due in 2 days**

How students retrieve the work missed during an absence is part of your classroom management plan.

REHEARSE

Students will need to role-play this procedure. Pick one pair to take turns playing the absent student and the responsible partner. Ask the absent student to stand in the doorway, so he can see what's going on in class. Tell the class, "Let's pretend Jason is absent today. What should his seat partner, Jerome, do?" Wait for the class to reply.

Wait for Jerome to go to the front of the class to pick out an Absent Folder and place it on Jason's desk. Announce, "I'm handing out some homework now," and pass worksheets across the row. Everyone in class should be paying attention as Jerome takes two copies —one for himself, and an extra one for his absent buddy. Remind the class that the extra copy should be placed in the Absent Folder immediately—so there's no chance of it getting lost. If Jerome stumbles with the procedure, have his classmates prompt him on the correct procedure.

Have Jason step into class. Announce to the class, "Jason's returned to school today," and ask him, "Where do you go to find copies of the work you missed while you were absent?"

Everyone should see how easy it is for Jason to walk confidently to his desk, pick up the Absent Folder, and say, "All the work I missed is in here."

Ask Jason, "What do you need to do with it?"

Jason should respond, "Do the work, put it back in this folder, and return it to you in three days."

After a successful rehearsal, have Jason and Jerome switch roles so that the class gets to see the correct procedure played out again. Or choose another pair to role-play the procedure.

Depending on your grade level, you may have to repeat this process several times before students feel confident about what to do.

REINFORCE

Tell students that this is a buddy system. Seat partners look out for each other by ensuring that all work missed during an absence is neatly gathered in the Absent Folder.

In the first month of school, every time a student is absent, gently remind the class of the correct procedure for using the Absent Folder.

The procedure helps build class camaraderie because students appreciate having a buddy system they can rely on.

Names are written with water-based markers on folders with make-up work. Absent students check the basket upon return to class. The folder is returned to the teacher with the completed make-up work inside.

Accessing Assignments on the Internet

Create a web page to post the work and assignments of your class or classes. Wiki is an easy web tool to use to create your web page.

Your class web page allows students who are absent to obtain make-up work before they even return to class. It also allows students in class to check that they have completed all assignments.

A class web page shows parents what students are learning in class. Updates can be made daily to reflect the work that was done in class. Updates can also be made at the beginning of each week to show what students will be working on in the week ahead.

Accommodation needs to be made for students without Internet access at home. Displaying the web page on a class computer gives students access to the information. They may choose to copy the information in their notebooks or do a print screen. These students are still responsible for locating their missed assignments.

Remind students that it is their responsibility to check the class web page and complete all missed assignments within the allotted time.

 14 •))

Learn how to create a free, class web page, so your students can access their work.

Organizing Homework

Maintaining an organized folder or binder makes it quick and easy for students to locate homework and refer to assignment responsibilities. Students who are organized use time wisely from the moment they enter the classroom and at home.

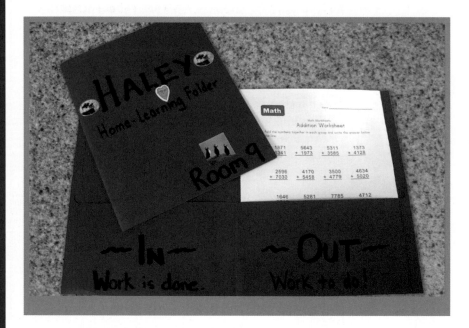

THE **SOLUTION**

A "Homework" or "Home-Learning Folder" and "Weekly Assignment Sheet" will help keep students organized. They are effective communication tools between school and home, keeping parents in the loop on a daily basis as to what students are learning.

This procedure provides these opportunities:

1. Teaches students how to be organized with their homework
2. Eliminates time wasted searching for homework papers
3. Keeps the home informed on school assignments

THE **BACKGROUND**

Teachers use an assortment of materials to help organize their students—folders, spiral notebooks, binders, portfolios, calendars, and electronic devices. The organizational tool can hold anything from class and school policies and procedures to discipline rules, school and class handouts, schedules, classroom notes, activities, tests, projects, assignments, and homework.

Equip students with tools to become organized and stay organized. A homework organizer and assignment sheet will become indispensable to a student's daily routine.

THE **PROCEDURE STEPS**

Organizing the homework folder will depend on the method used. If you are using a folder, use two-pocket folders of various colors, one for each student. Label the cover of the folder with the student's name, room number, and "Home-Learning Folder."

Open the folder and label the two inside pockets with pairs of words such as "In" and "Out" or "Done" and "To Do."

The work to be done is put in the right side marked "Out," for work to be done outside of the classroom. The completed homework is put in the left side marked "In," for work to be turned in the next day.

TEACH

1. Ask students to put their **Home-Learning Folder** on their desks and open it, so the two pockets are showing.

2. Ask students to point to the Out pocket of the folder. Tell students to put their homework in the Out pocket of the Home-Learning Folder. This is work that is done outside of the classroom.

3. Ask students to create their **Home-Learning Assignments** page. Students write one week's worth of assignments on this page. The listing consists of the name of the assignment, when it is due, and a means for marking it as completed. Allow students time at the end of each lesson, period, or day to check that all assignments are written on the page.

4. Put the Home-Learning Assignments page in the Out pocket of the folder. Tell students all work goes behind the assignments page in the pocket.

5. When students are ready to do their homework, they open the folder, check the assignments page, and look for the work to do.

6. Ask students to point to the In side of their folders. This is where work goes after it is done.

7. As students complete their homework, tell them to place the finished work on the In side and check off the task on their Home-Learning Assignments page.

8. Tell students to put the folder in their backpack and when they get home, the homework will be in the folder.

9. Remind students to take the Home-Learning Folder home each day and to bring it back to school each day.

An assignments page lets students keep track of work to do and when it has been done. Some teachers ask adults to initial the page signifying they have reviewed the work completed at home.

REHEARSE

Ask students to take a single sheet of lined paper and label it with "Done," "Assignments," and "Due." Remind students that this paper keeps all homework assignments in one location for easy reference. Together as a class, have students place the assignments page in the Out side of their folder.

Write an assignment task and the due date on the board. Ask students to copy the task and the due date on their assignments page. Add additional assignments to the page throughout the day. Each time an assignment is added to the board, ask students to get out their folders and copy it to their assignments paper.

The assignments page typically lasts a week before being replaced with a fresh sheet. Tell students to make another sheet if they need more space and add it to the existing one for the current week.

When the first homework worksheet is given, remind students to place the paper behind the assignments page in their folder.

Check each student's folder for correct placement of the worksheet behind the assignments page, as well as listing of the task and the due date on the assignments page.

Tell students to take their homework folders out at home and work on their Out assignments.

As each assignment is completed, place a checkmark under the Done column on the assignments page and put the completed work in the In pocket.

Tell students that when all the homework is done, to put the homework folder in their backpack and place it by the door, ready to take to school the next day.

REINFORCE

At the end of as many days as necessary, conduct a homework check. Ask students to put their homework folders on their desks and open it to the pockets. Walk around and check that students have their folders and their work placed properly. Acknowledge students who bring their completed homework back to school in the In pocket of their folders.

On subsequent days, conduct spot checks, as needed, while saying goodbye to students.

Trashing Ceremony

At the start of each week, host a Trashing Ceremony. Students who have completed all of the homework from the previous week are invited to grandly rip, tear, crumple, and toss the page into the recycling bin. This symbolizes a successful week of learning and the start of a fresh, new week.

A new assignments page is created to replace the trashed copy. Students put this in their homework folder in preparation for the assignments of the week.

Home-Learning for Secondary Students

In a secondary classroom, you may opt to have students keep an organized three-ring binder. Prepare a model binder to share with the students. Ask each student to bring to class a three-ring binder. Provide binders to those students who are unable to bring one to class.

Students in Oretha Ferguson's classes keep an organized binder that includes a tab for Homework.

Determine how the binder is organized for your class. For instance, students in an English class may have these divider pages:

- Homework
- Daily Grammar Bellwork
- Vocabulary
- Writing Journal
- Notes

No matter the method used to keep track of assignments, the procedure needs to be taught, rehearsed, and reinforced to help students keep track of the work to be done outside of the classroom.

Tweaking the Process

My Homework Binder procedure has evolved over the years. I had to figure out the most effective way for students to get homework between school and home, as well as to keep parents updated on daily assignments.

I started by giving my students a two-pocket folder, but these fell apart quickly. Since they are smaller than binders, the folders got lost easily. Assignments were constantly damaged from being carelessly stuffed into the folder pockets.

I also tried giving large manila envelopes to each student. Students would use these to carry their work to and from home each day; but students and parents were unable to find work quickly and easily in these envelopes.

Now I have a binder with a divider system. One of these dividers is Homework. Homework can easily be located, completed, and turned in when it is placed behind the divider in their binders.

Sarah Jondahl ■ Brentwood, California

15 •))

This is a Homework Checklist to help students establish a consistent routine.

THE **PROCEDURE**

Paper Headings

A consistent paper heading helps students remember to include the important details you require for assignment identification. You will receive far fewer mystery papers and will spend less time identifying the mystery authors.

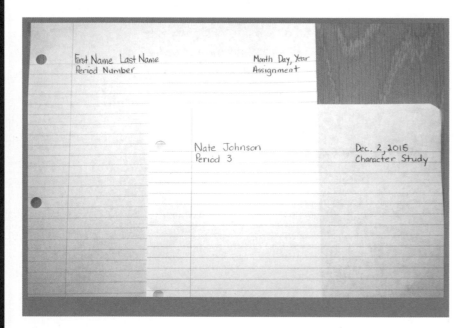

THE **SOLUTION**

Posting an example of a paper heading for students to follow will result in consistent information on every paper and reinforces for students the importance of identifying their work. **When a paper heading procedure is in place, students are less likely to omit their names from an assignment.**

This procedure resolves these problems:

1. Missing names and other important information on assignments
2. Wasting time trying to identify mystery papers with no identification

THE **BACKGROUND**

With the multitude of subjects taught and the many students that teachers encounter each day, a procedure for identifying papers is helpful for teachers to keep track of student work. A consistent format can be used on a classwide, grade-level-wide, or schoolwide basis. Putting a heading on work becomes a natural part of any assignment and eliminates the scribbling of a name and date in a random location on a piece of paper.

THE **PROCEDURE STEPS**

Create a sign showing how to head all papers. Create a sample of what a paper heading should look like with the requested information in the right locations on the paper. Post these samples in the front of the classroom. Include the information you want put on each student's paper:

- Student's name
- Student's number
- Date
- Subject
- Period
- Assignment title

Sarah Jondahl created a poster to remind her students of the paper heading for all of their work.

Decide on the placement of the heading on the student's paper. Headings are usually at the top left or right side of the paper. Determine whether you want it to start in the top margin or on the first line. Whatever placement you choose, **the heading needs to be in a consistent format, with a consistent heading location for every assignment**.

Make It S-T-A-N-D

Many secondary teachers use **S-T-A-N-D** as an acronym for heading a paper:

S – Subject and class period

T – Teacher

A – Assignment

N – Name

D – Date

TEACH

1. Before the very first assignment is given, model the correct procedure for writing paper headings.

2. Show students the premade poster at the front of the classroom. Explain that students can refer to it as a reminder of the correct procedure for writing paper headings.

3. Point out where each part of the heading goes on the piece of paper.

4. Have students take out a blank piece of paper to practice writing the heading.

5. Ask students to write one piece of information at a time on their papers.

6. Walk the room and check that the information has been placed in the correct location on the paper and that the information is what it should be.

7. Announce the next piece of information to write as part of the paper heading.

8. After each direction of what to write, check for accuracy.

9. Ask students to help and check each other's papers for accuracy.

10. Continue the process until all parts of the heading are on the paper.

11. Practice writing the heading again, checking for accuracy each time.

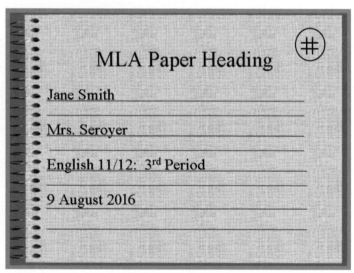

MLA Paper Heading

Jane Smith

Mrs. Seroyer

English 11/12: 3rd Period

9 August 2016

Chelonnda Seroyer's students use a modified MLA format to head their papers. She wants students to include their unique number on every paper.

REHEARSE

When handing out the first class assignment, practice the correct procedure for writing paper headings. Walk students through each step of the procedure again. As the class is doing this, walk around the room and check for accuracy. If a student is not following the procedure, stop and gently redirect the student.

Continue to model this procedure to individuals as needed and at small-group or whole-group instruction settings. Acknowledge students who are following the procedure.

Name Check

If papers are still being turned in without headings, simply say "Name Check" in a neutral tone before the papers are turned in. For a particular student who consistently leaves a name off the paper heading, a quick, verbal "Name Check" serves as a prompt to check that the heading has been done.

Ask students to place a checkmark next to their names as confirmation during the name check. Or, look for a visual confirmation from students with a thumb up, pencil up, or hand up, and respond with a thumb-up to cement the procedure.

REINFORCE

With practice, the procedure for writing paper headings will quickly become a routine. If the procedure is forgotten, remind students to refer to the poster at the front of the class.

For some students, an example of the proper paper heading—a paper taped to the desk—aids those who are slow to catch on to the procedure. With the correct format in close proximity, it's easier for students to mimic this procedure.

District-Wide Consistency

The schools of the **Flowing Wells Unified School District** in Tucson, Arizona, have adopted a culture of consistency for the headings students put on papers. In this K–12 district, the expectation is in place in all classrooms that a paper heading is used on all papers.

Every teacher in the **Flowing Wells** schools requires a heading for all papers. However, the format of the heading is left up to the individual teacher.

A progressive component list for paper headings has been agreed upon and is in place in all of the classrooms throughout the school district.

- **Kindergarten**
  Students write their first names and the first and last names by the end of the year
- **1st–2nd grade**
  Students write their first and last names and the date
- **3rd–6th grade**
  Students write their full names, date, and assignment
- **Junior High and High School**
  Students write their full names, date, assignment, and class/subject

Many of the teachers customize the paper headings with a student number. Teachers assign students a unique class number and then require the number to be part of the paper heading. Assigning each student a number aids in collecting papers, putting papers in order to record scores, and calling on students to assist in the classroom.

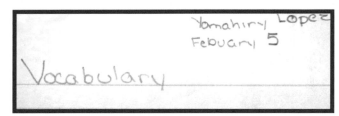

Brie Barber, Third-Grade teacher

Whitney Weigold,
Second-Grade teacher

Ashley Robertson,
High school teacher

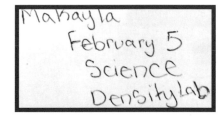

Bridget Betterton, Sixth-Grade teacher

The progressive plan is in place, simply because it makes sense, but teachers are not required to adhere to it. As long as the teacher is teaching students to include headings on papers, it is acceptable to customize the heading routine.

Unfinished Class Assignments

A simple-to-manage system for unfinished class assignments helps students stay on top of their work. The practice also allows the teacher to keep track of unfinished class assignments.

THE **SOLUTION**

Time often runs out for some students to complete assignments in class. **A File Crate system or a "Work In Progress" (WIP) folder can be used to manage these unfinished class assignments.**

This procedure resolves these issues:

1. Unfinished assignments being misplaced or lost
2. Time wasted trying to locate unfinished assignments
3. Students not being held accountable for their assignments

THE **BACKGROUND**

Students tend to keep unfinished class assignments inside their desks. This can quickly result in a mess. A central spot, where students can keep and find their unfinished assignments, helps everyone stay organized. You are able to keep track of who needs to finish assignments, and students have no excuse for misplacing their work or submitting crumpled papers.

Beth Featherston of Monroe, Louisiana, uses a Work In Progress Folder. When time is up and students have not completed an assignment, the work goes in their WIP folder until the student can return to work on the assignment.

Students check their personal WIP Folder, kept in their desk, every day before leaving. Work in the folder is taken home as homework and returned the next day to class.

Sarah Jondahl uses a File Crate system for students to keep their unfinished work. Folders are arranged in numerical order based on each student's unique number.

THE **PROCEDURE STEPS**

Place a File Crate at the front of the classroom. Create a hanging file for each student in class. Arrange files in a logical order, so students can quickly and easily locate their files.

TEACH

1. Show the class the File Crate and explain that each student has a personal hanging file. Students are to keep any unfinished classroom work in their files, but should have no more than three pieces of incomplete assignments inside at any given time.

2. Remind students that it is their responsibility to stay caught up on assignments, and that they should regularly check their files.

3. Tell students that all work in the folder is due the next school day. If there are more than three assignments in a student's file, they must use time at recess to get the work done. Otherwise, the unfinished work becomes homework due the next day.

4. Emphasize that everyone in class begins each day with a clean file folder.

REHEARSE

Introduce the File Crate system along with the first class assignment. When it is time to transition to another activity, tell students to stop working. Ask who has not completed the assignment.

Ask those students to demonstrate how to use the File Crate system.

Call on students by groups to walk their assignment up to the File Crate. Instruct students, one at a time, to locate their individual files. Remind students to be careful to place their work in the correct file.

Acknowledge students who file their papers in the correct folder. Assist students who are taking too much time to file the papers. Explain the organization of the files in the crate and help the students find their folders.

REINFORCE

At the end of each assignment, remind students to put their unfinished work in the File Crate.

Remind students that it is their responsibility to complete the work and return it to class the next day. Tell them to use any available class time during the school day to work on their assignments.

Check the File Crate at the end of the day for any papers still in folders.

Remind students of their responsibility to collect the papers and for completing the work.

Incomplete Work

Shelly Pilie of St. Rose, Louisiana, gives students a Work In Progress folder. They are told to keep the folder at their desks.

The students not only put their incomplete assignments in it, but also keep several tasks in the folder to do if they finish early and need to wait for the rest of the class.

Students are responsible for gathering their incomplete assignments to take home and returning the work completed the next day.

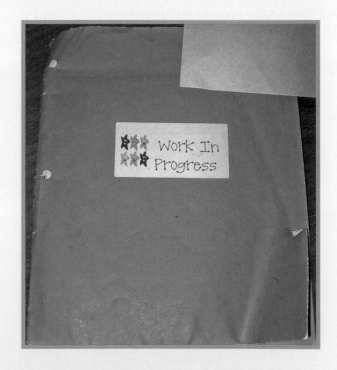

I Am So Excited to Go to School Each Morning

I began teaching fresh out of college. I was twenty-one years old, single, and had no clue as to what I was getting into. I began as a high school teacher, teaching three classes of consumer math and two classes of Algebra II.

I went through a year of TOTAL chaos! I gave serious thought to not returning in the fall. I had no order in my classroom. I posted classroom rules but did not place much emphasis on them.

The next three years were no better. Last year was awful! Pregnant with my second child, I found myself sick and put to bed thirty-one weeks into my pregnancy. My students suffered greatly.

When I was able to return part time, I found there was NO organization in my classroom. Needless to say, when my students completed the semester, I truly believed I was a failure as a teacher.

I was not looking forward to returning in August . . . until I heard you speak to our county teachers at a preschool meeting. I decided to make some major changes in my classroom structure. It wasn't too difficult to improve, since I had no structure at all.

I never knew what the _one simple thing_ was that was missing from my classroom—until that teacher workshop session in August.

I went home that night and started writing. By the time I was finished, everything I expected of my students was written out and ready to be distributed on the first day of class. I spent the first two days of school doing nothing but discussing and practicing my policies and procedures. Then, I used the second week of school to reinforce my classroom procedures.

I am having a wonderful year! My students follow my policies and procedures without any gripes. The greatest thing is that my students are really learning this year! They walk in the door and stay on task for ninety minutes every day. My first block students are even in class before the first bell—they do not wait until the second bell anymore.

We were on a testing schedule last week, and my students were disappointed that they would not be in class. Can you believe students being disappointed about missing Algebra II? I am totally sold on procedures and routines. They work! You saved my career as a teacher.

I am SO excited about going to school each morning and _teaching_ my students!

Jamie Davis ▪ London, Kentucky

Emergency Preparedness

Ensuring the physical safety of the students is one of your major responsibilities. Everyone being prepared is the best defense in the face of adversity.

THE **SOLUTION**

Being prepared to manage and direct students in an emergency is critical and saves lives. Having a special transition activity ready to implement after practice has taken place eases students back into the flow of the classroom with minimal wasted time.

This procedure provides these opportunities:

1. Prepares students and teachers to deal with a crisis
2. Eliminates confusion and panic during an emergency
3. Allows the teacher to resume instruction upon returning to the classroom

THE **BACKGROUND**

Tornadoes, earthquakes, fires, bomb threats, and intruders are emergencies that could happen at your school—yes—even at your school. These incidents unexpectedly interrupt the calm and security of your classroom environment. When you're prepared for anything, nothing fazes you or your students.

Students tend to be indifferent or become too excited when something occurs that is out of the ordinary—like a fire alarm going off. This excitement or indifference is likely to manifest itself as panic in a real emergency. Students need to know how to respond swiftly and safely in a crisis.

Having a frank discussion with them about the value of staying clear-headed and alert will remind them of the importance of respecting and adhering to emergency procedures.

THE **PROCEDURE STEPS**

When every moment could be the difference between life and death, preparation is vital for the safety of everyone. Students need to be able to respond to an emergency situation with calm and assuredness that they know what to do.

1. **Prepare an Emergency Evacuation Binder.**
2. **Post a school map with the highlighted evacuation route.**
3. **Prepare a transition activity to help students return to learning mode after a drill.**

1. **Prepare an Emergency Evacuation Binder.**
   Prepare a binder that contains this basic information:

   - Emergency procedures
   - Map with highlighted evacuation route
   - Class rosters
   - Required administrative procedures

Keep the binder in an easily accessible location and make sure the students and any substitute teachers know where it is kept.

2. **Post a school map with the highlighted evacuation route.**
   Posting the map on the classroom door, or near it, for quick and easy reference can be a lifesaver for students and teachers.

Class Roster

Laurie Jay of Saskatoon, Canada, has her class roster attached with Velcro® by the door jamb. The students are taught that the last person leaving the room is to take the class roster with them. Class attendance is taken with this list at the designated assembly point. Any time there is a drill, this procedure is practiced.

Lakeridge School Gr. 2/3 – Mrs. Jay

FIRE DRILL

Dear Guest Teacher,
Please take this sheet with you for attendance.
Thank you!

1.	ALLAN,	M.			
2.	BABB,	N.			
3.	BELL,	S.			
4.	COUSINS,	T.			
5.	DARLING,	B.			
6.	HASSAN,	T.			
7.	HE,	T.			
8.	HOEPPNER,	K.			

3. **Prepare a transition activity to help students return to learning mode after a drill.**
Prior to an emergency drill, consider how the class is to transition back into learning mode. After the excitement and activity of a drill, how can you help students settle down and get back to work quickly?

These are some ways to get students to focus back on learning:

- Class Meeting
Hold a class meeting to discuss the events that just happened. Point out what went right and how students can improve. Ask students what they noticed and for recommendations for improvement.

- Journal Activity
Show a writing prompt and ask students to respond in their journals.

- Word Wall
Keep a list of interesting words for students to define and use in sentences, provide antonyms and synonyms for, and so on.

- Resume Lesson
Pick up from where the lesson was disrupted.

TEACH

1. Discuss the dangers of an actual emergency with students. Emphasize the importance of an emergency drill procedure and how it saves lives.

2. Teach students the evacuation procedure as prescribed by your school. Explain the purpose of each step so that students understand why they are being asked to do something in a certain way. This ensures student cooperation.

3. Use a school map to show students the evacuation route. Ensure all students know how they are to evacuate. Include these detailed instructions, as necessary.

- Students must keep to the right-hand side of hallways and stairs.
- Students are to stay in a single file.
- Students are to keep moving and are not to wait for friends in other classes.
- Students must remain quiet and listen for directions from adults.

Students need to know this essential information:

- Which route to take
  - If stairwells or hallways are numbered or named, ensure students are familiar with these designations.
  - If cardinal directions are used in instructions, ensure students are orientated and know how to distinguish between north, south, east, and west.
- Where to assemble
  - If a student gets separated from the class, the student will know where to rejoin the class.

4. Assign one student and a backup for these tasks:
- Lead the class out of the room in an emergency.
- Be responsible for switching off the lights, shutting the door, and taking responsibility for being the last individual to leave the class.

5. Teach students to line up in class order at the assembly area. If you use a class number system, then students are already familiar with which students come before and after them. This allows you to walk down the line of students at the assembly area and quickly determine whether all students are present by calling off numbers instead of names.

6. Once attendance is taken and a clear signal is given, walk students back to class. Upon returning to class, immediately launch into the prepared transition activity. Resume the day's lesson once the class focus is back on learning.

7. Tell students that although this is only a practice, in a real emergency situation, they must carry out the steps, so they will be safe and their classmates will be secure. We all know how serious emergency preparedness is when a disaster or other dangerous event occurs. You cannot afford to waste time reviewing directions in a real life-threatening situation.

REHEARSE

After explaining the procedure, take class time to walk students through the procedure:

- Lead students down the correct side of the hallway, stairwell, and exit door.
- Show students where they are to meet during a drill.
- Have students line up in class order.
- Take attendance.
- Walk students back to the classroom.
- Commend students for following the procedure.
- Launch immediately into a transition activity.

REINFORCE

Talk to students about what you observed during the procedure—what was done well, and what can be done better. Repeat the drill until all students understand what they are to do in an emergency.

Do a dry-run of the emergency evacuation procedure at the start of some marked interval—the first day of the month, quarter, or term. Responding to an emergency situation should become a routine for you and your students.

If a new student joins the class, review the emergency procedures with the student, and consider using this occasion as an opportunity for another classwide emergency evacuation rehearsal.

Emphasize to students that although an emergency drill may seem like a waste of time, knowing what to do during a crisis can save lives. Also, explain that just because there is a practice drill, this does not mean the rest of the period is lost. **The transition activity helps students refocus on learning and allows the teacher to resume the day's lesson.**

Students cooperate more readily when they understand the purpose of emergency preparedness is to save lives.

Bring Confidence and Calm

In the aftermath of the many tragedies schools have experienced the past few years, additional safety precautions have been put in place. Some schools keep their outside doors barred during school hours; classroom doors are locked, and the student nearest the door asks, "Who is it," when there is a knock on the door.

Others outfit classroom doors with pull-down shades and require students to move in pairs. Some schools practice a drill each month—fire drills, intruder drills, bomb drills, tornado drills, and earthquake drills.

By teaching, rehearsing, and reinforcing what to do in an emergency, you help students stay calm and remain safe.

Present drill information to students in an age-appropriate context, so the procedure does not unduly frighten young children. The level to which students can execute the emergency preparedness plan with confidence and calm will ready them for what to do should a catastrophe strike.

16 •))

Check your emergency preparedness information against what others do.

Surviving a School Active Shooter

Tornado, earthquake, fire—these are the mandatory drills we conduct to keep students safe in schools. Sadly, **Lockdown** and **Active Shooter** are new drills being added to the list. National Violent Intruder Preparedness Solutions (National VIPS)—offers some procedures to help protect teachers and students from the unthinkable.

Far too often, the sounds of screams and gunfire ringing through hallways and echoing between classrooms has become commonplace in schools. Despite countless hours of media coverage, innumerable expressions of surprise, anger, and grief by government officials, and demands by concerned citizens, students are far from safe in schools.

Sadly, in most cases, inadequate procedures, training, and drills have left school staff ill-prepared to prevent attacks or protect students. Police will respond when called but are often only able to intercede after substantial casualties have already been inflicted. **The greatest predictor of surviving an active shooter attack in school is what staff and students are trained to do before police arrive**.

At one high school in a progressive, well-funded school district, administrators were asked what students had been instructed to do if a shooter was rampaging on campus. They answered that students should go into classrooms and lock the doors.

When asked what students should do if the doors are all locked and they find themselves in the same area as the shooter, administrators said students should lie on the ground and cover their heads with their hands. This would make students fixed targets and is obviously a completely inadequate and dangerous procedure.

Administrators were questioned why students would not be told to run off campus, away from the shooter, to a safe location. The answer: that to allow students off

campus during school hours would constitute truancy and truancy is not permissible. Reducing truancy is a laudatory goal, but **saving lives is paramount**. A crisis situation is not the time to prioritize school rules.

The procedure should be simple:
Run Away from Gunfire.

In many schools, active shooter drills are conducted mid-period. A part of the drill is locking and barricading classroom doors. Designated personnel check the doors and declare the exercise a success. However, the training and conditioning accomplished by this drill is valuable only if an active shooter appears on campus mid-period. It does not take other times or other circumstances into consideration.

Evidence of this was at a school where the shooter pulled a fire alarm to cause teachers and students to leave their classrooms so they could be shot in the hallways. Because students and teachers had no other training, they instinctively tried to run back into their classrooms, which they could not enter or secure quickly enough, and so became easy targets for the shooter.

The administrators were asked what students should do if they are outside on school grounds and a shooter is inside, roaming the school buildings. They advised that students should run toward the classrooms and find a room to lockdown. The administrators admitted that this plan meant students would run toward, rather than away from, danger and gunfire.

Ask yourself these tough questions about the procedures in place at your school in the terrifying event of an active shooter. The answers could be the difference between life and death.

- Do they prescribe running away, evading, and escaping as important and viable options? If not, they should. **Moving away from danger is, in most cases, the most logical and safest action to take.**

- Do they say to lockdown in places that cannot realistically be secured against an intruder? **Never consider a place safe that cannot be truly secured.**

- Do the procedures prepare for actual and different situations? **Simplistic drills dictating a single response action will cause more chaos and danger, rather than safety and escape.**

Surviving an Active Shooter

- **Report suspicious people or circumstances.** Many attacks have been stopped by people who trusted their instincts and reported their observations. Follow through to make sure your concerns have been addressed.

- **Know the escape route options,** not just for the classroom or school but in any public gathering space—theaters, shopping centers, supermarkets, stadiums, places of worship, playgrounds, museums, convention halls, meeting rooms. Practice the escape routes, if possible. At the very least visualize how you would exit the space.

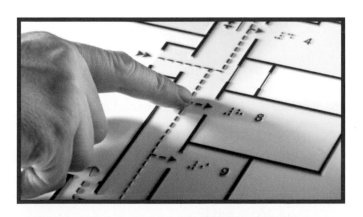

- **Routinely** consider the options available in any given situation at any given moment.

- Learn how and **practice locking down** the classroom with available resources. Stack chairs, desks, and furniture to barricade; use belts, ties, and electrical cords to secure; push rulers, erasers, markers, and books into doorjambs to block.

- Assume loud, unexpected noises are gunfire—until informed otherwise. **Take rapid action to evade or secure.** Don't waste precious seconds waiting for an announcement.

- Break a window to escape or open the door that says, "Don't Open Alarm Will Sound." **Flee first and worry about the damage later.**

- If in danger, do whatever is needed to survive. **Never give up.** Continue to resist. Maintain the will to survive.

- **Finally, treat everyone with kindness and respect.** More than one active shooter has spared the life of someone because the person was nice to the shooter in the past.

The National Violent Intruder Preparedness Solutions team (www.nationalvips.com) offers assessments, training, and other services to keep schools safe places for learning.

THE **PROCEDURE**

Getting Students' Attention

Teaching students a predetermined signal for coming to attention saves time and prevents yelling, begging, and pleading at students to get their attention.

Getting Your Attention

1. The teacher will say, "**Ladies and gentlemen, thank you for listening**," "**Listen up,**" or "**Are you ready**?"

2. In some cases, teacher will also raise a **finger**.

3. When you hear (or see) this signal, please **stop** what you are doing and **listen** for instructions.

 **The class noise level must be silent.**

THE **SOLUTION**

A **consistent method of getting your students' attention minimizes classroom confusion and brings an elevated noise level down quickly.** The students' dignity is kept intact because they are not demeaned into coming to attention. The teacher's dignity is kept intact because the cue is delivered in a professional, caring manner.

This procedure provides these opportunities:

1. Remaining calm while the class comes to attention

2. Using a consistent signal so anyone can bring the class to attention

3. Wasting little time while the class comes to attention

THE **BACKGROUND**

Too often, getting the class' attention is a battle of wills. With your patience wearing thin, you raise your voice, hoping to drown out your students' noise in order to get their attention.

It makes no difference which signal you use to get your students' attention; just have a signal and teach the procedure to follow the signal. It can be as calm and simple as, "May I have your attention, please?"

Students respond well to simple verbal commands such as, "Please listen up," clapping, ringing chimes, or issuing a visual command such as a raised hand.

Teach students the signal to come to attention. **Give the signal with confidence and the expectation of quiet.** Wait for silence. Once the classroom is quiet, thank students, and then proceed with instruction.

Depending on your classroom environment, you may need more than one method for bringing the class to attention. Whatever the signal, use it exclusively for achieving this purpose.

Teach others who work with your students about your technique and encourage them to use it whenever they work with your students and require their undivided attention.

THE **PROCEDURE STEPS**

Select a signal that you can deliver with confidence and that students associate as a simple request to come to attention. This signal will vary according to students' grade level and subject area. A simple way to quiet a class and get students' attention is to announce, "May I have your attention, please," or "Everyone, (boys and girls, class), please listen up."

TEACH

Introduce the attention signal. If you are using a verbal command, explain to students that when they hear the teacher announce, "Everyone, please listen up," they must do three things:

1. Immediately stop what they are doing.
2. Look at the teacher.
3. Listen for instruction.

If you are using a non-verbal command, show the students what the signal is and ask them to follow the same three steps.

Deliver, Then Wait

Once I saw my principal quiet an entire auditorium of students without a microphone. I was so impressed! The principal told me, 'When you want to get the students' attention, stand firmly, and ask for their attention in a strong, commanding voice—then wait.'

That was a revelation for me. It is a simple thing, but it took twelve years for me to really get it. I wouldn't ask for attention firmly enough, or I wouldn't wait long enough, so I would end up talking over them.

Once I chose to deliver the cue with firm conviction, and waited, I got it—and got results consistently.

Karen Rogers ▪ High School Teacher, Kansas

 17 ◾))

"Give Me Five," made famous by Cindy Wong, is a classic technique used across grade levels.

REHEARSE

Lead the class in practicing the procedure. Invite them to turn and talk to their neighbors. At an appropriate time, give the cue with a clear, assured tone, "Everyone, listen up." Verbally lead the class through the steps and ask them to stop what they are doing, get themselves into a position where they can see you, and then listen for your instruction.

When students are slow to respond, assist them with guidance on how to practice the procedure correctly.

Thank those students who follow the procedure.

Practice again, with some students out of their seats. Deliver the cue again, but this time, do not lead them through the steps. Monitor the students and correct those who need assistance. Wait for the students' attention. This is the key to the procedure's success. Do not speak again until the class is completely silent and all eyes are on you.

If students are taking too long to quiet down, remind them of the procedure and why it is important for everyone to follow it.

Rehearse again until you observe the students properly following the procedure.

Use the next opportunity—when students are doing group work—to practice this procedure again.

REINFORCE

Thank the class for coming to attention so quickly. At the end of the day, remind them how well they followed this procedure. Let them know this is the procedure you will use every day when you want their attention.

Signing Quiet

Mike Reed of New Jersey teaches middle school and uses sign language to communicate with his students. Many teachers have discovered that the less they speak, the more the class gets done. Students sign to the teachers with letters for their basic needs—"B" for bathroom, "W" for water fountain, "H" for help, and "S" for pencil sharpener. The teacher responds with a simple nod, or a sign "Y" for yes or "N" for no.

Students flash their needs with a B and an H to communicate silently in the classroom.

 — **Index finger held in the air tells me that you have a question**

 — **Two fingers held in the air mean you need to leave your seat**

 — **Three fingers held in the air lets me know that you need my help**

 — **Fingers crossed mean you need to use the bathroom, get a drink, go to your locker, or go to the nurse**

The consistency in his classroom and school prompted his inclusion teacher to comment after his recent absence that she had never seen a class act that well in all her twenty-five years as a teacher.

How do you know when I need your attention?

- I will ring the bell on my desk once to let you know to look up at me because I need your attention.
- If the noise level is inappropriate, I will ring the bell two times.

Your Attention, Please

There is no single "right" way to **call a group to attention**. Consider the environment, the setting, the group's age level, and your personality when selecting the procedure you will use.

SALAME

When the teacher says, "SALAME," the students recognize what this word means and carry out the action.

Stop And Look At ME.

School Mascot

At assemblies, the leader of the assembly holds up a stuffed animal of the school's mascot—in the story shared, it was a lion. The group looks at the lion and lets out one big roar. Then the mascot is taken away and the group is quiet and focused on the leader.

Please and Thank You

The simplicity of a "please" and "thank you" are sometimes all it takes to bring the class to attention. Confidently say, in a questioning voice, "Please?" and wait for the students to respond by coming to attention. After the students have come to attention, reply, "Thank you," and continue explaining the purpose of calling the group to attention.

Hand Signal

Beverly Woolery is director of an award-winning alternative certification program, the Educator Preparation Institute (EPI), at Polk State College in Winter Haven, Florida.

Beverly uses a procedure called **"Yakety Yak,"** a call and response technique, for getting the participants' attention. She poses her hands in a yakking/talking gesture.

1. Beverly gives the hand signal for "Yakety Yak" and says "Yakety Yak" at the same time.
2. Participants turn and face her.
3. Participants give the hand signal for "Back on Track," extend both arms toward the teacher with pointer finger extended, and say "Back on track" at the same time.
4. When everyone is quiet and facing Beverly, she has everyone's attention.

THE **PROCEDURE**

Classroom Jobs

Jobs give students a sense of responsibility and ownership of their home away from home—the classroom.

THE **SOLUTION**

When each student is in charge of completing a job, everyone takes ownership of the classroom. This instills responsibility, discipline, teamwork, and a sense of pride in their class and contributes to establishing a positive learning environment.

This procedure resolves these problems:

1. Doing the daily tasks necessary to keep the classroom clean
2. Ensuring that housekeeping is not done by the teacher
3. Encouraging responsibility and teamwork among students

THE **BACKGROUND**

Introduce the class to the concept of classroom jobs by reading the book, *Miss Malarkey Doesn't Live in Room 10*. After reading the story, discuss with the class that you don't live in the classroom. You have a home outside of the classroom and will need everyone's help to get their classroom home ready for learning each day. Each member of the classroom will contribute to getting the classroom ready with a job. It will take teamwork, responsibility, and accountability to get daily tasks and jobs done, so the room will be ready— beginning with the very first week of school.

A Job Wheel is a tool you can use as part of a fair and transparent method for assigning tasks. The Job Wheel rotates jobs weekly, so students can take turns carrying out different tasks.

The Job Wheel makes it easy to assign classroom tasks.

THE **PROCEDURE STEPS**

Each classroom is unique. Your classroom job list will differ from your colleagues' lists. Some tasks are daily routines, and some tasks are done once a week. You will need to create the job list for your class.

In the primary classroom, there is ample opportunity to have a job for every student every week. In the secondary classroom, ensure that students have a job at least once a month. No job is too small for the list.

- Teacher assistant
- Homework keeper
- Substitute assistant
- Pledge leader
- Flag holder
- Attendance monitor
- Paper passer
- Paper collector
- Line leader
- Morning Meeting leader

- Lunch runner
- Gardener
- Pencil sharpener
- Window opener
- Window closer
- Book monitor
- Board cleaner
- Library books monitor
- Lights monitor
- Supplies monitor

- Tally keeper
- Desk checker
- Cubby checker
- Sweater monitor
- Tech assistant
- Date changer
- New student greeter
- Pet tender
- Trash monitor
- Playground equipment monitor

Every task is important to a smooth-running classroom.

Create a **Job Wheel** with all the classroom jobs listed:

1. Cut out a large circle on tag board.
2. Divide the circle as you would a giant pie, with a wedge for each job.
3. Label each wedge with a job title.
4. Write each student's name on a clothes pin and then clip each pin to a job wedge.

Students will locate their names to find out which jobs they are responsible for that week. At the end of each week, move the clothes pins clockwise to the next job.

Post a **Job List** on the class notice board where students can quickly and easily reference it.

- Name of the job
- Description of the job
- What time of day the job is done
- How often the job is done

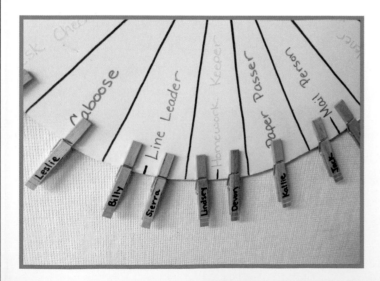

TEACH

1. Discuss with the class how a clean, inviting classroom is more welcoming and conducive to learning than a dirty, disorganized one. Tell them that everyone in the classroom will be working as a team to keep the classroom ready for learning.

Danielle Blonar's student job chart is a "Flutter of Helpers." Her students are responsible for their specific job for one week. If a student is absent, the Substitute helper does the absent student's job for that day.

2. Announce that each student will have a specific job for a certain length of time.

3. Introduce the Job List, describing what needs to be done and when it should be completed. Explain that every student plays an equal role in maintaining a clean and inviting classroom environment.

4. Show the class the Job Wheel. Explain how to read the Job Wheel and how the job responsibilities are rotated each week.

5. Read each student's name and the job that the student will be responsible for in the first week. Ask each student to verbalize the details of the job assignment. Clarify as needed.

REHEARSE

Role play and have students practice their different jobs, one at a time. Ask the class if the job has been performed correctly. Remind them that one day, they will be doing the same job.

Tell students the Job Wheel and Job List are available for them to check their responsibilities.

Thank students for doing a good job during practice.

REINFORCE

Build housekeeping time into the daily schedule. Most jobs are done at the end of the period or day. Be consistent with the time students are assigned to carry out their classroom jobs.

Students may need gentle reminders to start their jobs, check the Job Wheel, or refer to the Job List in the first week of school, but these will soon become routine.

S.O.S. Time

S.O.S. or "**S**uper **O**rganized **S**tudents" time is typically held during the final 10 minutes of the school day. The entire class participates in the time, whether they are doing a classroom helper job or organizing themselves and getting ready to leave for the day.

S.O.S. time is recognized by students as a time to help the classroom, the teacher, and themselves. When the teacher announces it is S.O.S. time, the students spring into action by organizing their classroom and themselves.

S.O.S
Super Organized Students

- Take out your binder.
- Do your classroom job.
- Check to see that your homework is in your binder.
- Pack up your backpack.
- Sit at your desk quietly waiting for dismissal.

THE **PROCEDURE**

Classroom Phone Ringing

With a set procedure for answering the classroom telephone, the teacher can stay focused on working with students, rather than taking the call immediately and disrupting the flow of the lesson.

THE **SOLUTION**

The teacher is not always able to answer the classroom phone when it rings. **Establish a procedure so students know who should answer the phone, what to say to the caller, and the appropriate noise level in the classroom.**

This procedure minimizes disruptions to teaching and learning and resolves these issues:

1. Who should answer the phone if the teacher is busy
2. The need for reduced noise level in the classroom when there is a phone call

THE **BACKGROUND**

When the phone rings in the middle of teaching a lesson or helping students, it is disruptive. Stopping to answer the phone is equally disruptive. Establishing a procedure lets students know how a phone call will be handled, so it will have little impact on the learning taking place in the classroom.

THE **PROCEDURE STEPS**

Keep a supply of paper and pencils by the classroom phone for anyone to use when taking a message. Put a small sign next to the phone, along with the appropriate voice prompt you want students to use.

- *Room ___, student speaking.*

- *Just a minute, please. Let me tell the teacher.*

- *The teacher is coming to talk to you.*

- *The teacher will call you back at the end of the class time. May I ask who is calling, please?*

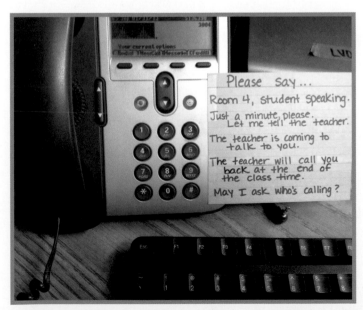

Students are reminded how to respond to a call should the telephone ring during class time.

Let students know you will always answer the phone unless you are working with students. This procedure is for the times when you are not able to answer the phone.

TEACH

1. Tell students that when the classroom phone rings, they are to lower their voices to a whisper if they are talking.

2. The student closest to the phone answers it. Students are not to race to the phone—it is not a competition.

3. Instruct the students to answer the phone with this prompt, "Room ___, student speaking."

4. After the caller identifies himself or herself and gives the message, instruct the student to tell the caller, "Just a minute, please. Let me tell the teacher."

5. The student goes to the teacher and passes the message forward.

6. Depending on the message, you can ask the student to tell the caller, "The teacher is coming to talk to you," "The teacher will call you back at the end of the class time," or, "May I ask who is calling, please?"

7. The student will write the number on the notepaper by the phone and deliver it to the teacher.

REHEARSE

Write the voice prompts on the board for the students to follow along as they rehearse answering the phone with you.

Model the procedure for a student answering the classroom phone using the script.

Ask the class to read the voice prompts aloud as you pretend to be a caller.

Ask a few students to play "telephone" and practice the exchange.

Remind the class that when they hear the classroom phone ring, they should continue to work, but to lower their collective voices to a whisper.

REINFORCE

When the first call comes through that you are unable to answer, stop what you are doing and focus your attention on the student answering the phone.

After the call is done, share with the entire class how the procedure was performed correctly or incorrectly. Reference what the student did well and highlight what needs to be improved the next time the classroom phone rings.

Script for Entering a Classroom

Good morning, I am Alex Chan from 5A, may I speak to Mr Holland, please?

Help students identify themselves before the classroom door is opened for them. A standard message posted outside of the classroom door, helps students relay the information you need to know before the student enters.

Students Live Up to Expectations*

I teach classes of Pre-AP and regular English, and I love to display the work of my regular students with the work of my Pre-AP students. The difference in the quality of work cannot be distinguished because I have the same expectations for all my students.

My colleagues often ask, 'Is this the work of your Pre-AP students?'

I am so proud when I reply, 'No, this project was done by my regular English students.'

Students live up to your expectations. Set the same standards for all students.

*Read the classic research on expectations in **THE First Days of School**.

Oretha F. Ferguson ■ Fort Smith, Arkansas

Teaching Procedures Becomes Routine

If you are reading this story now, you are almost one-third through the heart of the book—the Procedures. However, *THE Classroom Management Book* is not a novel. You probably have not read it in sequence from beginning to end.

THE *Classroom Management Book* was written with the same flow as its companion book, *THE First Days of School*. It was not meant to be read in sequence from cover to cover. It is meant to be used more like a vehicle's owner's manual. You will be able to turn to a section to solve a problem, learn a new technique, or have an Aha.

Every recipe in a pressure cooker cookbook repeats the same warning: "Open the lid carefully, tilting the lid to release the steam away from your face."

Every hot beverage from a retail outlet carries the same warning: "This beverage is hot and can burn you."

Every procedure in this book repeats the same three steps to teaching a procedure:

- **Teach**
- **Rehearse**
- **Reinforce**

Master the three steps to teaching a procedure, until the process becomes routine for you. Each step to teaching a procedure helps to make that procedure a routine for students. When procedures become routines, your time is spent focused more on the learning that takes place in the classroom and less focused on the management of your classroom. Procedures give you time to teach.

Bathroom Breaks

Classroom time is reserved for learning. Recesses and breaks are reserved for taking care of personal needs. Because emergencies do occur, a procedure is needed to minimize classroom disruptions.

THE **SOLUTION**

Constantly giving permission to students who need to use the bathroom during class time can interrupt the flow of your lesson. Keeping track of how often students leave class for the bathroom is also a waste of time. Make it a student responsibility. **Use a pass system to monitor bathroom use.**

This procedure provides these opportunities:

1. Manages students' use of the bathroom during class time
2. Prevents instructional time from being interrupted by students leaving the classroom
3. Encourages students to take care of personal needs during recess or breaks

THE **BACKGROUND**

Attending to personal requests from students, like asking permission to use the bathroom, does not have to interrupt the flow of your lesson. Using a class pocket chart gives students the responsibility of managing their own needs.

The class pocket chart is hung in the classroom. Each student is assigned a pocket, labeled with the student's class number or name. Inside each pocket, place a set number of bathroom passes.

The number can be calculated based on students' ages and how many days of school exist in the month. For instance, in regular school months, a student may be given four bathroom passes.

However, for shorter school months due to holidays and vacations, a student may only receive two bathroom passes.

These passes are the students' temporary tickets out the door for brief bathroom breaks.

Students, identified by their class numbers, have their own pocket of bathroom passes for the month.

The bathroom pass has the student's name and your class information on it.

THE **PROCEDURE STEPS**

Create a file of the bathroom passes using a table in Microsoft Word or a similar program. Once the file is created, it can be updated easily if necessary and printed each month.

Secure a chart with pockets. Label each pocket with the student's name or unique number.

Print, cut, and organize the month's supply of bathroom passes and place the appropriate number of passes for the month in the student's corresponding pocket. This monthly task can be assigned to an aide or classroom helper.

Ease students' minds on the first day of school by teaching them the procedure for bathroom breaks.

Patience

Have patience.
All things are difficult before they become easy.

Saadi ■ Medieval poet

TEACH

1. Show students the bathroom pass pocket chart. Explain that each student has a pocket labeled with the student's unique number or name.

2. Tell the class that at the beginning of each month, everyone will be given the same number of passes. These passes are their temporary tickets out the door if they need to use the bathroom during class time.

3. Remove a set of bathroom passes from a student's pocket. Point out that each of the passes has the student's name on one half, and that students can only use their own pass—not their classmate's.

4. Point out that they must keep the pass with them when they are excused to use the bathroom.

5. Teach students that when they need to use the bathroom, they should remove the pass from the wall pocket.

6. Quietly bring it to the teacher.

7. If it is a suitable moment during class for the student to leave and use the bathroom, you will tear the pass in half, keep the name portion, and then give the student the Bathroom Pass half. Tearing the pass signals that the student may leave the room.

8. If it is not a suitable time for the student to leave, you will hand the pass back to the student. The student then returns the pass to the pocket and waits until a suitable time arrives. Exceptions are made if the student has an emergency.

9. Explain that the procedure means there are minimal disruptions to the class learning time.

10. Students can go for bathroom breaks as long as they have passes left in their pockets.

11. Bathroom passes last for a month. If a student runs out of passes before the month is over, they must ask for permission to leave the classroom at an appropriate time during the lesson. Schedule a time to hold a conference with the student to check if there is a physical problem that needs attention and to make recommendations for better management of their bathroom needs.

12. If students have passes left over in the month, they can be saved toward earning a special activity. For instance, six passes could be rewarded with a ticket to a special movie shown during lunch time. Select an incentive that's appropriate for your students. Incentives encourage students to use the bathroom during recess, breaks, or lunch instead of during class time. Students are responsible for saving their unused passes.

13. Tell students that upon returning to class from the bathroom, they are to immediately go to their seats and resume the lesson. They are responsible for any missed learning.

14. The name portion of the bathroom pass you keep can be put on your desk as a reminder of who is not in the classroom if an emergency arises.

15. Limit the number of students to one boy and one girl leaving the classroom with bathroom passes at any given time.

REHEARSE

Model how students are to use the bathroom pass to request a bathroom break. Go to a pocket and retrieve a pass. Talk aloud as you demonstrate the steps of getting the pass, taking it to the teacher, and waiting to see if permission has been granted to leave the classroom for the bathroom.

Select a student to demonstrate the steps. Remind the class that when approaching the teacher with a pass, they should be quiet and careful not to interrupt the lesson or their classmates.

Students quickly get the idea of how the bathroom pass procedure works and when it is considered a suitable time to use the pass. They dislike having their passes handed back to them and will avoid approaching the teacher in the middle of a lesson or while the teacher is helping another student.

Students also grasp how important it is to use the bathroom during recess, breaks, or lunch. Having an incentive motivates everyone to try and save their passes.

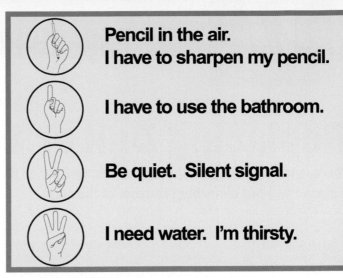

Pencil in the air.
I have to sharpen my pencil.

I have to use the bathroom.

Be quiet. Silent signal.

I need water. I'm thirsty.

At Alain L. Locke Elementary School in New York City, the entire school uses the same procedure for asking to use the bathroom. There are signs posted throughout the school that serve as reminders to the students.

REINFORCE

Some students will need to practice this procedure before they learn to be sufficiently quiet and discrete about seeking permission to go to the bathroom. Thank each student for remembering the procedure and following it properly.

If a student forgets the procedure, select a student to assist in helping the student recall the correct procedure.

The Best One So Far

Over many years of teaching, I tried different procedures for managing bathroom breaks in my classroom. I tried wall passes—one for the girls' bathroom and one for the boys' bathroom. I tried a log-out and log-in sheet by the door, where students had to record the time they left the room and the time they returned. I tried individual bathroom pages, which students kept in their desks and brought to me to initial before leaving the room.

All of these methods worked to some degree, but were never very effective at encouraging students to use the bathroom during recess.

However, using the wall pocket with the passes in the pockets ready to use has encouraged students to use the bathroom during recess because they know that unused passes can be saved for classroom incentives. In nine years of experimentation, this procedure has worked best of all the ones I have tried. It has been so successful in my classroom.

Sarah Jondahl ▪ Brentwood, California

THE **PROCEDURE**

Replacing Dull or Broken Pencils

There is no need to disrupt instructional time when a dull or broken pencil can be quickly and quietly replaced without disturbing the rest of the class.

THE **SOLUTION**

There is no need for long lines at the pencil sharpener or to lecture students on personal responsibility and the importance of bringing enough sharpened pencils to class. **Do not get upset and do not waste learning time.**

This procedure allows students to resume work quickly with a fresh pencil and solves these issues:

1. Lessons being disrupted by students sharpening pencils
2. Students not being able to locate a sharp pencil when needed
3. Dull or broken pencils piling up inside students' desks

THE **BACKGROUND**

Dull and broken pencils are a fact of life, but there is no need for students to wave their broken pencils in the air, saying, "I broke my pencil! I need a new pencil!" This disrupts other students, throws the class off task, and wastes learning time.

Some teachers allow students to use the class pencil sharpener. The problem with this solution is the resulting disturbance of grinding wood and lead throughout the day.

Students also tend to talk to one another while awaiting their turn—adding more distractions to the classroom.

A simple procedure ensures students can get replacements and resume work quickly without disrupting the class.

THE **PROCEDURE STEPS**

Establish a pencil station at the back or sides of the classroom. Locating the station in the front of the room can easily distract students, while classmates continually walking up to the station can cause others to lose focus and stray off task.

Place two cans at the pencil station. Label one can "Used Pencils" and the other can "New Pencils."

The Used Pencils can is a handy place for students to turn in dull or broken pencils. The New Pencils can contains sharpened pencils for students.

Students often keep handheld pencil sharpeners at their desks. These can lead to a mess of dropped pencil shavings in and around a student's desk. The sharpener can also be a distraction during class.

Personal Pencil Sharpeners

If students prefer to use their own pencils and want to sharpen them during class time, they are encouraged to bring personal pencil sharpeners to class.

Provide each student with a Ziploc-type bag to store the sharpener. Tell students the bag must be sealed at all times. The bag can be opened when a student needs to sharpen a pencil, but the pencil must be sharpened within the bag so that shavings fall directly inside it. The bag can then be sealed and stored until there is an appropriate time to empty the shavings.

As the pun goes, "Writing with a broken pencil is pointless." Provide multiple ways for students to stay on point in class!

Sharpened pencils are placed in the New Pencils can, ready for use.

TEACH

1. Show students the pencil station and point out the two pencil cans. Tell students that if a pencil is dull or broken and a replacement is needed, they are to hold the used pencil slightly above their head. Students must remain quiet and not wave the pencil in the air.

2. Tell students that you will acknowledge the student's pencil signal. A no shake of the head means the student must wait to exchange the pencil. A yes nod of the head means the student has permission to exchange the pencil for a new one.

3. Tell students to walk quietly to the pencil station, place the dull pencil in the Used Pencils can, and take a fresh pencil from the New Pencils can. Students are to quietly walk back to their seat and resume working.

4. Announce that all students will take turns acting as the pencil monitor. At an appropriate time, typically at the end of the period or day, the monitor will help sharpen pencils from the Used Pencils can and replace them in the New Pencils can.

Pencils Ready to Go

As part of an end-of-day procedure, some elementary teachers have students put a sharpened pencil in their mail cubby and retrieve it upon entering class the next morning. With their pencils sharpened, students are ready to work as soon as they enter the classroom the next day.

18 •))

Learn more about how praising a deed is more effective than complimenting the student.

REHEARSE

Select a few students to demonstrate the procedure for exchanging a dull pencil for a sharpened one.

Make positive comments and gentle corrections while students are demonstrating the procedure. Say things like, "Thank you for not disturbing others while you exchanged pencils." The students are encouraged to repeat the same action the next time a pencil is in need of replacement.

No Pencil Dilemma

Students who are unprepared for class can be given or loaned a pencil. Students can borrow a pencil from the New Pencils can. At the end of the class period or close of the school day, students who borrowed a pencil should return it to the Used Pencils can.

REINFORCE

Remind students that the objective of this procedure is to minimize disruptions to the lesson and to the class while making available to the students the tools they need to do their work.

It is their responsibility to bring their writing instruments to class each day and to have them ready to use. However, if they forget to bring a pencil to class, or if during the class period they need a new pencil, they must follow the procedure for getting one.

It Is Tragic to Lose Something

I feel like I have so much to share with educators and teachers about what my experience on "Survivor" in 2009 has given me as a leader. How many of us really know what it is like when a child comes to school starving and we ask them to perform academically? Well, I know now!

How many educators know what it is like when a child who has nothing loses their pencil? In the past, I would always just give them another pencil, hug them, and move on. Now, I truly know what it is like to have nothing and lose something. It is shattering.

This is just an example of how my experiences have changed me as a leader.

**Debra "Debbie" S. Beebe ■ Auburn, Alabama
"Survivor" Tocantins, Brazil**

18

Keeping Desks Orderly

Provide students with tools to keep their desks organized. A simple, one-minute procedure for keeping their workspaces orderly shows them it is not the onerous task they imagined it to be.

THE **SOLUTION**

Students who get into the habit of straightening their desks take pride in their workspace. They are also likely to carry these organizational skills over to other aspects of their lives. Once-a-week wipe-downs and one-minute cleaning periods during the day will keep the workspace neat and ready for learning.

This procedure provides these opportunities:

1. Workspaces kept clutter-free and orderly
2. Students able to quickly find their materials

THE BACKGROUND

Students can often be seen rummaging through their desks for supplies, unloading half the contents of their desks before finding the needed item, and finally chucking everything back in their desks again. This process creates a mess and is distracting to other students; it also has a tendency to become habitual. Students repeat the routine of rummaging through their desks multiple times during the school day. While these students struggle to get ready to learn, organized students are sitting and waiting, squandering learning time.

THE PROCEDURE STEPS

Create a model of what an organized desk looks like. Take a picture of this model desk and print a copy of the picture on a sheet of paper. Annotate the sheet with arrows pointing to specific parts of the desk and accompanying instructions. For instance, all loose sheets of paper belong in the binder; all pencils and pens belong in the Tool Pouch; all hard cover books, including all workbooks, must be kept together.

Provide students with various labeled folders, such as Homework folder or Graded Papers folder, to prevent loose sheets from cluttering up desks.

Provide students with a Tool Pouch or invite students to bring one from home. This can be as simple as a Ziploc bag or plastic box. All of the required supplies—crayons, scissors, glue sticks, pencils and so on—go in this container.

TEACH

1. Duplicate copies of the organized desk model and distribute it to the students. Talk them through the organized desk on the sheet. Emphasize that keeping an organized desk reduces the frustration of trying to locate things.

2. Explain that an organized desk saves everyone time during a busy school day because there is no need to wait while classmates fumble for misplaced textbooks, papers, or pencils.

3. Tell students that if they take one minute to quickly organize their desks throughout the day, they will find it much easier to keep their desks neat, than if they keep it messy all day and try to clean up just before the last bell.

4. Distribute the labeled folders, and explain the purpose of each.

5. Distribute the Tool Pouch and explain what goes in the bag. Tell students it is to remain closed unless they are retrieving an item.

6. Explain that cleanliness is a priority in class, and that every Monday morning, each student will receive a wet wipe for a quick wipe-down of their desks.

7. Explain that all unwanted papers from their desks go into the garbage.

MAJOR DESK CLEAN UP:

1. REMOVE ALL SCHOOL SUPPLIES FROM DESK.
2. ARRANGE NOTEBOOKS AND BINDERS ON ONE HALF.
3. ARRANGE TEXTBOOKS, PENCILS, ERASERS AND GLUE ON THE OTHER HALF.
4. LOOSE SHEETS NEED TO BE PUT IN THE APPROPRIATE BINDER OR DISCARDED IN THE RECYCLE PAPER BIN.
5. DESK NEEDS TO BE ORGANIZED IN THIS MANNER AT THE END OF EACH DAY.

Post a chart that leads the class in how to organize their desks.

REHEARSE

Immediately after explaining the procedure, distribute wet wipes to a few students and have them model wiping down their desks. Then, distribute wet wipes to everyone else in class and have them do the same. Observe students and redirect them as needed.

Ask students to refer to the model of an organized desk before taking a minute to get organized. Set a timer to count down the minute. Remind students of what goes into each folder and the Tool Pouch.

Walk around the classroom as students are organizing their desks, and validate the students who are doing a good job. At the end of the minute, tell students they may not have managed to get their desk entirely organized in the allotted time, but you can already see a positive difference.

Remind students that they can take a minute to organize their desks whenever they have a little down time—while the teacher is handing out papers, for instance, or if they finish a class assignment early.

Allow students another minute to complete the job while you continue to monitor their progress.

If any students are struggling to organize their desks, ask a classmate to help those who need an extra hand in following the model.

When all the desks are organized, distribute a wet wipe to each student to clean their desktops. Tell them to dispose of the wet wipe along with any unwanted papers as they exit the classroom.

The Amazing Mr. Frog

*Our class mascot is a frog. After the students have left for the day, I select a desk for the 'most organized desk' designation. I place a stuffed toy bullfrog, **The Amazing Mr. Frog**, on that student's desk. The students are eager to come to class the next morning to see whose desk has been selected.*

The Amazing Mr. Frog remains in the classroom for the day and then leaps to another desk after the students leave for the day. The students enjoy being recognized for keeping their work space neat and clean.

Sarah Jondahl ▪ Brentwood, California

REINFORCE

Ideally, one of the classroom jobs is the role of a Desk Wizard. (See Procedure 14.) During the last few minutes of the school day or class period, the Desk Wizard's job is to take a quick peek inside students' desks. If the Desk Wizard sees a disorganized desk, he or she gently taps the student on the shoulder to remind the student to tidy the desk.

As you work with students at their desks, commend them on how well their desks are organized.

If a student needs extra help in organizing, invite that student to meet you after class when you can help the student learn to become better-organized.

Everything Has a Place and a Purpose

Peggy Ervin of Kingsport, Tennessee, says a procedure for organizing a desk will help students keep the contents in order. She models how to stack the books in the desk. She discusses what happens to the soft-sided workbooks when stacked with the hard books. The students learn to stack according to size with the hard cover books on one side and the soft cover books on the other side.

> My students have a homework folder and a graded paper folder (to be signed by parents weekly). These folders and notebooks eliminate the paper clutter that is often found in a student's desk. I can quickly look in at a desk as I scan the class to check for messes. I make neatness a priority at the beginning of the year and then as needed. On Monday morning students get a wet wipe and clean their desk top and inside, to begin the week with a positive note, a clean desk.
>
> I think the greatest aid to the clean desk is the pencil pouch. Many years ago, I grew very tired of the noisy clutter boxes for crayons and supplies. As I strolled through a store, I saw a money bag! This was the answer to my noise problem. The bag costs about $2.00. It easily holds the required small box of crayons, scissors, glue stick, pencils, and erasers. Now the students have a "tool pouch" that will last several years.
>
> I always suggest that parents keep a tool pouch at home for homework activities. Using a procedure to have the students keep up with the necessary tools is important for success. This technique cuts down clutter.

People Expect Procedures

People expect procedures for everything they do in life: going to the movies, waiting in line to be served at a restaurant, using guidelines in the workplace, etc. Teaching children the procedures they need to follow in class gives them life skills and makes teaching less stressful.

When procedures are in place, the teacher can focus on teaching. Students know automatically what needs to be done. They know when and how to do it because you have taught them until they get it right.

Marie Coppolaro ▪ Queensland, Australia

Collecting and Returning Papers

Seating students in a predetermined order will assist in the process of collecting and returning papers. As students master the procedure, less instructional time is wasted on the process.

THE **SOLUTION**

Distributing and collecting papers can be a simple task. **It should not be a major undertaking that interrupts instructional time.** When students know how to handle papers, instructional time is not squandered.

This procedure solves these issues:

1. Collecting and returning papers quickly and easily
2. Keeping papers in order for scoring, recording, and returning

THE **BACKGROUND**

This is a request for a common task repeated many times in a school day, "Pass the papers, please." As routine as the process is, for many teachers the task is a burden. Regardless of your class size or the number of assignments per week, you are handling thousands of pieces of papers each year with a potential enormous amount of instructional time lost.

# of Students	# of Assignments	# of Pieces of Paper Handled		
		1 week	9 weeks	In a year
25	5	125	1,125	**4,500**
150	2	300	2,700	**10,800**

Some teachers have students place homework papers in a basket or tray as students enter the room. This does not waste instructional time, but it leads to more work for the teacher because the papers are in random order for recording scores or returning papers. Teachers who use this method of managing papers usually

1. walk around the room and distribute individual papers as students sit and wait;

2. return the papers to the trays and ask the students to find their paper as they exit the room—leading to chaos; or

3. ask students to return the papers to their classmates—creating distractions and unnecessary chatter as papers are returned one by one.

None of these methods are effective for the student—or the teacher. Yet, walk into most classrooms and on the teacher's desk are baskets filled with papers.

THE **PROCEDURE STEPS**

Arrange the classroom desks in columns and rows. Assign students to seats with a predetermined order—either alphabetical or with a class number. **Seat students in order across the rows, so papers will be in order when collected.**

Collecting Papers

Instruct students to pass their papers across the rows, not up columns. Problems arise when papers are passed up columns:

- The teacher cannot see what is happening behind each student's back. Papers are waved and backs of students are poked as the papers are passed up the column.

- There are usually more students seated in a column than across a row. The more students there are handling papers, the more time it takes, which detracts from instructional time.

Thus, passing papers up columns takes longer and may result in greater class disruption.

Papers are collected much easier and faster when they are passed across the rows rather than up a column.

Returning Papers

If papers are picked up in order, then returning the papers follows the same order. Piles of papers are set on each end desk, so the students can pass them across the row to its rightful owner.

When desks are grouped, students give their papers to one person within the group. The teacher or a designated student collects the papers from each group. Once reviewed, the papers are returned to the groups and distributed to classmates by the designated student.

Mailboxes

Many elementary classrooms assign cubbies or trays, one to each student. The classroom Postmaster delivers papers to the cubbies on behalf of the teacher. Students retrieve their papers at an appointed time, usually as they are packing up to go home.

TEACH

1. Show students how to place their paper on top of the stack before laying the stack on the desk of the student sitting next to them. Ask the left or rightmost student (depending on which way you choose to pass papers—to the left or to the right) in each row to **place the paper on the desk** of the student sitting at the desk in the adjacent column. To prevent students from flicking papers as they are passed, do not allow papers to pass from hand to hand.

19 •))))
Learn the methods and benefits of assigning each student in your class a unique number.

2. The next student places his or her paper on top of the paper received, then places the stack of papers on the desk of the person sitting at the next adjacent column. This procedure is repeated until the papers arrive on the desk of the left or rightmost student's desk.

3. Emphasize the importance of paying attention while papers are being passed, so there is no confusion or papers dropped.

4. Ask students in all rows to follow the same procedure—passing papers across the row, from column to column, until all papers reach the end of the row.

5. Ask the student sitting in the last seat of the last row to pass the collected papers to the student sitting in front of him or her. That student places the stack of collected papers **on top of the papers** received until all the papers reach the student sitting in the front seat of the column. The stack is now in alphabetical or numerical order.

6. Retrieve the stack of papers that are now in your predetermined order from the student in the front row corner.

With a big smile, the teacher collects the class's papers.

REHEARSE

Ask students to head a piece of paper, following the format for heading papers. (See Procedure 10.)

Review the passing sequence before collecting these papers by asking some questions and eliciting hand signals as a reply. Demonstrate what the hand signal should look like when responding to the questions.

1. Which direction are you going to pass the papers?

2. Where are you going to put your paper on the stack—on top or underneath?

3. What direction do the stacks get passed for me to collect them?

Ask students to pass in their papers according to the procedure. As students pass their papers from desk to desk, monitor the process. Correct or redirect students when necessary. Commend students who are following the procedure correctly.

Tell the students you are now going to <u>return</u> their papers to them. Remind them how to select their paper from the top of the stack and to check their names on the paper to make sure they have taken only their piece of paper. If there are five students in each row, give the first five papers in the stack to the student

sitting in the rightmost seat. That student keeps his or her paper—conveniently located at the top of the stack—and places the remaining papers on the desk of the student to his or her left. The second student keeps his or her paper—also conveniently at the top—and places the remaining papers on the desk of the student to the left. This process repeats until the final paper arrives on the desk of the leftmost student.

Practice collecting and returning papers until you feel comfortable that the students understand the process.

REINFORCE

Tell students that this procedure will be used each time papers are collected or returned.

Walk to the side of the room the first few times you collect or return papers and scan the rows to ensure students are following the procedure correctly.

As the students strive to complete the task without error, challenge them to accomplish the movement of paper more efficiently. Time how long it takes students to collect or return papers and chart their progress. Challenge each class to outshine the other classes you teach by taking the least amount of time to collect or return their papers.

Passing in Papers for Collection

6	→	5	→	4	→	3	→	2	→	1	↑
12	→	11	→	10	→	9	→	8	→	7	↑
18	→	17	→	16	→	15	→	14	→	13	↑
24	→	23	→	22	→	21	→	20	→	19	↑
30	→	29	→	28	→	27	→	26	→	25	↑

Pass papers across the rows putting each paper on top before putting it on the desk to the right. Once all papers are to the far right, pass the stacks of papers up the column of desks, putting each new stack on top. All papers are in order when they reach the desktop of seat 1.

THE PROCEDURE

Classroom Transitions

Class time lost by students in chaos can be avoided when students know how to move easily from one activity to the next.

THE **SOLUTION**

Seamless classroom transitions allow for the uninterrupted flow of learning throughout the school day. Learning time is wasted when students have no direction for ending one task and beginning another. **A transition cue guides students through a defined process so that time is used efficiently in the classroom.**

This procedure provides these opportunities:

1. Students transitioning seamlessly between activities inside and outside of the classroom

2. Learning time used efficiently for classroom transitions

3. Student and teacher preparation of materials

THE **BACKGROUND**

A transition is a bridge connecting one activity to the next throughout the school day. Transition is difficult for some students to handle because it requires students to do three things at once.

1. **Close** one task.
2. **Prepare** for the next task.
3. **Refocus** on the next task.

When a class of students can make these transitions seamlessly, more time can be spent working and learning, instead of constantly struggling to get back on task.

Refrain from announcing an instant transition.

Announce a transition at least two minutes before it occurs. This is especially important for autistic and ADHD students.

THE **PROCEDURE STEPS**

The key to a smooth transition is clarity and simplicity of instructions. Keep it short, simple, and easy to do.

1. **Plan smooth transitions within the classroom.**
2. **Prepare lesson materials ahead of time.**

1. Plan Smooth Transitions Within the Classroom.
Plan the transition cues you will use in your classroom to move students from one activity to the next.

Transition in Three

When it is time to transition from one lesson to the next or move from one area to the next, announce to the class, "**One.**" Let them know that the time is approaching to move on to the next activity. Announce, "In two minutes, I will say, 'Two, Change.'" This serves as a warning to students that a transition is about to happen.

After two minutes, say, "**Two, Change. Please put away your work and get ready for the next lesson.**"

After one minute, say, "**Three, Refocus.**" Give students the direction to begin a new task, like turning to a page in a book, numbering a sheet of paper, or assembling into groups.

In three calm minutes, students are led through the transition process.

Visual learners like to see what is going to happen after the transition takes place. Write on the board the activity that will take place after the transition. Remember, you are asking students to process multiple steps in performing the transition. Help them get to where you

want them to be after the transition takes place by posting what they should be doing at the end of the transition.

When the transition begins, do not talk during the transition time. Talking distracts the students' ability to switch properly. If directions are constantly being given, then your transition instructions are not short, simple, and easy to do.

Watch carefully, and if someone is not shifting properly, give a firm smile and a hand signal or point to the directions on the board. Help students get to where you want them to be at the end of the transition.

Introduce students to the transition cues you've created. There is no single, right transition cue. Select one that will be easy to use, keeping in mind that there are many transitions throughout the school day. These are some common transition cues:

- Playing music
- Ringing a bell
- Flashing color cues
- A hand-clap rhythm
- A verbal countdown
- A visual countdown

Select the most appropriate transition cues for the class and use them consistently.

Tell students they will always be told how much time they will have to work on an activity. Students should also be given a Time Remaining warning to bring closure to their work. A warning gives students a chance to tie up loose ends in a calm manner before the end time is called. An abrupt end to an activity causes panic and rushes students to find an ending point for their work.

At the beginning of an activity, announce how much work time students will have and how they should transition to the next activity.

You will have ten minutes to work on this math page with your seat partner. I will give you a one-minute warning before time to the last problem you are working on.

When the ten minutes are up, you will hear this song play (play the beginning of the song, so students know what to listen for).

At the start of the song, I expect you to quietly pass your math pages for collection and to pull out your Literature Circle books. The song lasts for three minutes, so you must start your transition from math to reading as soon as you hear the song begin.

There is no need to rush, since three minutes is plenty of time for you to pass your math page and to take out your Literature Circle books.

Again, I expect you to do this quietly so that we can all enjoy the song while it is playing.

Thank you. You may begin.

When students know how much time they will be given to work on an activity and are given a warning before the transition, it allows them to manage their work time better. They are also less likely to panic and more likely to transition from one activity to the next with ease. Provide students with fun transition cues, so they remember what they are listening for and can enjoy these transitions.

2. Prepare Lesson Materials Ahead of Time.
Organize lesson materials ahead of time, so you can efficiently distribute supplies, and students are able to retrieve needed supplies and start work quickly. Your method of distribution will depend on the size of the class, the room arrangement, and the materials being distributed.

TEACH

1. Explain to the class the purpose of transition time.
2. Tell them what cue you will be using to signal it is time to stop one activity and get ready for the next.

Brain Break

A Brain Break allows students to take a brief pause from working before getting back on task. Bodies welcome this pause to refresh, and it gives you a moment to get ready for the next lesson. Students can use this time to

- get a drink of water;
- sharpen a pencil;
- talk productively with another student; or
- stretch.

Practice by setting a timer for one minute. When the timer beeps, students are to stop what they are doing, complete tasks like sharpening pencils, and return to their seats immediately. Do a countdown for students to indicate the seconds remaining for them to sit and begin the next activity.

3. Let them know how much time they will have between activities.

4. Provide a visual checklist of steps for students to follow to accomplish the transition successfully.

5. Demonstrate how you would like to see the students transition. Let them know what step you are doing and explain how the steps flow smoothly.

REHEARSE

Ask students to pretend they are working on a class assignment. Tell them your cue for a transition. Verbally pace the steps you've outlined as they do the step. Lead them and correct them through each step.

Ask students for understanding and readiness to transition on their own.

Ask students to pretend they're working on an assignment again and give them the cue for transition. Tell them this time they are to do the transition themselves. Watch and correct students with a hand signal or point to the directions on the board as needed. Do not talk during transition time. Talking distracts the students' ability to switch succesfully.

At the end of transition time, thank the students for following the procedure.

REINFORCE

At the first opportunity for the class to do a transition in a real setting, remind the students of the cue and what the procedure is when they hear the cue. Monitor progress and thank students as they follow the transition procedure.

A thank you at the end of every transition time reminds students you are aware of what they are doing and how they are doing it.

Transitions for Preschoolers

Transitions guide children gently through the day and help children move smoothly from one area of the room to another.

Teach the students your transition cues:

- Flash the lights.
- Clap your hands.
- Play music or sing a song.

Most importantly, move to the area where you would like the children to gather and begin the task or talk quietly. The children will quickly come to where you are to see what you are doing.

Singing Jingles

I always greet my students and others who pass by in the hall as they come into class. It sets the tone for the period and builds positive relationships.

I sing jingles to my students (juniors and seniors) as transitions to new activities. They soon learn the jingles and sing with me. They love singing the songs, which simultaneously segue quickly from one activity to another, because they know the routines. It makes transitions easy, simple, and fun.

I am completing my 40th year of teaching in June and have totally enjoyed it because I know I am an effective teacher!

Dave Allen ▪ Mt. Shasta, California

20 •))

Learn how to keep materials organized to ease the confusion experienced during many transition times.

Keeping Students On Task

Establishing a clear procedure for over-active engagement in activities reminds students to adjust their activities to established classroom norms if their actions are unacceptable.

THE **SOLUTION**

Some activities prompt students to become overly exuberant and unable to manage their actions while performing the work. **The STOP strategy is very effective for returning the classroom atmosphere to one that's suitable for learning.**

This procedure provides these opportunities:

1. Eliminates noisy, off-task class behavior
2. Returns the classroom to an appropriate learning atmosphere

THE **BACKGROUND**

Students can become overly excited about exploratory or hands-on activities and have trouble following classroom procedures. Sometimes, the day before a school holiday or a special event triggers high-spirited, over-energized student actions. Whether students are being loud and disruptive, or just silly and off task, you need a quick signal to let them know their actions are inappropriate, and they need to get back to work.

THE **PROCEDURE STEPS**

This technique is only effective when the majority of students are engaged in off-task behaviors, not with individuals who are disrupting the rest of the class.

Teach this procedure as needed, not in advance. Teaching this procedure in advance sends the message you expect students to be noisy or to go off task.

To solve this problem, write the word STOP on the board in large block letters. Each time the class engages in off-task behavior, draw a line through one letter. If you have to mark out all four letters, stop the activity and change to something more structured.

Mark out a letter to signal to the class they need to STOP their current actions and refocus on the activity at hand.

Have a back-up activity ready at all times. The activity is one the students do on their own while they recompose themselves. A back-up activity could be

- completing a worksheet,
- reading in their choice of books, or
- writing in their journals.

You may never have to deploy your back-up plan, but you should have one ready.

TEACH

1. Introduce the STOP strategy only as a last resort. If students become noisy and stray off task, first use the established quiet signal to get their attention. (See Procedure 13.) Remind them it is important to work quietly and to stay on task.

2. If students continue to stray off task, write the word STOP on the board and explain to the students you will mark out one letter of the word each time the class is engaged in noisy or off-task behavior. Ask students to help each other keep the noise level in check.

3. Tell them if all of the letters are marked out, you will stop the activity and continue with a quiet learning activity. There is no need to explain the back-up activity, just be sure you have one ready!

4. Each time the class is too noisy or off task, use the established quiet signal to get students' attention. Deliberately mark out one letter from the word STOP, and gently but firmly announce, "Class, you just lost a letter." There is no need for you to raise your voice or to explain why a letter has been erased—the students know the reason.

5. When only the final P of STOP remains, remind the class that they have one last chance to prove their ability to stay on task. Do not hesitate to mark out that last letter. The most ineffective thing you can do is repeatedly threaten to mark out the letter and not do it.

6. If students improve their behavior, circulate in the classroom and thank them for improving and leave the remaining letters on the board.

7. If the last P is marked out, deploy the back-up activity. Emphasize that the class needs to work in silence and that whatever work was not completed in class that day is to be completed as homework.

8. Refrain from lecturing the class. If you feel something must be said, a simple, "The noise level and your actions for this activity were not appropriate. Maybe we can try it tomorrow," will suffice.

REHEARSE

Tell students there is no rehearsal for the STOP procedure. This procedure happens in real time and will only be used if the noise level or activity level in the classroom needs to be refocused on learning. Anytime they see STOP on the board is an indication that their actions are not appropriate for the learning activity.

REINFORCE

The next day, attempt the activity again. Expect to see a big improvement in the students' ability to stay on task and keep their noise levels down.

You will find that implementing this procedure in its entirety just once ensures the final P will never be marked out again. The loss of hands-on activity time—to be replaced by individual work and homework—is too high a cost for most students.

THIS IS A
PROFANITY
FREE
ZONE

Tone Is the Key

Individual outbursts can be just as disruptive to a class as groups not focused on a task. At times, all it takes is a single word—by the student—to change the learning atmosphere in the classroom. Help students control a sudden slip of the tongue and make it a learning opportunity.

Profanity-laced conversations can deflate a carefully constructed learning environment. Whether said intentionally or said in error, profanity is not suitable language to use in the classroom.

Janene Palumbo teaches 7th- and 8th-grade English in an urban school district. She knew the conditions would be challenging, and she knew that she would encounter profanity on a rather frequent basis. She thought about how she could de-escalate the situation when she heard the profanity. Even though many students, because of their cultural upbringing, need to "save face" when confronted by the teacher, she knew she could not allow profanity in her classroom. She was proactive, not reactive, to the problem she knew would surface in her classroom.

Special Guideline

This classroom is a

"Profanity Free Zone."

That means that there will be no cussing, for ANY reason.

Respected scholars use academic language to accurately describe what they are thinking.

Profanity Procedure

1. Teacher will remind you of our

   "Profanity Free Zone"

   by saying **"Language."**

2. Student will respond by apologizing and restating what they said in academic language.

3. Student will say, **"Sorry. What I meant to say is . . . "**

Janene uses the text on these PowerPoint slides to teach the no profanity procedure to her students.

Janene explains to her students that she expects academic language in class at all times. However, she tells them she understands that they have been out with their friends all summer and may not be accustomed to using academic language every day.

She also understands that many times, cursing is a habit, and "you may not even realize you are doing it." The use of the word "understands" helps Janene come across as empathic to their habit and not as someone lecturing or sanctimonious.

She then shows them a picture of her fiancée and explains that he, too, struggles with profanity (which he really does!). She assures them he is trying to fix his problem, but explains that bad habits are hard to break. Although her fiancée is an intelligent person, some people may not believe it when they hear him swearing.

With that as an introduction—the part about the fiancée makes it very real and personal—Janene explains the procedure to the class.

Janene says, "If I hear you swearing, I will say, 'Language.'" She says this in a neutral tone and says that the neutral tone is the key to the effectiveness of this procedure.

Try saying "language" in several tones. It's amazing how effective it is when said in a neutral and non-judgmental tone.

Janene tells them that they are not in trouble when she says "Language." But, she expects them to follow the procedure and correct themselves.

To correct the swearing, the student says, "Sorry. What I meant to say is . . ." This teaches the use of academic language when the students substitute the correct words.

Be vigilant the first few weeks about consistently enforcing this procedure. Every time profanity is heard, even if it is whispered, say, "Language."

Janene says, "It Works! The students are so responsive to the procedure. They immediately apologize and restate what they meant to say. In fact, students often censor their own language before I even say 'Language' to them. Many have broken the habit altogether and have not used profanity after the first few weeks. I now hear students say 'Language' to each other!"

The most important part of this procedure is for the tone of voice to remain neutral and non-judgmental.

THE PROCEDURE

Finishing Work Early

Help students get the most out of their learning time with a list of things to do should they complete their work before the rest of the class.

THE SOLUTION

When students finish their work early and have nothing to do, productive class time is wasted. The likelihood of misbehavior increases. While Silent Reading is used by many teachers to fill this time, there are other ways to engage students in learning while they wait for classmates to complete an assignment.

This procedure resolves these issues:

1. Students not working when they are done with their assignments
2. Ineffective use of time in the classroom
3. Redirecting students who are off task
4. Avoiding the question from a student, "I'm done. What do I do now?"

THE **BACKGROUND**

The individual who is working is learning. If students are off task while waiting for the next assignment, or waiting for other students to finish the current assignment, the teacher is usually the one working—running around the classroom trying to keep students busy.

A Start Off and Finish Off chart will keep early finishers working while the rest of the class completes the assignment. Your time is free to continue teaching rather than finding work to keep students busy.

Start Off	Finish Off
1. Do your assignment. 2. Check your work. 3. Turn it in.	1. Check your unfinished file. 2. Work on writing in your folder. 3. Choose a free time activity from the shelf. 4. Read your chapter book.

The Start Off and Finish Off keeps students on task and learning at all times.

THE **PROCEDURE STEPS**

Prepare a T-chart that will be large enough for posting in the classroom. Label one side Start Off and the other side Finish Off.

In the Start Off column, list a number of activities or assignments for students to do when they finish their work. Number them to indicate the priority in getting the tasks done.

In the Finish Off column, give a numbered or bulleted list of activities or assignments. Students can choose what they wish to do from the list once they finish all the tasks in the Start Off column.

Post the chart in the classroom.

TEACH

1. Show students the Start Off and Finish Off chart and explain each column.

2. Point out that the numbered assignments in the Start Off column must be done in sequential order.

3. Explain that students may choose from any of the other tasks in the Finish Off column once they have completed all the tasks in the Start Off column.

4. Explain that students can only work on the tasks on the Start Off and Finish Off charts when they have finished their assigned class work and only while they're waiting for others to finish.

5. Tell students the lists will not always be the same. Some items will be added and some will be taken away as the school year progresses. Let the students know you'll point out changes as they are made.

REHEARSE

Once the students have moved on to their independent practice, remind the class that as they finish, they should look at the Start Off and Finish Off chart.

Watch as students complete their work and move on to their Start Off assignments. Acknowledge students who follow the procedure correctly and remain on task.

If a student is done, but is not following the procedure, catch the student's attention, smile, and point to the chart. Nod with approval as the student follows your request.

REINFORCE

At the end of the assignment time, and before moving on to the next lesson, acknowledge the students for using their time effectively. Let them know that the Start Off and Finish Off chart will be posted every day, and will remain posted for their reference as they finish their work.

What's in a Name?

The Start Off/Finish Off chart is adaptable to any grade level or subject taught. Give the categories a name that relates to the personality of your classroom.

Alternate Names for		Type of Classroom
Start Off	Finish Off	
A	Z	For primary grades
1	2	
Mr. B's Choice	Your Choice	
P¹ Priority 1	P² Priority 2	For a Math class
Chapter 1	Chapter 2	For a Literature class
Appetizers	Desserts	For a Home Arts class
Touchdown	Extra Point	For a PE class
Uno	Dos	For a Spanish class
Salutation	Signature	For a Writing class
Core	Crust	For a Science class

No Chaos

I had a preservice teacher observing my classroom. I welcomed him and encouraged him to monitor the students, watch the day's events, and help with the lab activities of the day.

The following day I asked him, 'So, what do you think of this whole business of becoming a teacher?'

I was not prepared for his response.

He calmly replied, 'There isn't the stress involved with teaching like I thought there would be.'

I asked what he was expecting to see in the classroom.

'I expected there to be more conflict, argument, and chaos. It's what I remember when I went to middle school, and I expected to see it here. There just weren't any of those things in your classroom.'

I shared with him that all of the teachers teach classroom procedures the first week of the school year, and I tell the students everything they need to know, right down to the dreaded— what to do if you think you'll be sick in the middle of class. Nothing is left to chance. I have a plan and a procedure for everything that happens in this classroom.

The students know exactly what to do when they walk into my classroom. There is no chaos because they KNOW the procedures. There is consistency, not only in this classroom, but it is repeated in every classroom here at Sisseton Middle School.

Tammy Meyer ■ Sisseton, South Dakota

Creating a Learning Zone

Fifth-grade teacher **Elmo Sanchez** knows about whining and yelling. His first year of teaching was filled with it. Elmo's students spoke throughout the class period. They were disruptive, whined, and lacked direction. Elmo found himself yelling in response.

That entire first year, **Elmo** was frustrated. He was unhappy in his profession, and it affected his family life. During the summer, Elmo attended a workshop sponsored by the Miami-Dade school district where he heard the Wongs talk about classroom management. It was his "light bulb" moment. Elmo began to visualize how he could improve his classroom management.

It took him about a month to create a PowerPoint presentation (in Spanish, too) that conveyed his new classroom policies and procedures. **Elmo created a Learning Zone—a place where his own students could soar, a place free from the distractions of whining and yelling.**

In the new school year, he warmly greeted each one at the door. "Welcome to our class," he said as he shook each student's hand. "I'm glad you are here."

When the students entered the classroom, there was an opening assignment, and the students immediately began to work. When Elmo entered the class, his students were busy working.

He introduced his students to the procedures that would create their classroom learning zone. His students, many who are ESL students, had absolutely no problems understanding what was expected of them in his class. They learned how to ask permission to use the restroom, what to put at the top of papers they turn in, what to do when they finish an in-class assignment early, and how to appropriately treat their fellow classmates.

When the bell rang at the end of the day, Elmo's students remained in their seats for the teacher to dismiss them, not the bell. They all left with smiles. Elmo's smile was pretty big, too!

There's no more whining, no talking back, no shouting in Elmo's classroom. Parents tell him that their kids complain about missing school when they are sick. Elmo just smiles. He knows that he has created a strong learning zone based on classroom management strategies that enable him to create calm where there was once chaos. He is happy; his family is happy; and his students are happy, too.

Missing Assignment Slip

With a responsibility card, students become accountable for reporting their reasons for missing work, and you receive documentation to keep on file for the missing work.

Student Responsibility Card

For students who _do not_ have the assigned homework

Fill it out.

Sign and date it.

Turn it in with the homework papers.

Student Responsibility Report

Date: _____   Printed Name: _____   Subject: _____

Completing your homework or assignment is your responsibility as a student.

Missing Assignment: _____

I do not have my homework today because:

_____ I did the assigned homework, but I did not bring it to class.
_____ I chose not to do my homework.
_____ I forgot to do my homework
_____ I did not have the appropriate materials at home.
_____ Other reason is _____

Explanation of checked item above (provide detailed explanation).

_____
_____

Signature: _____

THE **SOLUTION**

A **responsibility card keeps track of excuses for missing student work** and dramatically improves a student's homework turn-in rate. It provides excellent documentation at Parent-Teacher conferences because you do not have to scramble to explain why a student received a failing score on an assignment.

This procedure solves these problems:

1. Lack of documentation for missing assignments
2. Lack of responsibility for missing assignments

THE **BACKGROUND**

It is impossible to remember why students don't have their assignments in class, unless you have a tracking tool to assist you. A student responsibility card is a lifesaver for gathering data from students and provides documentation for underperformance.

With a form for students to complete, teachers can continue their routines without interruption because the students are responsible for recording the details on the card.

The student responsibility card as a "Pink Slip" has gained some notoriety in teaching circles because **Chelonnda Seroyer** shares it when she speaks and when people look at the video, *Using THE FIRST DAYS OF SCHOOL*, at www.EffectiveTeaching.com.

The Pink Slip came about when a veteran teacher was cleaning out her supply cabinet and offered a package of pink copy paper to Chelonnda. Because it was near the end of her first year of teaching with that looming prospect of being pink-slipped, the pack of pink paper was a vivid reminder of what could happen to her.

Fortunately, those thoughts took a more positive outlook and soon she birthed the "Pink Slip."

As Chelonnda says,

> *I initially 'stole' this procedure from another teacher, **Karla Henson** of Liberty Middle School in the Madison City School District. Eventually, I modified it and adapted it so that it fit the specific needs of my classroom. I called the adapted version the 'Pink Slip.'*
>
> *This has been an extremely helpful procedure because it has provided me with valuable documentation, it encourages the students to take responsibility for their work, and it also allows the students to share valuable information with me that I might not know.*

When I go to a meeting and attempt to explain why a student has a zero for an assignment, it makes me feel organized, competent, and professional when I am able to provide documentation for each missing assignment. This takes the guess work out of why students miss assignments.

I also think that it is important for students to be able to explain why they do not have their assignments. This gives them a voice, and it lets them know that I am genuinely concerned about what is going on with them.

One of the options on the form allows them to admit that they chose not to do the assignment. I let them know that we all make conscious choices each day. When they make a choice not to do their homework, they must accept responsibility for that choice.

I have found that students truly appreciate this gesture and are generally very receptive.

On the other hand, I have also found that they will do even a small portion of the assignment, just so they won't have to fill out a form. This works well because anything is better than a zero in the grade book!

THE **PROCEDURE STEPS**

The Pink Slip is taught to students on the first day homework is assigned. The procedure is applied if the student comes to class the next day without the homework assignment.

21 •))

Watch Chelonnda Seroyer tell how the Pink Slip saved her life and a grandmother's life.

Print the Pink Slip on pink-colored paper. Include prompts and fill-in blanks for these things:

- Date
- Name
- Class Section
- Missing Assignment
- Checkboxes for the student to indicate the reason for not doing the homework:
  - I did the assigned homework, but I did not bring it to class.
  - I chose not to do my homework.
  - I forgot to do my homework.
  - I did not have the appropriate materials at home.
  - Other—Please explain below. (provide space)
- A student signature line
- A parent/guardian signature line (optional)

TEACH

1. Introduce the Pink Slip to students.

2. Distribute a Pink Slip to each student to have in hand while you explain how it will be used and when it will be issued.

3. Tell students that when they choose not to do a homework assignment, they are to complete a Pink Slip and submit it to you when homework is collected.

4. Let them know you record an "M" (for missing) for the student's missing assignment, with the understanding and encouragement to complete the work and replace the "M" with an appropriate grade.

5. Emphasize to students that there is no penalty for filling in a Pink Slip—other than the loss of credit for the missed homework assignment.

6. Ensure students understand that completing their homework is their responsibility. You will not punish students if they do not complete their homework.

7. Tell them you will keep the Pink Slips on file while they are students in your classroom. These will be produced during Parent-Teacher conferences if there is a pattern of missed homework assignments.

Pink Slip Variations

A Pink Slip is a form of documentation; it is not a form of discipline. With a multitude of students, this slip is essential for establishing patterns for missed work in a non-judgemental way.

- If a student has been Pink-Slipped, but later turns in the missing assignment in a timely manner, you may choose to award the student partial credit for the assignment.

- You may send the Pink Slip home for a parent to review and sign.

- If a student refuses to complete the Pink Slip, complete the form with the student's name, date, and assignment that is missing. Note on the Pink Slip that the student refused to complete the form. Keep this as documentation for the incomplete assignment.

Date: _____
Printed Name: _____
Class Section: _____

You've been *Pink-Slipped*!

Completing your homework or assignment is your *responsibility* as a student.

Missing Assignment: _____

I do not have my homework today because:

_____ I did the assigned homework, but I did not bring it to class.
_____ I chose not to do my homework.
_____ I forgot to do my homework.
_____ I did not have the appropriate materials at home.
_____ Other—please explain below.

_____
_____
_____

Signature _____

A Pink Slip gives students the opportunity to explain why they chose not to do their homework.

REHEARSE

Model how a Pink Slip will be issued. When a student does not have a homework assignment, you will do the following:

- Place a Pink Slip on the student's desk.

- Ask the student to complete the form and turn it in with the rest of their homework.

- Record an "M" to document the student's missing assignment.

- File the Pink Slip as documentation.

Ask students to practice completing the Pink Slip as if they have not done their homework.

Select Pink Slips to read aloud and demonstrate to the class that the student's form was done correctly.

Collect the Pink Slips as you would homework.

Check them for accuracy and conduct one-on-one conferences with those students who need additional direction in completing the form.

REINFORCE

Walk students through the procedure steps for the Pink Slip the next morning. When it is time to check or collect homework, ask the class if anyone needs a Pink Slip for not completing their homework. Distribute a Pink Slip to those who need one. Allow an extra minute to complete the form before the homework is collected. If time permits, check the forms for accuracy.

Why Not a Zero

Assigning a zero to work requires an enormous amount of effort to counteract such a low grade.

Imagine grading on a percentage scale from zero to 100 with A = 90%, B = 80%, C = 70%, D = 60%, and F = 50%. In a 100-point scale, there is typically a 10-point break between the passing grades, whereas there is a 60-point spread between a zero and barely passing, a D or 60%. Assigning zeros as grades is illogical and mathematically incomprehensible.

If a student receives a zero and then on the next assignment or test the student scores a perfect 100, that only averages out to 50%, still a failing grade.

It would take a student two perfect 100% scores to reach a C and four perfect 100% scores to climb up to an A.

Rather than a zero, any letter or symbol would work. If you feel the need to record a number, consider 50%. The climb back up to a passing grade is more reasonable for students to accomplish.

 22 •))

Read Thomas Guskey's article, "O Alternative" for other scoring options.

THE **PROCEDURE**

Daily Closing Message

At the end of the school day, review the events that occurred and the learning that took place with a Daily Closing Message.

Class Recap
These are some of the things we did today, Wednesday, Decem

In Reading, we
1. started reading *2030: A Day in the Life of Tomorrow's Kid*.
2. looked for common nouns and the adjectives that made ther
   plasticized blocks, smart trampoline, and magnetized hoverir

In Math, we learned how multiplication and division are related

For Writing, we worked on using adjectives to improve our writ

Tonight for homework, please
1. read the next 10 pages in our *2030* book.

THE **SOLUTION**

A school day recap eliminates the scenario, whereby students go home and claim they did nothing in school that day. **This technique allows you to share with students and parents the daily activities, lessons, and homework in a matter of minutes at the end of each day.**

This procedure provides these opportunities:

1. Reviewing the day's events with students
2. Reminding students of upcoming events and homework
3. Conveying to the parent the activities of the school day
4. Opening a line of communication for the parent and child

THE **BACKGROUND**

Every school day is packed with activities and lessons, so that when a child goes home and tells a parent that nothing happened all day, the teacher can establish the facts.

> Parent: *What did you do in school today?*
>
> Child: *Nothing!*

A Daily Closing Message is a half-page memo that is prepared by the teacher during the school day and then read aloud in class before dismissal. **It is a quick way to review the day's lessons and activities, give reminders about upcoming events, and reinforce the homework for the evening.** It is also a valuable communication tool between the school and home.

The Daily Closing Message is kept as brief as your time permits. Only the highlights of the day are shared. Create a template so that preparing the Daily Closing Message each day is a simple task.

This is the text from one of Sarah Jondahl's Daily Closing Messages.

Daily Closing Message
January 15

These are some of the things we did today:

This morning, we held our reading group sessions.

1. We read a new story and learned new vocabulary words.
2. We also learned about adjectives. We know that an adjective is a word that describes a noun.
3. Continue to read at home with your parents.
4. Tonight, as you read your book, look for all of the adjectives in the story.

In math, we continued to work on our multiplication tables.

1. Today, we focused on division.
2. We played division games in small groups.
3. Continue to practice all of your math facts at home with flash cards.

We are learning how to write paragraphs.

1. Today, we worked on writing a topic sentence, followed by details that will support it.
2. Of course, we can't forget that every paragraph needs an ending sentence.
3. We know that a paragraph needs to stay on one subject.
4. You can practice writing paragraphs at home.

This is your homework tonight:

1. Please do the math page about division and multiplication.
2. Also, work on the page about adjectives.
3. Study your spelling words and don't forget to read with a parent.

Have a great rest of the day!

THE **PROCEDURE STEPS**

Create a template for your Daily Closing Message. This will make the process go quickly each day. Adapt a format to suit your needs.

Daily Closing Message

Date

These are some of the the things we did today:

In Reading, we

In Math, we

For Writing, we worked on

Tonight for homework, please do

Don't forget to

I'll see you tomorrow!

Class Recap

Date

Today, in **(Subject)**, we

1.

2.

3.

Homework for tonight is

1.

2.

3.

A project due soon is

I'll see you tomorrow!

Using a template for a Daily Closing Message allows you to fill in the blanks throughout the class period or school day.

TEACH

1. At the end of the first day of school, give a copy of the Daily Closing Message to every student. Explain that the Daily Closing Message will be read every day.

2. Model the correct procedure for reading the Daily Closing Message. Tell the class that different students will be selected to read the message. Everyone must follow along, so they are able to read the message at home.

3. Once the Daily Closing Message has been read aloud, instruct students to place it with their materials to take home. Tell them it is their daily responsibility to read the Daily Closing Message to a parent when they get home.

4. Tell students that in your letter to their parents, you shared that a Daily Closing Message would go home each day. Thus, students can expect their parents to ask for this slip of paper every day.

REHEARSE

Select a few students to read the Daily Closing Message aloud after you have read it. Explain that as their classmates read, everyone should follow along.

Thank the students who read the Daily Closing Message and for showing the class how to do the procedure correctly.

Remind students to place the Daily Closing Message with their take-home materials and to share it with a parent when they get home.

REINFORCE

If students are not following along as the Daily Closing Message is read aloud, remind them by asking, "What is the procedure for the Daily Closing Message?"

Check their understanding of your expectation for how the procedure is to be done.

Rehearse the procedure again with one or more of the students until the Daily Closing Message procedure is demonstrated correctly.

In your first communication to the home after the start of the school year, remind parents that the Daily Closing Message has been going home with their child each day.

Communication on a Weekly Basis

Marco Campos is an elementary teacher in the Houston Independent School District where 99 percent of the students qualify for free or reduced-price lunch, 85 percent live in government-supported housing, and 42 percent are considered "at-risk." Yet, in past years, 100 percent of his students have passed the Texas Assessment of Knowledge and Skills Test in Math. How is this done?

Marco introduces his students to his classroom procedures beginning on the first day of school. He tells his class that the procedures are for their benefit. "If you follow our procedures, school will be less confusing for you."

One of his procedures is the **Homework Conduct Control Sheet**. He devised it to maintain involvement with the adults who are at home and responsible for the students. Each week the students take home a task list that they are asked to work on with their parents or guardians. The task list includes their daily home learning in reading, Spanish, math, and English.

Their daily home learning reinforces what the students have learned in class that day. When they have finished working together, the parents or guardians must sign the task list. The Homework Conduct Control Sheet is also used as a vehicle for two-way communication between

Marco and the adults. Marco provides daily feedback on classroom conduct. In return, the adults at home can easily communicate with Marco.

Marco was asked to participate in Project Aspire—a study of highly effective teachers sponsored by the school district. The teachers were brought together to share their effective teaching methods. At first, Marco was awed by what he called the real experts. But, he soon realized that every teacher there had several things in common. Every single teacher was a motivator. Each of them understood the importance of building solid relationships with their students and the home. Every single teacher agreed that the most important ingredients for teaching success are motivation, perseverance, compassion, and procedures!

In Marco's words, "To be an effective teacher you must make a conscious decision to be positive and to set high expectations—for your students and yourself."

Guideline Infraction Notice

When a student chooses not to follow a classroom guideline or rule, have a procedure in place to immediately address it. This allows the teacher to acknowledge the infraction while preserving instructional time.

Guideline Infraction Notice

Please correct your behavior ☐

Please return to task ☐

See me after class!

Signature_____

Offense_____

Conference results_____

As conceived by Lawana Welt – Liberty Middle School

THE SOLUTION

With a Guideline Infraction Notice, you can deal with potentially disruptive behavior without embarrassing the student in front of the class. You are able to meet privately with the student, express genuine concern, and work out a solution with the student.

This procedure solves these issues:

1. Wasting instructional time due to inappropriate student behaviors
2. Getting into a confrontation with a student or making incorrect assumptions about why a student may be acting inappropriately

THE **BACKGROUND**

Teachers will typically do one of two things when a student acts inappropriately in the classroom. They either ignore the behavior, or they address it in a confrontational way in front of the entire class. Both actions waste instructional time.

Ignoring the behavior causes the teacher to lose valuable instructional time because the behavior disrupts the class.

Ignoring the behavior communicates that it is not inappropriate. It can also communicate to the students that the teacher does not know how to handle the situation. Therefore, ignoring inappropriate behavior often leads to more elevated infractions, which typically leads to office referrals and almost always results in lost instructional time.

In contrast, having a proactive procedure in place often prevents students from escalating their negative behaviors and will ultimately help to maintain a healthy and stress-free environment for the teacher and the students.

Addressing the behavior in a confrontational way and attempting to embarrass a student never has a positive effect for the teacher or the student. Ultimately, it ends up as a demeaning situation and leaves the student and the teacher feeling frustrated, angry, and resentful. These are toxic emotions that poison the classroom atmosphere and inhibit learning.

Exposed students have much more to lose from demeaning situations than do teachers. There are times when students would rather suffer disciplinary action and "save face" in front of their peers than allow a teacher to "win" a confrontation in the classroom setting.

This procedure allows you to address the behavior by discretely sharing your concerns with the student and asking them to see you after class so, together, you can discuss it calmly.

Oftentimes, there are underlying reasons that cause students to act out in class. They may be sleepy and stressed from a difficult home life, exhibiting avoidance behaviors, or doing things to gain attention from peers. These things are sometimes evidence of deeper problems that need to be addressed by parents.

Do not assume that students are exhibiting these negative behaviors simply to make your life miserable; this can lead you to develop resentments toward a student instead of finding out what is really going on with the student.

A conference with the student after class helps you gain a better understanding of why the student is acting out in class.

Depending on the grade level or the infraction, you may choose to send home a "Guideline Infraction Notice" in the student's Take Home folder on the day of the occurrence.

THE **PROCEDURE STEPS**

Create a Guideline Infraction Notice on cardstock or colored paper and print a supply to have readily available. Choose from the ideas on the list to include on your notice:

- Checkboxes to indicate your instruction to the student. For instance, "please correct your behavior," or "please return to task."
- Space for filling in details of the offense
- A notice to the student to see the teacher after class
- A student signature line
- A parent signature line
- The date
- Space for filling in the results of the student-teacher conference

```
Name_____    Date _____

☐ Please correct your behavior.  ☐ Please return to task.  ☐ See me after class!

Guideline Infraction _____

Conference Results _____

_____

Signature_____  ☐ Parent Signature _____

Notes:
```

A Guideline Infraction Notice calmly identifies misbehavior and minimizes instructional time spent on the issue.

TEACH

1. Distribute a copy of the Guideline Infraction Notice to each student.

2. Explain how the notice will be used and when it will be issued. When a student chooses to act inappropriately, you will do the following:

   - Place a check mark in the appropriate boxes.
   - Note the offense.
   - Place the notice on the student's desk without saying a word.

3. Emphasize that when a student acts inappropriately in class, instruction and learning time are lost. You understand that there may be underlying reasons why the student is choosing to act in certain ways. You will not embarrass the student in class, but will meet with him or her after class to discuss the issue, if needed.

4. Tell students that repeated offenders and blatant disregard of classroom guidelines will result in a conference. The need for a conference is up to your discretion.

5. Tell students that when they choose to act inappropriately, they will be issued a Guideline Infraction Notice. The notice will be silently placed on the student's desk, and you will resume the lesson.

6. The student must see you after class for a conference if the box is checked and discuss the infraction to arrive at a resolution.

7. The student will acknowledge the infraction by signing the card.

REHEARSE

Select a student to role-play breaking one of the classroom rules.

Model how you will mark the infraction notice. Ask students to follow along on their copy of the notice.

Show students how you will place the Infraction Notice on the student's desk.

Ask for a response to the next step. Elicit an answer from the student that confirms they will see you after class. This can be a simple nod of the head.

Tell students the Guideline Infraction Notice will be filed as documentation, and that it may be produced during Parent-Teacher conferences.

Ask for questions about the process and the notice.

Model the procedure again if necessary.

REINFORCE

When the first infraction occurs, go through the procedure. If the student reacts with a puzzled look, respond with, "And what's the procedure for the Guideline Infraction Notice?"

After class, follow up with the student at your individual conference with clarification as needed.

 23 •))

Listen to Chelonnda Seroyer share how she uses the Guideline Infraction Notice.

Preparation and Consistency Are Key—A Mother's Advice

Tena Hubble is an elementary teacher in Virginia. Her daughter has followed in her footsteps and has become an elementary teacher. Like all good mothers, Tena has shared her years of wisdom and experience with Rhiannon.*

I have been using what the Wongs teach for nearly twenty years. I instilled some of the most important and useful tips from the Wongs in my daughter, Rhiannon.

The Wong concepts that Rhiannon used made her student teaching experience, and her first year of teaching, enjoyable for both herself and her students, and have earned Rhiannon excellent evaluations from her supervisors.

Here are some of those tips.

1. Know what you want your students to do from the moment they arrive in the morning until they leave your classroom in the afternoon. Plan procedures for every situation you can think of, such as entering the room, unpacking, morning assignments, lunch count, transitioning from one subject to another, rotating in learning stations, turning in homework and classwork, going through the lunch line, hallway procedures, and packing up to go home. Have your management plan thought out and written down before the first day of school so that you are ready to present, model, and practice.

2. Demonstrate how each procedure should be done and how it shouldn't be done. Guide students through practice until they have the procedures down pat. Be prepared to revisit, rehearse, and reinforce periodically throughout the year, especially after extended vacations such as winter and spring breaks. Don't be afraid to tweak a procedure if it isn't working the way you envisioned.

3. Create an atmosphere of mutual respect and comradery in your classroom through morning meetings. Model cooperation and respect towards your students and their parents, and to your own supervisors.

4. Read *THE First Days of School* and follow the Wongs' advice and methods. Reread the book (I have read it several times) because it will remind you of possible scenarios that necessitate having a procedure in place that you may have forgotten or not thought of at all.

5. Rethink your procedures as you gain experience or change grade levels. Procedures may need to be tweaked for different groups of students and different grades or ages.

6. Be consistent with your procedures and expectations. **CONSISTENCY IS THE KEY TO SUCCESS**.

I have read some of Rhiannon's evaluations and all of her supervisors have been very complimentary of her classroom management. Her student-teaching supervisor even commented that the second-grade class in which she student taught was better behaved at the end of her student teaching than when she began.

Rhiannon now teaches fifth grade in Virginia. Her current principal commented that her classroom management skills far exceed those of many seasoned teachers.

It's all due to having a classroom management plan and taking the time to have the students practice procedures until they become automatic.

*Read Rhiannon's response to her mother's advice on page 173.

Morning Meetings

Starting the school day with a class meeting brings the teacher and students together to practice communication skills in a trusted setting. Meeting time is spent answering concerns, outlining the learning objectives of the day, and announcing future events.

THE **SOLUTION**

Morning Meetings allow the teacher to model discussions and teach effective problem-solving techniques that will serve students well throughout their lives. **Meetings regularly foster class spirit and give students the chance to deal with conflicts in a gracious and non-confrontational manner.**

This procedure provides these opportunities:

1. Gathering the class together to connect
2. Discussing the daily schedule or calendar
3. Discussing any issues the students may have
4. Previewing upcoming events

THE **BACKGROUND**

Morning Meetings can take place at any time and as often as needed, so the class can connect as a team.

Morning Meetings are usually held after the morning opening activities and typically last no longer than 10 minutes. During the meeting, the schedule for the day is shared, as well as important upcoming dates and events.

The Morning Meeting is a time when students can bring up any relevant issues that may be bothering them. These may include conflicts on the playground or a classroom procedure that is not being followed. Discuss these issues as a class, without mentioning names. Talk about how these issues can be resolved.

At the end of the Morning Meeting, wrap up with a discussion of the opening assignment and set your positive expectation that it will be a great day for all.

Creating Harmony

I use Morning Meetings to create a community of learners. This premise is based on creating cohesion among the students, so they care about each other and accept one another for who they are.

This has been a very important step in my classroom because I have special needs students who require in-class support.

A classroom that runs on procedures and students that respect each other leads to a harmonious environment.

Laura Keelen ▪ **Brick, New Jersey**

THE **PROCEDURE STEPS**

Establish a time for the Morning Meeting to take place and the location for the meeting in the classroom. Determine how and where students will sit. The ideal arrangement is in a shape (oval, circle, or square) where eye contact is possible among all the group members, and everyone feels a part of the group.

Decide on the flow of the Morning Meeting and keep it consistent. Post it for students to follow:

1. Greet each other.
2. Read morning message.
3. Review the daily schedule.
4. Reminders of upcoming events.
5. Discuss student concerns.
6. Review the opening assignment.

TEACH

1. Explain the purpose of a Morning Meeting and what the class will gain from it. Emphasize that students should not mention names when discussing issues.
2. Ask students to gather for the Morning Meeting in your predetermined location and seating arrangement.
3. Introduce the flow of the meeting chart and tell students that all Morning Meetings will follow this outline.
4. Tell students that all meetings will begin by sitting close together in their formation, followed by a friendly greeting.

5. Start the greeting by turning to the student on the right and saying, "Good morning, Chris." Chris returns the greeting by saying, "Good morning, Mrs. Jondahl," before turning to the classmate on his right and greeting the classmate. The greeting continues around the circle until it returns to you.

6. Read an opening statement to the students. It can be an interesting fact, why today is going to be a great day for learning, or something they will be learning today.

7. Share the day's schedule, as well as any important upcoming dates or events.

8. Open the discussion for students to share issues. Remind students not to mention names. Model this by starting with an example. Keep discussions short and brief so that everyone who has an issue gets a chance to bring it up. Don't allow the class to get carried away with any one issue or by repeating issues.

9. End the meeting with a review of the opening assignment.

10. Conclude by wishing everyone a great day.

11. Instruct the students to return to their seats in an orderly fashion.

REHEARSE

The first time the class gathers for a Morning Meeting, make sure students are spread out as evenly as possible before complimenting them for arranging themselves correctly.

Show them where the outline of the meeting will be posted, and encourage them to anticipate each part as you move through it during the meeting.

Remind students not to mention names before opening the discussion to the floor. During the discussion, identify students who do a good job of talking about incidents in an effective manner. Highlight what the

student said. For instance, "Mary did a great job using her words to express her concerns about . . . ."

Tell students you will be the leader of the Morning Meetings at first, but everyone will have an opportunity to lead the meetings.

REINFORCE

Follow the flow of the meeting you have posted, so students will feel comfortable when it is their time to lead the meeting.

It may take students time to get a grasp of talking about issues effectively, without mentioning names. Remind them that one of the purposes of the meeting is to discuss and resolve issues without hurting other's feelings or confronting them.

As you feel confident in turning over the leadership of the meeting to the students, remain a part of the meeting circle and participate as if a student.

Morning Meetings Modifications

Instead of opening the discussion to the floor, a Praises and Concerns Board can be used to facilitate discussions and keep them in check. A portable whiteboard can be divided in half with a line drawn down the middle. One half is reserved for Praises and the other half for Concerns.

Students can note under Praises someone in class who did something nice or for someone who was helpful. Students can note under Concerns an issue they want to discuss.

During the meeting, place the Praises and Concerns Board where everyone can see it and discuss students' praises and concerns for the week.

The Meeting Leader can share a piece of interesting information as an opening or end-of-meeting activity.

Preparation and Consistency Are Key—A Daughter's Reflection

Rhiannon H. Richards is an elementary teacher in Virginia. Her mother's insights and the application of that wisdom in her classroom have earned her excellent evaluations from her supervisors.

I have just ended my first year of teaching, and I would like to reflect on what made it such a success. One of my professors required **THE First Days of School** for a classroom management course. Because I saw what my mother did as a teacher, I've always known that classroom management was the most important characteristic of an effective educator and what most new teachers struggle with.

I know that students thrive on consistency and routine, so planning my first year, and especially the first few weeks of teaching, was critical.

I used a strong (well-organized) classroom management plan because I have a very busy classroom, full of transitions which are made easy by the routines we have practiced and mastered. Each transition is the same; however, I play a different chime to indicate which activity we're transitioning to.

These are some other typical procedures from my classroom *management* plan.

Greeting

I greet each student entering the classroom. I have the morning routine posted each day.

Start of the Day Routine

Students review the morning routine on the SMART Board, which includes a thinking point and activity.

Morning Meeting

The morning meeting usually lasts twenty minutes and is meant to be quick and to the point to keep students engaged.

Walking in a Line

- All students face the same direction
- Students keep one pace behind the student in front of them
- There is no leaning or rubbing against the wall
- They keep their hands to themselves
- They walk quietly

Midday Routine

An alarm is set for the amount of time we have before lunch for students to

- Check their binder
- Prepare their math materials, which follows lunch
- Complete any unfinished work from earlier in the day
- Wait for lunch instructions when the alarm goes off

End of the Day Routine

- Write their homework and daily points in their planner
- Check for mail to take home
- Pack up their book bags
- Stack up their chairs
- Stand quietly by their desks waiting for the dismissal bell to ring

I am very pleased that my students have performed well and met 75 percent and 70 percent for reading and math, respectively, in the standardized state assessments for achievement in the state of Virginia. I know this is my calling in life, and I am so thrilled to help shape the students that will lead our future.

Class Discussions

Define how students participate in class discussions to encourage all students to feel confident about sharing their thoughts and ideas. Students learn when it is appropriate to speak or listen, and to do so respectfully.

THE **SOLUTION**

All students should feel comfortable participating in discussions without anxiety that their classmates will talk over them, interrupt them, or disrespect them. **When students know how to truly listen to what others have to say, they will learn more and acquire greater benefit from a lesson.**

This procedure resolves these issues:

1. Uneven student participation in class discussions—students speaking out of turn, monopolizing the discussion, or not contributing at all

2. Students not respecting their classmates during discussions

3. Students' lack of confidence in public speaking

4. A classroom where students do not feel they are in a safe and trusted environment

THE **BACKGROUND**

Areactive teacher is preoccupied with stopping students from speaking out of turn. The proactive teacher is more concerned with having all the students take turns speaking in class.

The classroom is a safe space where students feel comfortable participating in class discussions. There will always be students who are more confident with public speaking than others, but they must not be allowed to monopolize class discussions. Quieter students must be encouraged to share their perspectives and are more likely to do so when they are assured that their classmates will listen when they speak—without interrupting, ignoring, or belittling them.

The age level of your students will dictate the technique you use for calling on them. With younger students, providing a Talking Tool—a Koosh Ball, a bean bag, or a stuffed animal—is an effective way to encourage mutual respect. A student can talk only when in possession of the Talking Tool. Everyone else must be quiet, with their eyes and ears focused on the speaker. Discussions are more productive when there is a tool that helps signal to students who can speak and when it is a person's turn to share.

Employing a Talking Tool has the added benefit of providing a visual aid for the teacher to track student participation. When a Talking Tool is passed around the room during a class discussion, it becomes very obvious if some students are participating more than others. The reassurance that the Talking Tool provides also tends to motivate students to participate and get more out of the discussion.

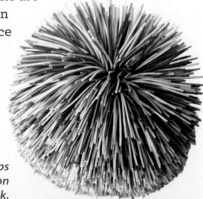

Using a Talking Tool helps the students focus on whose turn it is to talk.

The Teacher as a Model

Students observe the teacher listening and participating in classroom conversations on a daily basis. The effective teacher models

- proper eye contact;
- upright sitting posture;
- how to paraphrase an idea that someone has shared; and
- how to use classmates' contributions as a springboard to their own.

These are valuable communication skills that students learn quickly, demonstrate in school, and use throughout life.

THE **PROCEDURE STEPS**

If you are going to use a Talking Tool to facilitate discussions, be sure it is safe for the students to use in tossing to one another. Class discussions or small-group discussions need guidelines. These guidelines can include any from this list:

- You may speak only when holding the Talking Tool.

- Eyes and ears must be on the person speaking.

- Mutual respect—respect the person speaking, and he or she will be respectful in turn.

- The classroom is a safe space—everyone should feel comfortable participating in discussions.

- Raise your hand and wait to be in possession of the Talking Tool before speaking.

- Pass the Talking Tool gently with an underhand toss.

- Announce the recipient's name before passing the Talking Tool so that he or she is ready to catch it.

There are other techniques for calling on students. Put names on a craft stick or in a fishbowl, and then simply pull the stick or slip of paper to call on the student.

Craft Sticks

Select names for participation from a container holding the name of every student

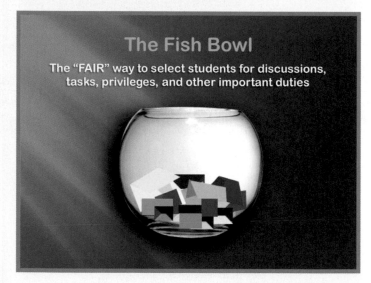

The Fish Bowl

The "FAIR" way to select students for discussions, tasks, privileges, and other important duties

A stack of index cards with student's names on each card can be carried around the classroom as you moderate the discussion and call on students to participate.

24))

Learn a card trick from a college professor and how she calls on students in her classroom.

TEACH

1. Students sit at their desks or on the floor so that they are facing each another and can always see the speaker.

2. Introduce students to how they will be selected for participating in the discussion. Show the device you will be using—Talking Tool, craft sticks, fishbowl, index cards, or other.

3. Remind students that when someone is speaking, all eyes and ears must be focused on the person who "has the floor." Only the person who "has the floor" can speak. Include any other parameters you want to establish for class discussion.

4. At the start of a class discussion, the teacher holds the Talking Tool and explains the topic of discussion. A student who wants to share something must raise his or her hand and wait for the Talking Tool to be gently tossed over. Once the Talking Tool is in his or her possession, the student may speak. In this way, the student is assured that no one will talk over him or her and ensures that the class is listening. Once the student has shared, the Talking Tool is gently tossed to the next student who wants to participate.

5. The teacher can encourage quiet students to participate by saying, "For the next few minutes, I'd like to hear from students who have not had a chance to share yet."

6. Or, at the beginning of the discussion, the teacher can say, "I'd like to encourage everyone to share at least once. So, if you see that there are classmates who haven't spoken yet, and you've already spoken several times, allow others to share their thoughts by not taking another turn yourself."

7. The teacher can also prompt student participation with an invitation to speak or a leading thought.

- "Jonas, since you have been such a good listener, won't you please share some of your ideas?"

- "I'm going to start the sentence. Can you share your thoughts on how to complete the sentence?" Give a sentence related to the topic that allows the students to finish with their personal thoughts.

8. To wrap up a class discussion, thank students for participating and sharing their ideas. Also, thank everyone for respecting one another and using the Talking Tool correctly.

REHEARSE

Invite the class to gather for a class discussion. Before the discussion begins, review the steps for a successful class discussion.

Ask the first question, say a student's name, and toss the Talking Tool to begin the discussion.

Special Places for Special Speakers

Rocking chairs, stools, recliners, or other special "speaking chairs" in the classrooms are special spots for students to perch upon while sharing ideas, projects, or presentations. Other students have no difficulty seeing and hearing the speaker, and they understand that when a classmate is in the special chair, everyone else must be excellent listeners.

A plastic, resin patio chair can be dubbed the speaking seat. This type of chair is easy to paint and personalize. At the beginning of the year, students bring in items to attach to the chair. These items may be related to the subject, or signify teamwork, respect, integrity, and other positive traits.

When a student sits in the leather rocker, he or she knows to use their "teacher voice." Listeners in the classroom display the 3 R's: Respect, Relationships, and Responsibility. If the speaker in the chair sees classmates talking or not listening, the student pauses and says, "I'll wait for you guys to be ready." This is a powerful message when it comes from a peer!

If there is a particular student who tends to distract others during class discussions, the teacher can sit next to or directly across from him or her. Establish a non-verbal cue that can be used to remind the student to be respectful of his or her classmates and to participate in an appropriate manner.

- A lowering of the hand to signal, "Please lower your energy level."
- A time-out sign
- Putting fingers to the lips for silence
- Motioning the zipping of lips for silence

For students who tend to dominate class discussions, sit down with them at another time and suggest that they limit themselves to sharing only three times per discussion. Encourage them to work hard on listening and learning from their classmates. If at the end of the discussion there are still items to share, ask students to write them out for you to read later.

When it is time to change speakers, ask students to recall the procedure.

Continue to practice until all students have participated in the discussion.

If a student forgets to use the Talking Tool, or is being disrespectful, ask a classmate to prompt the student on the correct procedure.

Thank students for holding a successful class discussion that allowed all students to speak and be heard.

REINFORCE

The next time the class gathers for discussion, observe if students are following the correct procedure. Comment and redirect students if necessary. At the end of every class discussion, thank the students for holding such a respectful and interesting discussion and for following the procedure.

Practice Makes Perfect

I have coached basketball for a number of years and the phrase 'practice makes perfect' transfers from the basketball court to the classroom.

We practice the procedures until they become routines and are performed correctly. I provide hand signals to go along with my expectations. This eliminates the use of my voice, especially when I need to be quiet as well. Eventually my students pick up on the hand signals and begin to use them, too.

Throughout the year, the routines need to be revisited, especially after winter and spring breaks; but it doesn't take long before they are in the swing of things again.

Christine Chang ■ Port Angeles, Washington

25 •))

Learn the value of wait-time and how it improves students' responses.

I Know the Answer!

Monica Burns teaches in New York City and uses a silent method in class discussion where all students are actively engaged in the discussion 100 percent of the time.

Monica teaches this signal at the start of the year when they begin having whole class discussions at their seats or on the rug. Instead of blurting out, "I know the answer," students pat the top of their head when they concur with the answer being given by classmates who have been called upon. This visual agreement is a quick check for Monica to see who is engaged in the discussion, who understands the information, and who may need additional help.

The pat-on-the-head technique keeps all students engaged in the discussion, regardless of who is answering the question. These are the reasons Monica finds this signal effective:

- Gets less outgoing students involved in a discussion.

- Keeps the whole class actively engaged even when they are not providing an answer themselves.

- Supports responsible talk prompts such as, "I agree with ____(name) because . . . ."

- Adds to a discussion by identifying students who do not support another student's answer ("I noticed that you do not agree with ____(name).").

- Combats a student's frustration from not being called on; an alternative to slamming one's hand on a desk or sighing heavily.

- Stops students from calling out, "I knew that!" or, "I had that answer!"

- Identifies who is not paying attention and holds every student accountable for participation.

- Transfers to discussions in all subject areas.

For instance, Monica is teaching fact families. She asks students to describe the fact family for 3 + 4.

Student 1: "4 + 3"
(Monica looks to make sure everyone has tapped their head in agreement.)

Student 2: "4 − 3"
(If a student does not tap his or her head, Monica follows up by asking a clarifying question.)

Monica: "Ali, I saw that you did not agree that 4 − 3 is part of this fact family. Could you explain your thinking?"

(Student should be able to support why she agrees or disagrees with another student's answer.)

Her technique helps students learn to listen and respect others when someone is sharing. It also gives students an opportunity to disagree in a non-confrontational way.

Working in Groups

Getting students into groups efficiently and quietly will set the pace for how productively students work in groups. The less time students spend transitioning into groups, the more time there will be for learning.

THE **SOLUTION**

Working in groups promotes teamwork, camaraderie, and practical experience for future employment. Students work in groups throughout the day, so having a procedure is a must for minimizing the time it takes for students to transition to an activity.

This procedure resolves these issues:

1. Chaos while students rush about, forming their own groups
2. Less popular students being left out of groups
3. Inefficient use of teacher and class time

THE **BACKGROUND**

Being able to work effectively in a group, learning to compromise to attain common goals, and assuming shared responsibility for teamwork are skills that students need to learn to be successful in school, at work, and throughout life. The procedure for forming groups and transitioning from a classroom setting to a group work setting must be well-rehearsed and hassle-free.

THE **PROCEDURE STEPS**

The success of this procedure will be determined before it is even played out in the classroom. The more thought and planning that goes into this procedure, the more effective it will be. There are many questions you will need to answer before you can ask your students to form groups.

- How will students be assigned to groups?
- Where will the groups work?
- How will the group work together?
- What will be the consistent transition cue to alert students it is time to end their work as a group and come together as a class?

ASSIGNING STUDENTS TO GROUPS

The purpose of a group is for everyone to work together as a team. Therefore, everyone in the group must have a job to do as a functioning member of the team. Preassign students to groups, rather than letting students pick their teammates. This eliminates students feeling left out, chaos in the classroom as students search for potential teammates, and grouping students with incompatible learning levels or disparate behavior patterns.

The size of a group is determined by the activity you wish the group to perform. Some groups could have three members, while other groups may have seven members.

Consider this when determining the groups' composition:

- Will everyone have a task to do while working in the group?
- Will the members of a group be able to help one another?
- Will the members learn from each other?
- Will the members work effectively together?

Group composition and size will change with each activity. Students will get a chance to work with all of their classmates and won't be stuck in a group, working with someone with whom they would prefer not to be teamed.

GROUP WORK LOCATIONS

Decide where the best locations are in the room for groups to meet and work together. Assign groups to these locations. Depending on the dynamics of the class, the type of activity, and the set-up of the classroom, students can either move desks or chairs, or themselves to their group's work location.

You assign the place for the group to work. It is not a free-choice decision.

If the group will be meeting for an extended period of time, make a class map that shows where each group is expected to meet and work together. Post this map on the class notice board next to the group list.

GROUP WORK PROCEDURES

Establish a set of procedures for students to follow while working in groups.

- You are responsible for your own work and behavior.
- If you have a question, ask your fellow group members for help.
- If your group member asks for help, try your best to help the person.
- Ask the teacher for help only if the entire group is stumped and everyone can agree on the same question.

These procedures encourage students to help one another, rather than relying exclusively on you. Your time is more effectively used because you need only attend to a group when all members are in doubt.

USING A CONSISTENT TRANSITION CUE

Depending on the grade level, use a suitable cue to facilitate students' transitions to and from groups and back to the classroom.

Giving a verbal cue to transition to the group work is appropriate. A simple, "Please begin your group work," works well.

Use a countdown timer to signal when it is close to transition time.

Playing music to signal when it is time to transition back is a commonly used cue. A song can provide the class with a set amount of time to bring closure to the task and resume working as a class. Music can also help keep the noise level down during transitions—tell students that any noise they make has to be softer than the music that's playing.

Counting down is also an effective verbal cue. Give students a set number of seconds and count aloud, or set a timer. This tells students how much time they have to transition and reestablishes when they have to be in their designated places.

A well-rehearsed cue for transitioning in and out of groups maximizes the time the students will spend on the group assignment.

26 •))
Learn some ways to quickly form groups without using any cards, marbles, candy, or other objects.

27 •))
Browse these free countdown timers to alert students to get ready for transitions.

TEACH

1. Explain to students that you have preassigned them to groups.

2. Explain that this group is for this one activity and that the next time they are asked to work as a group, it may be with different classmates and a different number of members.

3. Announce the members of your first group.

4. Point out the location where each group is to work.

5. If applicable, show students the group list and class map, and tell them where they can find it.

6. Demonstrate the signal for gathering in groups.

7. Explain to students while they are in working groups that there are procedures to follow:

   ▪ You are responsible for your own work and behavior.

   ▪ If you have a question, ask your fellow group members for help.

   ▪ If your group member asks for help, try your best to help the person.

   ▪ Ask the teacher for help only if the entire group is stumped, and everyone can agree on the same question.

8. Model the transition cue for coming back to the class. Share that it will always be the same cue.

9. Explain what the procedure is when the transition cue is given. For instance, when the teacher starts the countdown timer, the procedure is to

   ▪ bring closure to what they are doing as a group;

   ▪ return materials;

   ▪ return furniture to its original location; and

   ▪ be back in their respective seats when there is no time left on the timer.

REHEARSE

Appoint a few students to be the first group and point out where they are to work.

Give them a simple task to do that requires them to interact.

Ask the rest of the class to act as monitors for the procedure.

Give the cue for breaking into groups.

Once they are in their group and have begun working, stop the process and ask the monitors for feedback on how well their classmates performed the procedure. Correct mistakes and address problems as needed.

Ask the students to resume their work. Approach the group and ask what the procedure is for when they have a question. Allow the class to determine if it is the right or wrong answer. Correct them as needed.

Ask the students to continue working. Give the cue for transitioning back to the classroom.

When the students are back in their seats, ask for observations from their classmates. Correct mistakes as needed.

Thank the students for participating in the first group to model the procedure, pointing out the highlights of your observations of whether the correct procedure was followed.

Reverse roles—the students who participated in the first practice group are now the observers, while the rest of the class has been assigned into groups and their meeting locations.

Give the cue for group work to begin. Stop the process at the same points as before and allow the observers to respond. Correct problems as needed.

Continue prompting at points throughout the rehearsal process until you are sure the students know what the procedure is for going to groups, working in groups, and coming back as a class after group work.

REINFORCE

Before the first real-time group work begins, review the procedure for group work. As the students are going through the process, thank them for successfully following a specific part of the procedure. "Shoji, thank you for moving to your group without talking to your classmates." This affirms the specific action and is more useful than, "Shoji, you did a good job moving to your group." Your specific words of encouragement help the student to understand what your expectations are in carrying out the procedure.

When students have returned to their seats after the group work, give them feedback on how the process went. Affirm and correct the procedure as needed.

Working Together in Groups

For group work in the laboratory, there is a procedure, so each student is prepared to contribute equally to the group's work. I determine the lab groups at the beginning of the year, but will change them from time to time, if necessary. Students will decide which role they wish to complete for the first lab, and will then rotate through the jobs of Researcher, Supply Gatherer, Safety Person, and Recorder.

For group work in the classroom, students will work in groups of three. All students fulfill the role of Researcher for the group. Students will rotate the roles of Recorder, Time Manager, and Fact Checker, depending upon the group activity.

Jancsi Roney ▪ Clermont, Georgia

Note Taking

Students who master the skill of effective note taking learn how to identify important information and gain a better understanding of concepts.

THE **SOLUTION**

A pplying the Cornell Note-Taking Method eliminates disorganization in students' lesson notes. This method aids in capturing important information that can be used in preparation for tests. It helps to focus students' attention on the relevant content and minimizes distractions.

This procedure provides these opportunities:

1. Ensuring students take notes that are accurate, complete, and relevant

2. Teaching students to condense concepts into key words, phrases, or sentences

3. Transforming the passive student into an active learner

THE **BACKGROUND**

Research shows that students who take notes in class perform better on assessments than students who do not take notes. However, most students interpret note-taking as transcription—they madly scribble down every word the teacher says. As a result, their notes lack structure, are difficult to reference, and hard to study. Worse, students who are frantically transcribing a lesson tend to disengage from the lesson—they are no longer paying attention, thinking, asking questions, and learning.

Students need to be taught how to identify and organize essential information while note taking without disengaging from the lesson. **Students who understand how to efficiently take meaningful notes are transformed from passive listeners into active learners.**

THE **PROCEDURE STEPS**

The Cornell system for note taking helps students efficiently record important information. Once the ideas are recorded, they are further reduced by condensing the concepts into key words or phrases. Then these notes are summarized in one or two sentences for review.

To eliminate disorganization, the Cornell Note-Taking Method organizes notes into three specific sections: Record, Reduce, and Review.

1. **Record**, where students record notes on the important information.

2. **Reduce**, where the notes are reduced to a descriptive word or key point.

3. **Review**, where the notes are summarized to a concept and where questions that remain unanswered for further research are stated.

1. RECORD

Show students how to divide a sheet of note paper into the three sections with these dimensions:

- 2½-inch section from the left side of the page
- 6-inch section from the right side of the page
- 2-inch section at the bottom of the page

Show students how to label each section with Record, Reduce, and Review.

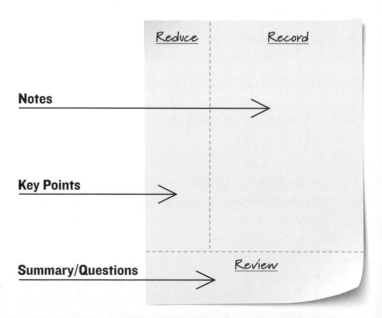

Teach students to take notes by recording meaningful information in the section labeled Record. Emphasize that organization is important for effective note taking. Help students record notes with these tips:

- Omit information that is unnecessary for understanding the material.
- Eliminate repeated information.
- Use abbreviations.
- Write brief phrases.
- Leave spaces between thoughts.

2. REDUCE

In the Reduce section, teach students to write a simple phrase, cue word, or key point based on the notes taken. Brevity and simplicity are important.

Words written in the Reduce section are cue words for reviewing and reflecting on the material that is being taught.

3. REVIEW

Review the information in the Review and Reduce sections to write a one- or two-sentence summary of the concept in the Review section. Students can also use this space to write points for clarification, questions unanswered, or an Aha for further research.

Students who have difficulty writing this summary have not fully grasped the material and need to revisit it. You can gauge your teaching effectiveness by observing students' ability to produce coherent summaries.

Teach students how to study using their organized notes.

- Instruct students to use index cards to cover the notes written in the Record section. This leaves only the notes in the Reduce section exposed.
- Based on the cue word or words in the Reduce section, students recite as much information as they can remember from the Record section.
- Reviewing their organized notes in this way will help them retain the information learned when test time comes around.

TEACH

Explain how the Cornell Note-Taking Method works and why it is more effective than writing down the lecture word for word.

Teach a lesson and use the white board, LCD projector, or document camera to walk students through the process of taking notes using the Cornell method.

Highlight relevant information from the lesson and note it in the Record section. Allow students to copy this for reference.

Suggest cue words and write them in the Reduce section.

Reread the information in both sections and write a one- or two-sentence summary in the Review section. Point out that this section can also be used to write unanswered questions, points that need further clarification, and suggestions for further research.

REHEARSE

The next day, review the Cornell Note-Taking Method with the class.

While teaching the lesson, stop and ask students to identify important information that needs to be recorded in the Record section.

Ask for volunteers to suggest cue words for the Reduce section.

Invite students to share the summary they have written in the Review section.

Show how using the notes can increase retention of information. With a piece of paper, cover the notes in the Record section. This leaves only the notes in the Reduce and Review sections exposed.

Based on the cue word or summaries in the Reduce and Review sections, ask students to recite as much information as they can remember from the Record section.

Ask for questions throughout the lesson as students practice taking notes.

REINFORCE

Regularly review the Cornell Note-Taking Method with the class. Take the time to occasionally walk students through the note-taking process.

Emphasize that by being organized now, students save themselves future work. Also emphasize that the Cornell Note-Taking Method makes studying for tests far more efficient.

Note-Taking Guide

Help younger students learn how to take notes. Create a Note-Taking Guide—a prepared set of notes with strategically-placed blanks. Students will not be overwhelmed by the responsibility of having to organize information and listen for the important information.

A Note-Taking Guide looks like this:

The teacher says, "Class, when the Constitution was written, the framers wanted to make sure that no government group had too much power. They divided the government into three different branches, the Legislative, Executive, and Judicial, each with its own duties. The Legislative branch makes the laws, the Executive branch carries out the laws, and the Judicial branch decides whether or not a law has been broken or misinterpreted."

As the lecture is delivered, a PowerPoint slide recaps the information.

The 3 Branches of Government
Legislative = Makes laws
Executive = Carries out laws
Judicial = Determines if the laws have been followed

This is how the student's Note-Taking Guide reads:

There are _____ branches of government. The Legislative branch _____ laws. The Executive branch carries out _____. The Judicial branch decides if laws have been _____.

The teacher briefly pauses for students to fill in the missing words before moving on.

As students progress in school, a Note-Taking Guide will become the Cornell Note-Taking Method where the students become responsible for all of the content.

30 THE PROCEDURE

Reading a Textbook

Showing your students how to use the SQ4R technique (Survey, Question, Read, Recite, Review, Reflect) helps them gain a deeper understanding of the material and allows them to use the method in all of their classes.

THE SOLUTION

The "SQ4R" method requires students to invest a significant portion of their time, but it helps students learn, recall, and use information. **Teach students how to read a textbook to help them navigate through all of the detailed information presented in it.**

A plan of attack for reading will solve these problems:

1. Poor comprehension of the information presented
2. Low retention of the facts

THE **BACKGROUND**

Most students read a textbook the same way they read a novel in an English class. They start at the beginning of the book and continue reading until they finish the last page. Although this method is appropriate for reading fiction, it is not the best way to read a textbook.

Highlighting is a commonly used method to emphasize text. However, this technique usually boils down to coloring a page, rather than critically thinking about the information and selecting the salient facts for recall.

The "SQ4R" method reduces the textbook information to bullet points for future study.

THE **PROCEDURE STEPS**

Teach students the SQ4R process for reading textbooks to help them better understand textbook material and retain the information. Prepare a wall chart with the steps for reading a textbook. Keep the chart posted throughout the school year.

1. Survey
2. Question
3. Read
4. Recite
5. Review
6. Reflect

Survey
Question
Read
Recite
Review
Reflect

The poster serves as a visual reminder of the steps in the process.

TEACH

1. Introduce students to the SQ4R method and discuss how it helps them gain and retain information.

1) SURVEY

- Briefly look through the chapter to gather information about the content.
- Read the title of the chapter to get an idea of the topic being presented.
- Read the chapter's introduction or summary. This introduces the reader to the chapter's main points.
- Read all section headings. These headings help the student understand how the material is organized.
- Read all boldfaced, italicized, highlighted, and boxed text.
- Examine the visuals and read the captions. Visuals are used to call out specific material and aid understanding.
- Read all definitions, objectives, and study guide questions at the end of the chapter.

2) QUESTION

- Think about the material being surveyed.
- Think of the chapter headings as questions that give purpose to reading and increase comprehension.
- Create questions to be answered from the reading material.
- When readers are actively searching for answers, they are engaged in the reading process.

3) READ

Surveying and questioning builds a framework for understanding the material. This step, Reading, fills in the information around the framework the student has built.

Reading is like building a house. The walls of the house cannot be finished before the framework is complete. Students should not begin to read before they have surveyed and created questions for the chapter.

- Look for the answers to the questions created.
- Take notes of the answers in the student's own words.
- To avoid information overload, focus on the main idea of the reading rather than all of the minute details.

4) RECITE

Encourage students to quiz themselves at the end of every chapter. Have them ask, out loud, the questions they created, and then have them answer the questions in their own words. When students can recite the material in their own words, they are more likely to understand and retain that information for later use.

5) REVIEW

The last phase of building a house involves a final inspection by the city. Similarly, just because students have finished the chapter—surveyed, questioned, read, and recited the material—it does not mean they are done.

When students get to the end of the chapter, encourage them to review and inspect their notes for details left out and information misstated. Reviewing the material enables students to retain the information.

6) REFLECT

- Encourage students to mentally manipulate the information they have gathered.
- Reflect on the questions created as a check for understanding.
- Look for relationships between the ideas and combine them for deeper understanding.

2. Choose a chapter from a textbook and use it to model the SQ4R method. Go through the steps as a class.

- Read the chapter title and summary.
- Show students the importance of reading the boldfaced, italicized, highlighted, and boxed text.
- Take time to examine the visuals and read the captions.
- Go over the definitions, objectives, and study guide questions.

3. Ask students what the chapter is about. Discuss questions that students should keep in mind when reading the text.

4. Ask students what the different sections are about. Discuss questions that students should keep in mind when reading each section.

5. Ask students to read the chapter with the appropriate questions in mind.

6. Ask for answers to the questions the students developed prior to reading.

7. Ask students to pause and think about the general concepts they just learned. Ask students to volunteer the information they gathered as a result of the SQ4R process.

REHEARSE

Instruct students to take turns quizzing their seat partners on the information from the textbook. Some students will ask questions from the textbook, and other students will use their SQ4R notes to locate the answers. Seat partners should alternate between asking and answering questions based on the text. Emphasize that students should use their own words as much as possible.

Observe student pairs and redirect them if necessary.

After quizzing themselves and reciting the material in their own words, students should review their chapter notes again. Emphasize that reviewing the information helps students retain what they have learned.

REINFORCE

At the next class reading, pair students again and ask them to work together on the passage using the SQ4R process. Monitor the groups and give assistance as needed. Use the pairing technique until the students feel confident in using the process on their own.

28 •))))

Jeff Gulle shares his SQ4R template with you to use with your students.

A SQ4R Guide

Prepare a SQ4R guide for students to use as they read their textbooks. **Jeff Gulle** of Danville, Kentucky, uses this guide to help his students record their thoughts.

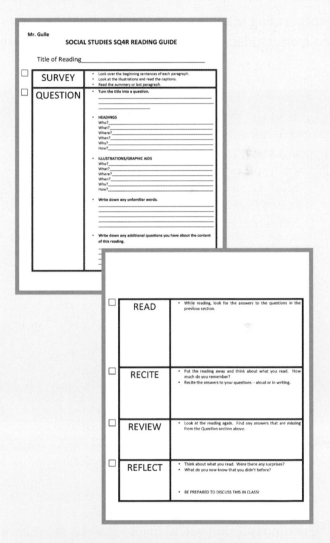

With a guide, students are able to follow the process and focus on the important information from the textbook. Once students know the method and become familiar with the steps, the process becomes second nature to them.

THE **PROCEDURE**

Read Any Place Time

Incorporating reading into the daily schedule gives students time to read for pleasure each day. The more students are exposed to reading, the more likely they are to be successful at it.

THE **SOLUTION**

Reading is a skill useful in all subjects. It is also a skill that brings great enjoyment. Being a strong reader opens doors to learning. **Read Any Place (RAP) Time encourages students to read.**

This procedure provides these opportunities:

1. Encourages students to read for fun
2. Motivates students to read independently
3. Allows for book sharing to encourage others to read

THE **BACKGROUND**

Encouraging students to read as a hobby or for fun provides a welcome relief to a home life of television and video games.

During RAP Time, students are encouraged to read any type of age-appropriate book of their choice. They are allowed to read anywhere in the room, as long as they are following the RAP Time guidelines:

RAP Time encourages independent reading.

- Students must sit at arm's length from each other.
- Silent reading only—no talking with classmates.
- Students take turns to use the special chairs and cushions.
- Books must be returned to their correct places when RAP Time is over.

When students are finished early, encourage them to take out their RAP books and to enjoy reading it while waiting for the rest of the class.

Categorize books by reading levels, genres, themes, and interests, and label the books and baskets or shelves to keep them organized. This way, students can easily find books that interest them, and it makes it easier for them to return the books to the correct places.

TEACH

Create a poster with the RAP Time guidelines and post it where students can easily refer to it. Teach RAP Time during the first week of school.

1. Introduce students to the inviting spaces for reading in the classroom.

2. Designate a time during the school day for RAP Time. Tell students when they can expect RAP Time in the schedule. Depending on your class structure, RAP can be a daily activity or done on certain days of the week.

3. Discuss the RAP Time guidelines and what they achieve.

4. Tell students that you will be participating in RAP Time with them.

5. As the activity comes to an end, allow for brief sharing of anything exciting they've learned or read.

THE **PROCEDURE STEPS**

RAP Time requires a variety of reading materials and levels of books accessible to all students. Put together a class collection of children's magazines and newspapers, comic books, picture books, and chapter books. Students should feel comfortable picking up the book of their choice.

Set up an inviting reading area in the classroom with easy access to the class book collection. Carpet squares, cushions, fun chairs, and a sofa help make students feel comfortable and cozy and contribute to their enjoyment of RAP Time.

REHEARSE

Model what RAP Time should look like. Show students how to choose reading materials and where to sit in the classroom. Remind them to sit at arm's length from one another. Ask a few students to model what RAP Time looks like.

As the class practices this procedure, remind students that RAP Time is for silent reading. Gently correct students who forget to read quietly and independently.

Announce a practice RAP Time, and allow half the students to stop their work and demonstrate how RAP Time works.

Ask the other half of the class to monitor their classmates and call out corrections to the procedure. Rehearse this procedure again, with the class reversing roles.

Ask for volunteers to share anything exciting they've learned from their reading.

REINFORCE

Acknowledge the students for following the procedure. If the procedure is not being done correctly, simply ask, "What's the procedure for RAP Time, please?"

If a student is idly sitting waiting for the rest of the class to finish an activity, ask, "What is an activity you can do while waiting for the rest of the class?"

Classroom and School Libraries

Research shows that having a wide range of quality books in the classroom contributes to students' academic success. Students who read also grow to be better writers, and students who write, learn to be better readers. Maintaining a **classroom library** is effortless once a procedure is in place.

Maintaining a classroom library gives students easy access to a wide variety of books. But, you'll need to establish some guidelines before the students can borrow books from the classroom library.

1. **Establish appropriate times for using the class library.**
   - Before and after class
   - Between classes
   - At lunch
   - At the start of RAP Time

2. **Develop a check-out and check-in system if the books are leaving the classroom.**
   - Use check-out cards placed in adhesive pockets in the front of each book. Students are given the responsibility of removing the card, writing their name, date, and class period on the card, and placing the check-out card in an alphabetized card box. When the book is returned, the student finds the card in the card box and returns it to the pocket in the front of the book.

- Use an electronic log. Create a Word document or Excel spreadsheet that students can access on the class computer. When students check out a book, they enter their name, book title, date, and class period in the digital document. When students return books, they insert the date they returned the book to the classroom library and save the document.

3. **Organize the books.**

- Books can be organized by genres or simply as fiction and non-fiction. Allocate specific sections on the library shelves for each category.

- Put colored tape or dots on the book spines to indicate the books that are grouped together on a shelf.

4. **Assign classroom jobs.**

- The class library can be run on an honor system, where students take on the responsibility of ensuring that books are properly checked out, checked in, and returned to their places.

- Alternatively, assign classroom jobs such as Librarian and Assistant Librarian. The Librarian checks books in and out of the library, while the Assistant Librarian returns books to the shelves. These jobs can be rotated so that all students share the responsibility of maintaining the class library.

5. **Keep the library open.**

- Encourage students to come in before or after school to browse the class library's collection.

- Familiarize yourself with the books in your classroom library, so you can recommend books to students. Use every opportunity to promote literacy.

The procedures of a classroom library are similar to the operation of a school's media center. **Joanne Ladewig, a Library Media Technician in Garden Grove, California,** believes **kids do behave better when they know what is expected of them and how to do it.**

In her library she differentiates between policies, procedures, and rules.

Policies are general management statements concerning how the library is run.

- Books due in two weeks
- Books brought in for renewal
- Damaged books must be paid for
- Limit of three items per person at any time
- Push the chairs in
- Keep the library clean

Procedures cover how things are done. They usually involve physical action. There is no punishment for not doing a procedure correctly, but the student will have to go back and do it properly. For example, someone who runs into the library will have to go back to the doorway, stop, and then walk appropriately into the room.

- Come into the library in a quiet and orderly manner.
- Sit where assigned.
- Scan in books and return them to the proper shelf (or book cart).
- Use a shelf marker.
- Before checking out, look through books and magazines and report any damage.
- Bring your library pass.

Rules refer to physical behavior, and there are consequences if they are broken.

1. Respect the books and other library materials.
2. Respect the library furnishings.
3. Respect everyone in the library.
4. Use your time wisely.
5. Respect the library as a quiet place.

THE **PROCEDURE**

Taking a Test

Test day can be productive when the teacher plans ahead to minimize unnecessary loss of learning time.

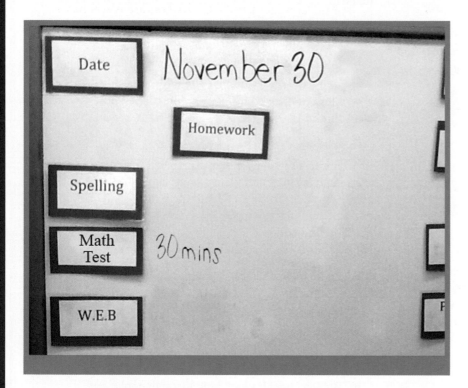

THE **SOLUTION**

Every minute is valuable in the classroom. Every day is a day for learning. Test day can be productive when students know what to do, and **the teacher is proactive about using every minute of classroom time effectively.**

This procedure resolves these issues:

1. Confusion on test day

2. Ineffective use of class time

THE **BACKGROUND**

The lesson plan book displays, in large print, "Test today!" Teachers view test day as a mini holiday from instruction, while students consider test day to be a pass from learning.

Students who finish early will fidget and look around, trying to find others who are finished as well. Mobile devices are checked and grooming gadgets miraculously appear—seldom does learning take place while early finishers wait for their classmates to complete the test.

Every minute in the classroom is an opportunity to learn. This is made clear to students with a posted agenda—even on test day. **With an agenda, students will always know what they should be working on next.**

THE **PROCEDURE STEPS**

Students have varied test-taking abilities, so plan ahead and post work or a silent reading assignment for students to begin as soon as they complete the test. By being proactive about not letting a single minute of class time go to waste, student learning is maximized.

Post an agenda with a schedule on test day. The schedule should show

- when the test will take place in the class period;
- how long the testing period will last; and
- what to begin working on upon completion of the test.

TEACH

Explain your procedure for taking a test. Include some of these steps for your students to follow:

- Keep your eyes on your own paper.
- Remain quiet during test time.
- You may not return to the test once you have turned your papers face-down.
- When finished, turn your test over and place all papers on the top-right corner of your desk.
- The test will be collected as soon as everyone has indicated they have completed the test.
- Remain seated and begin assigned work immediately.
- Have materials at your desk to work on when you are finished with the test.

REHEARSE

Tell students that on test day, all regular classroom procedures will be followed. On test day, students should enter the room quietly and begin their opening assignment as usual.

Model how students should indicate that they have completed the test by placing their papers face-down on the top-right corner of their desks. Remind students that once they have done this, they are not allowed to return to the test.

Emphasize that the agenda will be followed as usual. Students should remain in their seats and start on the assigned work as noted in the agenda.

REINFORCE

On the day of the first class test, discuss the test-taking procedure again to eliminate any misunderstandings.

Remind students that they should remain silent even after they have completed the test because their classmates may still be working.

Highlight the assigned work posted on the agenda and remind students to start on it immediately after completing the test. Clarify any questions students may have about the assigned work.

Creating a Personal Space

Students in **Beth Featherston's** classroom sit in clusters, with their desks touching each other. To create a personal space for students, without separating their desks, Beth glues the front of a file folder and the back of another folder together to form a three-paneled partition.

The students write their names on the folders and then write words of encouragement to personalize their folders.

Think smart	Do your best
Work hard	Focus
Check your work	Be positive

Beth laminates the folders to seal them together and then trims them.

The folders are stored in a special place in the classroom. On test day or with any activity that requires independent thinking, a student helper distributes the folders and students set up their partitions between themselves. Within a personal space, students are not easily distracted.

Be Strong

This saying was posted on the door of **Susan Green**, principal at Alain L. Locke School in New York City: "Today's struggles will bring tomorrow's achievements."

Students often complain, "This is so boring. Can we do something fun?" Their desire is to be entertained, not to work hard. Their attitude toward school is, "If I am not entertained, I don't want to be here." Working hard to get things done is a lost value among today's youth.

The origin of this story is not known, but the message is universal for being successful and effective in life. A man found a butterfly cocoon. One day, a small opening appeared in the cocoon. He sat and watched the butterfly as it struggled to force its body through that little hole. For several hours, it struggled. Then, it seemed to stop making any progress. It appeared as if it had gotten as far as it could and could go no further.

So, the man decided to help the butterfly. He took a pair of scissors and snipped away the remaining cocoon.

The butterfly then emerged easily. The man continued to watch the butterfly because he expected that, at any moment, its wings would enlarge to support its body and its body would contract to size.

Neither happened! In fact, the butterfly spent the rest of its life crawling around with a swollen body and shriveled wings. It was never able to fly.

What the man, in his kindness and haste, did not understand was that the restricting cocoon forced the butterfly to struggle and strengthen its wings. And emerging through the tiny opening was nature's way of forcing fluid from the butterfly's body into its wings. Only then, would the butterfly be ready for flight.

Obstacles and struggles are opportunities for everyone to grow and learn. The hard work to get through these difficulties strengthen us and boost our morale. An obstacle-free life might cripple us. We would not be as strong as we could have been. We would never learn to fly!

Be consistent, be strong, be vigilant in your efforts to teach children.

Harry K. Wong ■ **Mountain View, California**

Students Correcting Work

Not all papers need to be checked or scored by the teacher. Give some of the responsibility of correcting papers to the students.

THE **SOLUTION**

Seize the opportunity to lighten your workload. When appropriate, **students can assist in checking and correcting their classmates' work.** Your time spent on correcting papers can now be used on other professional responsibilities.

With careful teacher supervision, this procedure provides these opportunities:

1. Limiting the amount of items a teacher must correct

2. Teaching responsibility for peer scoring

THE **BACKGROUND**

This is not a procedure that can be done at every grade level or all of the time. But there are many assignments that can be corrected if students are taught the procedure for marking papers.

Students complete many assignments in a day. Not all assignments need to be graded, marked, or scored by you all of the time; however, it is important to review and grade the majority of assignments. There are certain pieces of work that must always be teacher-scored, such as pieces of writing, cursive handwriting, and most tests. However, there are many assignments that can be corrected by students during class time. In some instances, the grading process can be treated as a review of skills.

Students work hard on their assignments and take pride in their work. Explain to the class that when they correct another person's work, they must treat it with respect.

Students are taught responsibility when correcting their classmates' work.

THE **PROCEDURE STEPS**

Teach this procedure just before the first opportunity to correct papers occurs. Impress on them the importance of being fair and honest when correcting a classmate's paper.

Purchase a set of class marking pens. All pens are the same color and are reserved for correcting papers.

Let parents know that any papers corrected with the color you've chosen for the year are ones that have been corrected by students.

TEACH

1. Pass out student work, making sure each student has another person's assignment.

2. Distribute the colored marking pens.

3. Have the student who is correcting the work sign his or her name on the bottom right-hand corner of the page. This stresses the importance of taking responsibility for accurately correcting the paper and treating the work with respect.

4. Tell students to only make marks next to the incorrect answers. Instruct students to place an "X" (or any symbol you choose) next to incorrect answers. No other marks are to be placed on the paper.

5. Recite the answers, so students can correct the papers.

6. Ask if clarifications are needed as you give the answers.

7. Tell students to tally the total number of marks on the paper and place that number next to their name written at the bottom of the page.

8. Collect all of the corrected papers to review and check for accuracy.

9. Collect all marking pens.

REHEARSE

The first time papers are corrected as a class, double check the accuracy of students' corrections by exchanging the corrected paper with a seat partner's.

Ask the seat partners to sign their names next to the name of the person who just corrected the paper.

Remind students they are checking each other's work. Go through the corrections once more.

Repeat how to mark the papers if they find something incorrect. The mark used in this second round should be different than the mark used in the first round of checking.

Tally the number of incorrect answers on the paper and note the number next to their name at the bottom of the page.

Ask partners to compare their findings with each other.

Collect the papers and the marking pens.

Review all papers and compute the final score.

REINFORCE

Upon inspection of the student-corrected papers, inform the class of your findings and thank them for helping with checking this work. Affirm that the actions were followed correctly and encourage them to do the same the next time you need their help.

Reteach the procedure with students as necessary.

The next time papers are corrected as a class, review the procedure for correcting the work of others.

Adapt to Be Successful

Jeff Smith of Pryor, Oklahoma, was like so many new teachers. He knew his subject matter inside and out but had no classroom organization. Every day was a struggle, until he was almost fired. And then he was introduced to *The Effective Teacher* video series and started to plan.

Jeff sets up his students for success by using solid lesson planning, organization, and management skills. Every one of Jeff's students had experienced failure of some kind before they came to him. Yet, his students are successful because he plans for their success.

On the very first day of school, Jeff outlines his classroom policies and procedures for his students. He is clear and firm. His procedures teach industry standards, which enables the students to learn the behaviors and attitudes required to be successful in the real world.

Jeff's classes hold the record in Oklahoma for the most career tech students to pass the industry standard welding certification test in one day—an awe-inspiring thirty-three students. In addition, the Department of Career Tech has shared with Jeff that his former students have the highest pay average for high school graduates in the state.

Jeff's classroom practices are not unique. He has learned how to adapt the techniques of other effective teachers, so his students have the opportunity to succeed.

From being almost fired, to now guiding students to success, Jeff was honored as the first inductee of the American Welding Society Hall of Fame.

Making a Momentary Connection

Learn how to make momentary connections if you want to persuade a student to do better in an assignment, to help a student who seems to be having a bad hair day, or to defuse a potential classroom rage. Quick, sincere connections with students take care of many of these situations. It allows you to acknowledge the event and then to move on.

1. **Listen.**

   The most effective way to persuade someone is to listen. Pay careful attention to what the student says. Acknowledge the discussion with "I hear you," or a similar comment. Nod your head.

2. **Present positive body language.**

   Stand up straight, with shoulders back and chest out. Look positive; you want to help someone who is not feeling positive. Don't fidget. It's distracting and shows you are uncomfortable or unsure of yourself. Do not cross your arms in an authoritative, defensive posture. Rather, hold both palms up. This is a message that states, "I have nothing to conceal, and I am open to you."

   If you sit, assume a straight-backed position. Leaning back translates into boredom and leaning forward could make you appear over solicitous.

3. **Maintain eye contact.**

   Never be the first to break eye contact. When you use strong eye contact, people are more drawn to you.

4. **Smile.**

   Smiles show the student that you are friendly and confident. A genuine smile not only feels good to you, but will also put the student at ease while you create that moment of connection.

5. **Observe something.**

   Make a positive comment about something you observe, such as a piece of clothing, a book on the desk, a crazy pencil being used. Your words will let students know you are in their moment and are attentive to them and their needs.

Cultivating Social Skills

Social skills are essential to a positive classroom environment and are central to a student's success in life. Create a classroom where everyone practices courtesy and treats one another with dignity and respect.

THE **SOLUTION**

Teaching suitable social skills facilitates a positive learning environment. Teaching students to be cooperative and courteous are skills that will prepare them for a successful adult life. Model these skills in all your interactions with students.

This procedure provides these opportunities:

1. Effective communication in spoken and body language

2. Increased productivity in the classroom

3. A positive classroom atmosphere

THE **BACKGROUND**

Students can experience difficulty in the classroom and problems working in teams if they lack the social skills to work cooperatively. This lack of social skills can be a major roadblock to a student's success, including effective communication, problem solving, decision making, and peer relations.

By helping students master basic social skills, you help students develop suitable abilities for use throughout their adult lives.

THE **PROCEDURE STEPS**

Students may be unaware of how important social skills are to become successful in school and throughout life. **Brainstorm a list of social skills the class will work on** and discuss the importance of using these skills in every situation.

- Listening
- Displaying good manners
- Being respectful
- Being cooperative
- Helping others
- Being patient
- Being courteous
- Sharing
- Participating
- Seeking attention appropriately
- Using quiet voices
- Being verbally polite (e.g., saying "please," "thank you," and "you're welcome")

Students may not recognize some of these behaviors as social skills that are essential to a productive classroom.

Do not assume your interpretation of these skills is the same as the students' interpretations. Discuss what it means to have good manners. For instance, the tone and manner in which the phrases "please" and "thank you" are said are just as important as remembering to use the phrases themselves.

Model and demonstrate appropriate behavior in classroom situations, so they are not taught exclusively in isolation. For instance, before students are assigned to work in groups, ask the class what it means to work cooperatively. Brainstorm. If listening is the target social skill, ask students to list the qualities of "a good listener." What does a good listener do when the teacher or a classmate is speaking?

Role play scenarios, so students can practice desirable social skills. This will give the visual, auditory, and kinesthetic learner an opportunity to understand the differences between desirable and undesirable behaviors.

Teach students how to be good listeners as their classmates present to the class.

As a class, develop How-To lists for each target social skill. For instance, good listeners will

- sit up in their seats without slouching,
- focus on the speaker at all times, and
- limit movement so as not to distract the speaker or other listeners.

As definitions are developed, put together a guide that students can keep in their class notebooks for easy reference.

If a student has forgotten the social skills of a good listener, approach the student and say, "Kelsey, please reread the section in your notebook on how to be a good listener." After class, ask Kelsey if she has any questions on how to be a good listener.

Model social skills as you interact respectfully with students and treat them with the same social skills you expect them to exhibit to others in the classroom. Show the social skills you wish your students to develop.

TEACH

Each day, choose a specific social skill to include in the lesson and have students demonstrate that skill throughout the class period.

Tell the student what social skill will be incorporated in the day's lesson.

Discuss how the purposefully practiced skill will create a positive atmosphere for learning in the classroom. Emphasize how that skill is used in a productive workplace and how the skill is used in society.

At the end of the class period, review the impact the targeted social skill had on the class atmosphere and the learning for the day.

Repeat the process and continue working through all the target skills on the list the class has created.

REHEARSE

Practice social skills as necessary until the social skills become routine for the class. Remind students of the social skills to use in a particular lesson.

If a class still has a difficult time with a specific skill, isolate and rehearse that skill until students have mastered the desired outcome.

Work closely with individual students who have difficulty mastering these skills.

REINFORCE

Acknowledge the class for their performance of a specific social skill and encourage them to use it again.

Helping students develop social skills creates an environment that is conducive to learning and equips students for life. Be consistent in the expectation that suitable social skills be used at all times in the classroom.

No Room for Ambiguity

I teach in the UK. Over the summer, I wrote a list of procedures and a classroom management plan.

We've been back at school for almost three weeks now. I spent a lot of time going through the procedures.

There is no room for ambiguity. Every student knows exactly how things are done.

The result of all of this?

These are the most productive classes I've ever had, the calmest start to a school year I've ever had, and the most fun my students and I have ever had!

Jon Eaton ▪ Devon, United Kingdom

Simple Procedures, Plus Courtesy

The students from a small urban community in New Rochelle, New York, reflect a typical American classroom with a full range of learning needs and demographics; however, these distinctions don't hold back the students in **Faye Freeman's** classroom.

Faye Freeman's third-grade class bubbles with energy and purpose. As the day begins, children enter smiling and ready for school. The day's work plan is on the board right above a row of engaging children's books on the shelf.

The class hums like a well-rehearsed orchestra as students move to their places in the middle of the room for meeting time. Faye has taught the procedures on how a class begins and the students respond. They are comfortable with the consistency, they have a sense of purpose, and they easily follow the routine.

To prepare for a story-writing assignment, the students brainstorm ideas about how to make their group work productive. Faye skillfully guides the discussion and writes their ideas on the board: "Everyone should share. Cooperate and work together. Sometimes we have to compromise. Respect everyone's ideas."

It is quite evident that Faye has created a culture of students who share and work in groups interdependently; they do not comprise a classroom of "selves."

As they work, they know the simple courtesy of saying, "Thank you," "You're welcome," "Excuse me," and "Please." Faye teaches respect along with hard work. She demands much from students and expects much of herself.

Parents request Faye Freeman, and students thrive in her class. The elements of good teaching are readily apparent:

- Clear procedures and structure
- Loads of interesting work
- Plenty of opportunities to practice and succeed
- Abundant opportunities to imagine and create

We met Faye when she was mentioned in a 1996 document published by the National Commission on Teaching and America's Future. We've communicated with her through the years and hearing from her always brightened our day.

Sadly, Faye passed away suddenly early in her career, but her work lives on in the young hearts and minds she taught. Thank you, Faye Freeman, for demanding so much of the profession as your legacy lives on.

The Special Needs Classroom

"Ours is not the business of producing doctors or lawyers, teachers or nurses, factory workers or sales associates. Ours is the business of putting smiles on young faces, hope in young hearts, and dreams in young minds. The rest will take care of itself."

Dan Seufert ■ Special Education Teacher, South Carolina

All Children Are Capable

Special education presents significant challenges to teachers. The work is emotionally difficult and physically draining. The stress is considerable, and the workload is profound. It requires teachers who have the patience to stay true to their task, with the skill to bring order to confusion. **It requires a kind disposition and understanding heart to see all children as capable and worthy.**

Special education also offers the most rewarding outcome—preparing a child who faces unique challenges to function in a demanding world.

A Day in a Special Education Preschool Classroom

Robin Barlak teaches pre-K special education in Ohio. She has eight special needs students and four typically developing peers in each class, and she sees twenty-four students throughout the day.

Robin's students face a variety of challenges—autism, speech and language delays, along with severe behavior issues, physical handicaps, and developmental challenges. More than any other group of students, special education students need structure—a consistent set of procedures and daily routines to make life familiar and non-threatening.

To give her students a caring atmosphere, safe environment, and positive learning climate, Robin has a classroom management plan.

She teaches her students procedures beginning on the first day of school, and she reinforces them hourly. Robin works with a teaching assistant, three nurses, and five therapists who float in and out of the classroom each week. They function as a team, ensuring that every child can say, "I like coming to school because everyone knows what to do. No one yells at us, and we can go on with learning."

Structure for the Day

Robin's students go through the day with a schedule for all to follow.

8:20–9:15 A.M. – Free Play

Students work on developmentally appropriate activities. The playtime is child-driven, and the teacher facilitates play that enhances language and social and cognitive skills.

- Working on an art or craft project
- Conducting TEACCH, a program developed by the University of North Carolina to help autistic children develop skills in a structured environment
- Practicing with speech therapy cards
- Role-playing
- Playing in the sandbox

Just before the end of Free Play, Robin gives students a two-minute warning, so students can process what they are expected to do next and transition smoothly between activities.

9:15 A.M. – Clean-Up

Robin sings the Clean-Up Song:

Clean up, clean up, everybody clean up.
Clean up, clean up, everybody clean up.

The class works together to put toys on shelves.

9:17–9:30 A.M. – Circle Time

Robin sings the same welcome song each day. The children sing along, readying themselves to participate in Circle Time:

Hello, so glad you're here; hello, so glad
you're here.

Hello, so glad you're here; one, two, three, let's
give a cheer. Hooray!

The structure of Circle Time is the same each day, with no surprises for the students.

- Sing the Calendar Song.
- Do a movement activity.
- Practice a social skill such as listening, courtesy, or sharing.
- Dance to a song.
- Learn a poem.
- Study the word of the week.

9:30–9:50 A.M. – Gym

Just before the end of Gym, Robin gives students a two-minute warning and reminds them where to line up. Some students need extra visual cues—a picture of students patiently waiting in line or a picture of a snack to indicate the next activity, Snack Time.

9:50–10:00 A.M. – Snack Time

Students wash their hands with help from adults in the classroom. Once students are in their assigned seats, the class sings the Snack Song.

It's time for our snack, it's time for our snack.
It's time for us to eat and drink; it's time for our
snack.

Everyone enjoys their snacks. Students may ask for second helpings by using their words or a picture communication board.

10:00–10:20 A.M. – Circle Time
The students come together for a different activity or lesson each day.

10:20–10:45 A.M. – Small Groups
Children rotate every seven to ten minutes and are assisted by classroom aides.

- Three students learn on the class computer
- Four students do a table or floor activity
- Four students do an activity by themselves such as playing in the sandbox, playing with building blocks, or working with Play-Doh.

10:45–10:50 A.M. – Dismissal
Students sing the Goodbye Song.

> *It's time to say goodbye to our friends.*
>   *(clap, clap)*
>
> *It's time to say goodbye to our friends.*
>   *(clap, clap)*
>
> *Oh, it's time to say goodbye, so just smile and*
>   *wink your eye.*
>
> *It's time to say goodbye to our friends.*
>   *(clap, clap)*

Students line up and are led to the correct school buses.

The agenda is posted in the classroom, so the students and assistants can anticipate the day ahead.

Transitioning Between Activities

Robin uses visuals, gestures, objects, and songs to help transition students from one activity to the next. The daily schedule is adhered to, and classroom procedures are constantly reinforced. Procedures provide consistency for the students.

Robin says, "In many special education classrooms, there are classroom assistants, therapists, and nurses that come and go throughout the day and the week. Having consistent procedures and a daily schedule ensures the adults and the children are on the same page.

"The same practices are reinforced without fail," she says. "This means I do not have to waste class time repeating myself."

Three Consistent Procedures

Robin consistently integrates these procedures into her classroom:

1. **Engaging students while engaging with students**
2. **Making sure all teaching materials are on hand**
3. **Giving two-minute warnings**

1. Engaging students while engaging with students
Preschoolers who face challenges like autism, cognitive delays, and behavior issues have a difficult time transitioning between activities. In addition to making use of transition cues like verbal warnings, visuals, and songs, Robin ensures that students look forward to activities. Class activities must be enticing and meaningful to students, so they are motivated to transition.

She moderates the pace of activities so that class energy levels are kept high. By engaging with students, she can sense when students are growing restless. Teachers must sense when students need to get up and move, and they must direct students' energy appropriately. Otherwise, students will get up and move around without waiting for your instructions.

2. Making sure all teaching materials are on-hand
Robin has all of the materials at her fingertips that are necessary for an activity. For instance, if music is to be played during Circle Time, the player and the desired

music must be easily accessible. You should not be walking across the room to access the music and spending time rummaging for the right song. These actions are a waste of valuable class time. Worse, you will lose students' attention in the first ten seconds.

Prior to the start of class time, all materials for teachers and students must be assembled and ready to use.

3. Giving two-minute warnings
Students do not perform well when given an abrupt order to stop what they are doing in order to do something else. Special needs students find it difficult to handle transitions because it requires them to do three things at the same time:

- End one task.
- Prepare for another task.
- Refocus on a new task.

To help students ease into a transition, Robin prepares them by giving a two-minute warning. This allows students time to process what the teacher expects them to do and then to transition in a stress-free manner.

Communicating with the Parents of Special Needs Preschoolers

Preschoolers with disabilities need to have an evaluation prior to starting preschool. The school psychologist and assessment team assesses the child in the areas of fine and large motor abilities, speech and language, self-help and cognitive skills. This process is completed through play-based assessment, observation, and parent questionnaire.

Once a child is tested and qualifies for a Special Education preschool program, parent cooperation and preparation starts before the first day of school. For many parents, if it is their first child going to preschool, they are very nervous and anxious for their child. Also, it may be the first time the parent sees in black and white that their child has a disability. It's the first time their child is on school transportation, as well.

Maintaining regular contact with the parents of preschoolers with special needs helps make the preschool experience as positive as possible for the

parent and the child. There are numerous ways for you to communicate with parents:

1. Welcome postcard
2. Parent-and-child orientation
3. Phone call prior to orientation
4. Phone call on the first day of school
5. Happy Gram
6. Phone call after the first week of school
7. Get-together
8. Weekly newsletter
9. Class website
10. Communication folder
11. Conferences
12. PowerPoint presentations

1. Welcome Postcard
Before school starts, send a postcard to students' homes. The postcard welcomes the student to the class, and simply states,

Hi, Susie,

I am looking forward to having you in class. We will do many fun activities in preschool. I will see you on September 1st.

Sincerely,
Miss Robin

2. Parent-and-Child Orientation
The school or you may consider holding a parent-and-child orientation before school starts. This brief orientation allows the student and parent to visit the school so that neither the parent nor the child is overwhelmed on the first day of the semester.

Use this opportunity to get to know parents and to address any concerns parents may have. Prepare an information packet for each parent to take home. Include this information in the packet:

- How the classroom is run
- Classroom procedures
- School procedures
- How to contact the teacher

Talk parents through the information while the children play in the classroom and familiarize themselves with their new surroundings.

3. Phone Call Prior to Orientation

Prior to the Parent and Child Orientation, call the parents of each student in class. Calling helps you

- introduce yourself to the parents,
- ensure that parents received information about the orientation,
- find out if parents are able to attend the orientation,
- ease parent anxiety, and
- learn information about the child, such as "Jayne got tubes in her ears over the summer," or "Gregory is on a special diet."

4. Phone Call on the First Day of School

Some parents are anxious about their child taking school transportation for the first time. These parents will appreciate a call or an email to let them know that their child has arrived safely at school.

5. Happy Gram

To further reassure parents, consider giving each child a Happy Gram to take home on the first day of school. The Happy Gram simply says

Chelsea had a great first day of school today.

6. Phone Call After the First Week of School

Parents appreciate a call from you at the end of the first week of school. The call

- allows you to tell parents about their child's first week,
- gives you a chance to ask parents if they have any questions or concerns, and
- gives you a chance to remind parents about important documentation that needs to be returned.

A phone call could go like this:

Mrs. Smith, I just wanted to let you know that Zari's adjusting well to school. She is getting used to the classroom procedures, playing with toys, and participating at Circle time.

Do you have any questions or concerns about Zari?

Also, please do not forget to send in the blue card and the emergency contact card.

7. Get-Together

In late September, consider organizing a Get-Together during the school day. This allows parents to meet other parents, get to know each other, and to exchange information to make arrangements.

- Carpooling ■ Play dates ■ Support groups

8. Weekly Newsletter

Create a newsletter and send it home every Monday to communicate this information:

- Theme of the week   ■ Birthdays
- Word of the week   ■ Special events
- Concepts of the week   ■ Days off

9. Class Website

In lieu of the weekly newsletter, consider creating and maintaining a class website. However, it is important to consider if parents have easy access to the Internet.

 29 •))

Access some templates for Happy Grams to send throughout the year.

10. Communication Folder

Establish a Communication Folder that travels between school and home each day. Parents can communicate with you via written notes placed in the Communication Folder and vice versa. You can also place important documents for parents in the folders.

11. Conferences

Explain to parents that they can contact you at any time via phone calls, email, or written notes. On top of that, schedule conferences during the months whenever students' Individualized Education Programs (IEP) are due.

Keep in mind that parents may work shifts; ask when the best time to meet would be. Sometimes, a phone conference may have to take the place of a face-to-face meeting due to parents' work schedules, home commitments, or lack of transportation.

Depending on each student's needs, you may find that more frequent conferences are necessary.

12. PowerPoint Presentations

During special events like Open House and Awards Day, consider creating a PowerPoint Presentation, showing parents the different activities their children have been involved in throughout the year and what a typical school day is like. Parents also derive great joy from seeing pictures of their child interacting with other children.

Reaching Greater Heights

Special education offers the most rewarding outcome—preparing a child who faces unique challenges to function in a demanding world. Each day, Robin Barlak and countless other special education teachers give their absolute best. They celebrate differences and encourage the way these children think out of the box—just as all great leaders, inventors, and discoverers do. This is the charge of all teachers—to realize the potential of every child and to help them on their journey toward greater heights.

30 •))

Learn to identify autistic and ADHD children and how to help them be successful.

Assigned Seats

One of my students goes to another class in the afternoon. The afternoon teacher shared that the student has a hard time sitting at Circle Time on the carpet.

I told the teacher the child does not have a problem sitting in my Circle in the morning.

Students have their own space to sit on the carpet each day at Circle Time. It is their 'assigned seat,' and this particular student has a 'purple circle' he sits on each day to remind him that this is his space.

The afternoon teacher shared that the students do not have assigned seats and can sit 'anywhere' on the carpet for her Circle. The student is squirming all around the Circle because there is no real place to sit, and there is no procedure for sitting.

It all has to do with procedures *and it makes my life so much easier, along with the student's life, too.*

Robin Barlak ▪ Parma, Ohio

Hand Washing

Hand washing is a good habit for students to develop in and out of the classroom. It promotes good hygiene. A procedure for hand washing uses class time and resources efficiently.

THE **SOLUTION**

Even minor processes need to be thought through and structured, so children feel successful at implementing them. A simple task, like washing hands, could turn into a classroom flooded with water and emotions unless there is a procedure in place.

This procedure solves these issues:

1. Pushing, shoving, and crowding around the one sink that is in the classroom
2. Students playing with the soap, water, and paper towel holder
3. Dirty or dripping wet hands

THE **BACKGROUND**

Washing hands is a procedure used through the day. It happens after handling messy items or before handling food.

Snack time is part of the morning schedule for preschool special education students. Children are reminded to wash their hands before touching food. This is a lesson children can take home with them every day.

Consistency is the hallmark for special needs students. Procedures provide necessary structure that allow children to function happily in the classroom.

THE **PROCEDURE STEPS**

Teach students the procedure for hand washing on the first day of school. As you teach the procedure, explain why they are washing their hands and the value of good personal hygiene.

TEACH

The first time hand washing is needed, announce to the students it is time to wash their hands.

Students are to line up and follow you as you lead them to the classroom sink. Ask the classroom assistant to bring up the rear of the line, ensuring that students at the back are following the walking-in-line procedure.

One at a time, students wash their hands. The first student in line approaches the sink, where you are waiting to help with these items:

- Turn on the faucet.
- Dispense a small amount of liquid soap to the student.

- Remind each student to thoroughly rub their hands together before rinsing the soap off (help the student if needed).
- Hand the student a paper towel.

These are the tasks for the student:

- Dry his or her hands on the paper towels.
- Discard the paper towels in the trash.

Thank the student for following the procedure for washing hands.

Ask the classroom assistant to show the student where to go for the next activity.

This procedure repeats until all the students have washed their hands and are at their next activity with extra assistance as needed.

REHEARSE

Role-play the procedure. Tell students to pretend it is time for a snack and line up to wait their turn to wash their hands.

Without using the soap and water or paper towels, have students pretend they are following the procedure.

Practice more than once, until you think the students understand the procedure. Acknowledge each student for what they did to follow the procedure correctly.

REINFORCE

Whenever students need to wash their hands, remind them of why it is important to wash their hands. Thank the students each day for following the correct procedure. Gently but firmly redirect students who deviate from the procedure and need additional guidance to follow the procedure correctly.

36 THE PROCEDURE

Snack Time

Snack Time promotes language skills, social skills, patience, and independence. Students are taught to sit and eat in a social setting and to ask politely for seconds.

THE SOLUTION

Snack time is a very important part of the preschool curriculum. It needs to take place in an orderly yet friendly manner. **It is a time for nourishment, but it is also a time for socialization and learning.**

Procedures for snack time solve these problems:

1. Students walking around the room with food and drink
2. Students placing their hands on food that is not their own
3. Students arguing about where a student is going to sit for a snack

THE **BACKGROUND**

Snack time promotes socialization and language, and requires expressiveness and self-help skills. In **Robin Barlak's** classroom, the parents of each student in the class are asked at the beginning of the school year to bring in healthy snacks (enough for the class for a week) on a rotating basis.

The classroom assistant sets up the snacks while the students are cleaning up. A cup and napkin are placed in front of each chair prior to snack time. The snacks and pitcher of juice are placed on each table.

THE **PROCEDURE STEPS**

The snack time procedure is taught on the first day of school. The procedure is practiced each day, so snacks can be enjoyed as a group.

With any student who cannot follow the procedures of snack time, modify the child's routine to one where success is experienced and snacks can be enjoyed.

TEACH

Remind students that before eating any food in the classroom or outside of the classroom, they must first wash their hands. Go through the Hand Washing procedure with them.

After students have washed their hands and are in their assigned seats at the snack table, teach students the Snack Song to sing before their snack:

It's time for our snack, it's time for our snack.
It's time for us to eat and drink, it's time for our snack.

Explain that you and the classroom assistant will pour each student a small cup of juice and hand out a small portion of the day's snack.

Students are encouraged to chat with the adults and their classmates during snack time. Students are also encouraged to use their words, picture board, or communication board to request second helpings.

Explain that if students do not like their snack, they may choose not to eat it. However, the classroom is not a restaurant, and students may not ask for a different snack. Students must remain in their seats until the teacher excuses them.

Once students have enjoyed their snacks, they must place their cups and napkins in the trash bin.

Then, they check the schedule board and proceed to the next activity, so you can start the lesson.

 31 •))

Listen to Robin Barlak's class sing the Snack Song.

REHEARSE

Model the procedure for your students. Begin at hand washing, and then move to the snack table. Pretend you are eating.

Tell students what to say if they want more snacks. "Mrs. Barlak, may I please have another slice of apple?"

Ask one of your students to follow along with you as you go through the steps again. Have them do as you do. Stop at each part and state what you are doing to follow the procedure.

If necessary, walk each one of your students through this process. Thank the student for following the steps to the procedure.

Then ask if anyone can show the class how it is done without help from you. If the student falters, step in quickly to keep the student on track following the procedure.

After a successful rehearsal, remind students that it is Snack Time, and everyone can now sit together and enjoy their snack.

Then share with the students how to respond once the extra snack is received. "Mrs. Barlak, thank you for the apple." Include the words "please" and "thank you" as part of your procedure.

When snack time is over, model how to pick up after you are done and how to check where to go next. Point to the picture schedule on the board and show students where they are on the schedule and what is next.

Model how to go to that area to transition from Snack Time to a new activity.

REINFORCE

Teach and remind students of the Snack Time procedure every day. By the end of the first week of school, Snack Time will have become a familiar routine to students and a time everyone will look forward to each day as they sing the Snack Time song and gather to enjoy the nourishment of the day.

Security in Consistency

The school year has gotten off to a great start. Much planning over the summer helped my assistants and me prepare for the first day of school.

Students with special needs thrive on structure and routine. Daily procedures and routines give students security and predictability, so they can focus on learning.

My students are very familiar with the routine and procedures, and it has only been seven days of school. No stress for them and no stress for me!

Robin Barlak ▪ Parma, Ohio

Morning Procedures for Middle School Students

Ronda Thomas, a middle school, special education teacher in Arizona, created a large, Morning Procedure poster that is posted by the door, so her students know exactly what to do from the time they first step into the room.

The procedures are listed in chronological order in words and pictures. Her Special Needs students can "read," or Ronda or her teaching assistant will read the actual words related to the pictures. Ronda's students know what they are supposed to do as soon as they get in from breakfast.

Ronda shares that as an experienced Special Educator and a parent of special needs boys, "Special Needs students require something like an agenda or morning routine to go by. They all need something simple, understandable, and definitely within a structured setting. This helps to maintain order and still gives the students the opportunity to learn something that will help them in daily life."

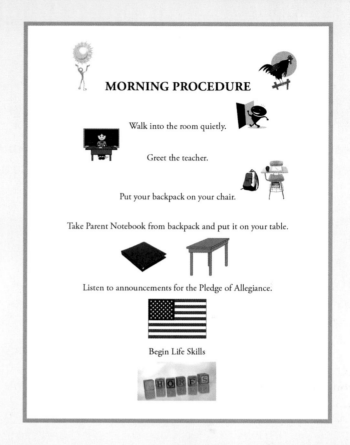

MORNING PROCEDURE

Walk into the room quietly.

Greet the teacher.

Put your backpack on your chair.

Take Parent Notebook from backpack and put it on your table.

Listen to announcements for the Pledge of Allegiance.

Begin Life Skills

Walking to Another Location

Teaching students to move orderly and efficiently through the campus keeps special needs students in the general flow of the school without calling attention to any of their behavioral issues or physical limitations.

THE **SOLUTION**

School life exists outside the Special Education classroom. Transitioning to a room outside of the safe classroom environment can cause anxiety and unrest for children. **Procedures keep students safe while moving about the campus and focused on moving from point A to point B.**

This procedure provides these opportunities:

1. Students walking orderly in the hallways without harming themselves, calling attention to themselves, or disturbing other classrooms

2. Efficient use of time preparing for transitions and during transitions

THE **BACKGROUND**

Although most activities take place within the classroom, children usually leave to engage in some type of physical activity, to go to an assembly, or to go to the media center. Using the same procedure each time to move from place to place provides consistency for the task.

THE **PROCEDURE STEPS**

Walk students through the procedure for moving from one room to another *before* the need arises. Break the procedure into small steps and teach it in increments, so children will have success at each part of the process. As each step is mastered, teach the next step, while building upon the last success, until the entire procedure is followed.

TEACH

When it is time to leave the classroom, make an announcement. The announcement is the cue for students to do the following:

1. Stand up (or come to attention for those children with physical disabilities).
2. Wait for the teacher to call out their names.
3. Move and line up by the door when called.

Once students are in line, announce that the class is going to go to the gym, auditorium, media center, or wherever the destination. Before the students begin to move, give them these reminders:

1. Stay behind the person in front of them.
2. Keep their hands behind their backs.
3. Be quiet.

Tell them these reminders before they begin to move, so they can focus on the act of moving and not listening to you at the same time.

Lead the line of students to the new location. Take care to walk at a slow pace. Depending on individual students' needs, place students with the most difficulty walking at the front of the line, and students with the least difficulty walking at the back. The classroom assistant stays at the end of the line and can help students who deviate from the procedure.

At the entrance, tell students that when this time outside of the classroom is over, students must do the following:

1. Listen for the teacher's instructions.
2. Line up at a designated spot.
3. Wait for the teacher to lead them back to the classroom.

Ask students to stand in the designated spot as if returning to their classroom to check for understanding.

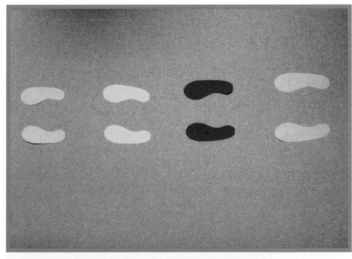

Feet attached to the floor help students know where to line up and how close to stand to one another.

Allow students to resume the activity they came to do.

At the end of the activity announce, "In two minutes it will be time to line up at our spot, so we can return to our classroom."

After two minutes announce, "Please line up at our spot, so we can return to our classroom."

Remind students of the transition procedure before walking back to the classroom.

1. Stay behind the person in front of them.
2. Keep their hands behind their backs.
3. Remain quiet.

Watch for any deviations from the procedure. Gently, but firmly, correct students as needed. Ask the classroom aide to assist in monitoring the students as they return to the classroom.

Thank the students for correctly following the procedure as they are returning to class. Once in the classroom, thank them again for correctly following the procedure and remind them this is how to do it each time they leave the classroom.

REHEARSE

Practice this procedure the day before you will need to leave the classroom as a group. Students will have much to remember on the first days of school. Waiting until the appropriate time will help students remember the steps.

Rehearse the procedure at a time when other students are in their classrooms, so there are no distractions for your students. They can concentrate on you while you model the procedure correctly for them.

Repeat the process until you feel sure they understand what needs to be done each time they leave the classroom and move to a new place on the campus. Be consistent in performing the procedure, and remain patient while you turn the procedure into a routine.

REINFORCE

As much as possible, observe the students while they follow the procedure and thank them for following it correctly. Each time the class follows the procedure, reinforce it with a smile and say, "Thank you for walking behind each other and not talking or disturbing other classrooms."

Tell students what it is they did correctly and encourage them to do it the same way next time they leave the classroom.

I Provide . . .

I provide knowledge and skills.
I provide security and a sanctuary.
I provide confidence and motivation.
I provide someone to look up to.
I provide respect and validation.
I provide success and a vision for the future.

Allie Hahn ■ Canton, Georgia

Everything in Its Place

Texas 2012 Teacher-of-the-Year **Stephanie Stoebe** works with students who are at risk of dropping out of school, students who are struggling to learn English, and students who receive special education services. Yet, she organizes all of her classes the same—with procedures.

" Students with autism need routines. There has to be a place, a procedure, a process for everything. The bathroom pass must always hang right under the American flag. The headphones must hang on the back of the computer monitor. If these things are not correct, there can be a full meltdown, crying, or persistent questions like, 'Why would someone leave the headphones on the table?' 'Can I go hang the headphones up where they belong?' 'Ms. Stoebe, do you think that the next person will be upset because the headphones are in the wrong place?'

If I have students with autism in my classroom, we as a whole class, must quickly learn to master the procedures and routines, or learning will constantly be interrupted. Driven to distraction by obsessions is not the frame of mind I need my students in when we are working on improving their reading skills.

Jessie is a young man with autism that I had for three years. At first, he had a paraprofessional attend all his classes with him. He felt comfortable in my class because the notebooks were always in the same spot, the tables labeled, and the agenda for the day on the board.

The first class that Jessie ever routinely went to on his own was my reading class. He turned one day to his aide and said, 'You know, I got it from here.' And from then on, Jessie came alone.

He first learned to maneuver my classroom, but he soon learned to maneuver the school. His third year in high school, Jessie became my student aide; he was responsible for running errands, posting the agenda for the day, and making sure that all materials were in order. And he would let me know if he was disappointed in a certain class for not following the classroom procedures! "

38 THE PROCEDURE

Handling Student Anxiety

Special needs students who are mainstreamed in a general education classroom can experience anxiety and frustration. With the proper support and structure, students can be successful.

THE SOLUTION

When special needs students are included in the general education setting, anxiety and frustration can occur during instructional lessons. These issues can manifest themselves as yelling, crying, withdrawing, or throwing objects.

Providing a procedure for students to follow when they feel overwhelmed revolves these issues:

1. Minimizes interruption to the instructional lesson

2. Allows the special education student to receive support without drawing negative attention

3. Reinforces the use of appropriate "replacement" behaviors

THE **BACKGROUND**

The need to fit in or a desire to start and complete a task like everyone else can be the cause of behavioral issues for the special needs student.

Out-of-control feelings can surface when the student feels "left behind" or wants to keep up with peers. Although these feelings cannot be totally eliminated, students can be taught an appropriate way to channel these feelings with minimal harm to themselves or others.

Giving the student a step-by-step procedure to follow when an anxious or frustrating moment occurs minimizes classroom disruption, allows the student to receive support without drawing negative attention, and reinforces the use of appropriate replacement behaviors.

THE **PROCEDURE STEPS**

Observe the student to pinpoint the specific behavior problem the student is experiencing. Use these questions to help you identify the problem and keep you making an incorrect assumption. Ask yourself these questions:

- What behavior is the student displaying?
- When and where are the behaviors occurring?
- What concerns does the student verbalize during these situations?
- Who is involved in these situations?
- How do these situations come about and why?

If appropriate, brainstorm with the student behaviors that are acceptable and appropriate for the classroom. Prior to the brainstorming session, prepare answers to these questions:

- What do you want the student to do instead of yelling, crying, or throwing objects?

- What will make the special needs student feel that his or her frustration or anxiety is being addressed?

Create a step-by-step procedure for the student to follow when he or she is experiencing anxiety or frustration.

For younger students, write the procedure in a first person narrative. For older students, write the procedure from a third person point of view. It is important that the procedure steps be positive, meaningful, and relevant to the student.

An example of a step-by-step procedure, written from the student's point of view, could look like this:

Sometimes, my teacher will ask me to do work at my seat or in a group.

I want to do well and to get all of my work finished.

Sometimes, I feel afraid and anxious that I will be left behind.

My teacher says that it is okay and that I will not get left behind.

My teacher says that everyone finishes their work at different times.

It is okay if I am working and my friends are finished.

If I start to become anxious,

1. *I will put my smiley face magnet on the side of my desk.*

2. *I will continue to work quietly until my teacher comes to help me.*

Value

How does one measure quality?
It is when one can add value to another's life.

Linda Lippman ■ Islip, New York

Abstract concepts such as anxiety and frustration can be represented through visual images. These visuals help support the easy-to-understand, step-by-step procedure. Take these pictures and insert them in the step-by-step procedure:

- The calm, reassuring teacher
- The frazzled student
- The student's peers offering positive reinforcement
- The frazzled student at his or her usual, confident best

Make copies of the procedure for the student and parents. Teach the student and the parent this procedure before the onset of frustration or anxiety. If necessary, make a condensed version of the steps and keep it in a place the student can see as a visual reminder of what can be done when these feelings happen.

TEACH

Read the procedure steps with the student. Walk the student through each step, explaining the rationale behind each step.

REHEARSE

Role play a situation where the student could get frustrated. Model for the student how to overcome those feelings by following the procedure. Verbalize the steps as you go through them.

Allow the student to practice the procedure steps in a non-threatening situation.

REINFORCE

Frequently revisit the procedure steps with the student. This can be done less frequently as the procedure becomes a routine. Tell the student you are there to help at all times and to never feel ashamed or afraid to ask for your support.

I Believe in You

I believe in you.
No matter what you've done . . .
  I believe in you.
No matter what's happened to you . . .
  I believe in you.

No matter what people say . . .
  I believe in you.
No matter if you are rich or poor . . .
  I believe in you.
No matter your age or size . . .
  I believe in you.

No matter your IQ . . .
  I believe in you.
No matter where you live . . .
  I believe in you.
No matter your position or lack of one . . .
  I believe in you.
No matter, no matter, no matter . . .
  I believe in you.

Melissa Dunbar ■ **Kerrville, Texas**

Effective Behavior Management Strategies

Prevention rather than intervention is what works best in the special needs classroom. Learn from skilled teachers what works and what doesn't work in the special needs classroom.

According to the results of a survey of special educators reported in *Preventing School Failure*, these are the least effective behavior management strategies:

- Sending a student to the principal's office for bad behavior

- Giving detention

- Having a class meeting to discuss problem behaviors

- Rewarding students with a point system for good behavior

These are the most effective strategies cited by special educators:

- Establishing classroom routines and rules

- Accommodating individual instructional needs by individualizing tasks and instruction

- Affirming or encouraging appropriate behavior

- Using verbal cues and prompts

- Modeling appropriate behavior

- Communicating regularly with students through conversations, notes, or journals

The report states that the same intervention strategies commonly taught in teacher preparation programs, are viewed by teachers as too complex to implement, and, in some instances, they are ineffective. When the costs of employing intensive interventions outweigh their benefits, teachers are unlikely to use those approaches.

The least effective approaches address problems after they occur; that is, conducting class meetings to discuss problem behavior, threatening students with loss of privileges, assigning detention or school suspension, or, calling parents to come and take a student home.

The report reveals one clear finding:

All of the most useful management strategies are intended to prevent or interfere with problem behavior at an early stage.

The solution?

Procedures, procedures, procedures

Marilyn Kaff, Robert Zabel, and Morgan Milham.
"Revisiting Cost-Benefit Relationships of Behavior Management Strategies: What Special Educators Say About Usefulness, Intensity, and Effectiveness."
Preventing School Failure, 2007, Volume 51, Number 2, pp. 35-45.

THE **PROCEDURE**

New Student Orientation*

Involving students in welcoming new students to class helps instill class spirit, allows the teacher to continue teaching without interruption, and focuses less attention on the new student.

THE **SOLUTION**

A **new student does not have to be a disruption to the flow of the day.** Instructional time is not lost trying to bring the new student up to speed with the organization of the classroom when a plan is in place to greet a new student. The daily routine is not disturbed; yet the new student feels welcomed.

This procedure provides these opportunities:

1. Introduces the new student to the way the class is run
2. Makes the new student feel welcome
3. Keeps the class on task with minimal interruption

*This procedure is not taught to students with the three-step approach. It is a teacher procedure with steps shared to show you how to do it.

THE **BACKGROUND**

Often, a teacher receives very little notice when a new student is assigned to a classroom. Typically, the office gives you a slip of paper or sends you an email with the new student's name before the new student shows up at your door.

Secondary teachers frequently add new students to class, with many new students arriving unannounced. Student class schedules change, classes are dropped and others added—all in a single day. A new student may arrive at the beginning of class or even in the middle of a lesson. This does not need to result in wasted instructional time. With a plan in place, the new student can join the class and receive all the information needed to succeed while you continue with instruction.

THE **PROCEDURE STEPS**

Welcoming the new student is a schoolwide endeavor. Enlisting the aid of your students allows you to keep teaching while the students help the newcomer fall into the established classroom routines.

Being prepared is the key to a smooth transition as you welcome new students to your classroom.

1. Keep a New Student basket.
Set up a basket with extra sets of the documents given to students at the start of the school year. These are some items to include:

- Classroom rules and procedures
- A list of required supplies
- Permission slips
- School maps
- A list of emergency codes and procedures
- A checklist for new students

Include empty folders or manila envelopes in the basket in case the new student does not have a notebook handy for keeping the handouts.

2. Train students to be New Student Greeters.
At the elementary level, have a dedicated classroom job for New Student Greeter. Each class member will have the responsibility of greeting new students throughout the year.

At the secondary level, assign a student in each period to be the New Student Greeter.

New Student Greeters are friendly and outgoing, and excellent communicators. They are responsible for retrieving a set of documents from the New Student Basket. Designate a place where the greeter can sit with the new student and discuss the material.

Assigning class members to help welcome new students allows the teacher to focus on teaching and gives the new student the opportunity to ask questions without interrupting the lesson.

In addition, it ensures the new student sees a friendly face in a new environment, as well as someone to sit with at lunch.

Encourage the Greeter to exchange emails or phone numbers with the new student should questions come up during the adjustment period.

Assign a classroom buddy to new students to help them acclimate quickly to the classroom routines.

3. Assign class numbers.

Most school rosters list and number students in alphabetical order. This number can be used for multiple tasks:

- As the student's ID number for paper headings
- For seating chart arrangements
- For computer terminal allocation
- For forming groups

Typically, when one student leaves the classroom due to a move or transfer, a spot is opened for a new student. There is no need to change the class numbers for the entire class when one student leaves and a new one joins the class.

When a new student joins the class, assign the student

- the next number after the last student in class, or
- the number of the student who left the class.

Think of your class roster as a numerical list and not as an alphabetical list of students.

4. Keep a digital photo seating chart.

When there are periodic changes to the class enrollment, a digital photo seating chart is a time-saver. Teach New Student Greeters how to help and how to maintain the chart:

- Use the class webcam to take a picture of the new student.
- Add the picture to the chart.

5. Prepare a New Student checklist.

Include a New Student Checklist for New Student Greeters to use. This checklist ensures all important information is relayed to the new student. The Greeter indicates that he or she has discussed the necessary material by initialing the checklist.

These are some things to include on the checklist:

- ☐ Give the new student a complete set of documents from the New Student Basket.
- ☐ Highlight the class website's address and the teacher's email address.
- ☐ Discuss the school rules.
- ☐ Discuss the classroom procedures.
- ☐ Discuss the list of required supplies.
- ☐ Show the new student how to set up the class notebook.
- ☐ Show the student how to head a paper.
- ☐ Tell the new student how the class number is used.
- ☐ Highlight and explain any required permission slips.
- ☐ Give the new student a school map.
- ☐ Show the new student the emergency procedures and exit routes.
- ☐ Review the class homework policy.
- ☐ Ask the new student if he or she has any questions.

Name of New Student _____

Date Checklist Shared_____

New Student Greeter's Name_____

6. Introduce the New Student to the class.

At a break in the instruction or at the end of the class period, introduce the new student to the rest of the class.

Welcome New Students

There is nothing more frightening than to transfer schools, leaving behind a familiar neighborhood, friends, school, and culture. The new school will be different, with established groups and cliques that may be hard to join. For adolescents, their peer group is the social "family" and is critical to their sense of well-being.

It is easy to develop new friends in a classroom where there is a culture of consistency and procedures are established to welcome everyone. A classroom handbook delivered to the student, along with a warm greeting, puts the new student at ease.

"Everything you need to know about how this class is run is in this booklet. Just watch how everyone does things in here and you will catch on very quickly. If you don't understand something, just ask someone near you or me and we will help you with the classroom procedures. We all know what is going on and you will soon know, too. So, welcome!"

When the new student is introduced to the New Student Greeter, an instant new friendship is created. It soon becomes very clear to the new student that everyone in the classroom is working together to make the new student feel welcome and successful.

In many schools, adolescent youth in particular, find it impossible to fit in and succeed in a classroom that is unstructured and disorganized. Bullying is feared and isolation and withdrawal set in.

Just as you have a classroom procedure for new students, schools need a procedure to ease the shock of the transfer.

- Create a handbook for students who transfer during the school year. It should include the school calendar, names and contact information for key personnel, and schoolwide procedures. If possible, give this handbook to the student and parents prior to starting the school.

- Create a committee of adults to meet with the new student to track progress in adjusting to the new school.

- Invite the Student Council to form a welcome group that assigns a school buddy to meet with the new student and share all of the clubs, teams, and organizations at the school and how to join the groups.

- Organize a gathering of all new students that week or month. The principal hosts the meeting and gives new students a chance to ask questions and get to know the leadership of the school.

New students need to feel welcome immediately in a classroom and in the school and this can only happen if there are policies, programs, and procedures organized in anticipation of the student's arrival.

THE **PROCEDURE**

The Angry Student*

Responding in anger to a student who is angry will only add fuel to the student's fire. Seek to understand and communicate effectively with the student, and you will help douse the flames of anger.

THE **SOLUTION**

The teacher who has a plan in place to deal with distressed students and is sincere about working with them to manage their emotions will be far more successful than the teacher who removes students from the situation by issuing an office referral. **Show you care, and the student will feel your concern.**

This procedure resolves these issues:

1. What to do when a student arrives angry or becomes angry in class
2. How to prevent additional confrontations with the angry student

*This procedure is not taught to students with the three-step approach. It is a teacher procedure with steps shared to show you how to do it.

THE **BACKGROUND**

Secondary students walk from one classroom to the next all day, usually with only three- to five-minute periods between classes. This leaves little to no down time throughout the day. Students sometimes need a moment to think and recover from an unhappy incident in a previous class.

Give the students a procedure to follow when they feel angry or frustrated. Let them choose their course or action before you intervene, if necessary.

1. Create a gesture that says, "I need some space." When the gesture is given by the student, respect the space before you check in with the student.

2. Create a space where the students can go to regroup. Set a time limit for staying and a one person at a time maximum. Respect students for knowing their need to utilize the space.

3. Create a signal that says, "I am having a bad day." Give students the parameters of what you will do when they are having a bad day.

Students will appreciate that you offer them a consistent plan for handling their emotional turmoil. Your plan says you understand and respect the student's need to regain composure and order to an oftentimes frenzied day.

It is your responsibility to maintain control of the class and to provide a safe learning environment for all your students.

THE **PROCEDURE STEPS**

An angry outburst is an emotional response; responding harshly to an angry student will merely aggravate the situation. By remaining calm, you can help soothe the angry student and get the class back on task.

1. Stay calm and remain in control.

Students who act out in school by displaying antisocial behavior such as whining, bullying, name calling, acting cool, or behaving stubbornly may be reaching out for help. It is easy to grow frustrated with the student who constantly displays these behaviors, but it is more effective to work with the student and gain the student's trust and cooperation.

Students who enter the room angry or unleash their anger in class expect the teacher to respond in anger. Angry students are prepared for, and may even desire confrontation. Stay calm. Do not

- threaten the angry student,
- return the student's anger,
- appear shocked or helpless, or
- yell at or argue with the student.

Any of these reactions will stoke the student's anger and reinforce his or her belief that they are in control. Remain professional. The teacher who is calm, understanding, and non-confrontational remains in control of the situation—and the classroom.

2. Be understanding.

Even effective teachers cannot compel students to do things. Students act appropriately, practice classroom procedures, and follow classroom rules because they

- respect the teacher;
- understand the clear rules and procedures; and
- have been taught socially acceptable behavior.

Respect the angry student as a person and attempt to empathize with his or her needs without condoning disruptive behavior. Writing a referral and sending the student to the office does not resolve anything. It may help you feel that you have won the battle, but how will the student react? The student will return to class eventually—either before the end of class or the next day. What will you do when the situation repeats itself? Will you write another referral . . . and then another?

The angry student will not be expecting a calm, positive response. The surprise factor may be enough to calm a student who is openly angry.

If the student persists with his or her anger, repeat that you do understand, and be sincere. Tone of voice is crucial. If a student enters the room openly angry, say, "I see that you are angry today, but please sit quietly, and we will talk after the class gets started on the opening assignment."

When inviting an angry student to sit, do not point. The angry student may interpret this as aggressive behavior from the teacher. Instead, make a gentle sweeping motion with the hand to invite the student to take a seat.

3. Give the student time to calm down.

Instead of requiring the angry student to begin the opening assignment immediately—which will seem confrontational—suggest that the student lay his or her head down on the desk or sit in an area away from the rest of the class.

In a few minutes, encourage the student to take out a sheet of paper and list everything that has gone wrong that day, everything that led to his or her anger. Give the student the option of using an electronic device to list his or her frustrations. Giving the student options will divert his or her attention from the source of the problem.

This process of lying down and writing gives the student a moment to evaluate his or her anger and to calm down.

For younger students, set aside an area in the classroom where they can use paper and crayons to illustrate their feelings. A kindergartner may not be able to express what he or she is feeling in words, but the student is able to color or draw. A typical fourth grader can verbalize and write, but an angry and frustrated student at this age may calm down faster and be better comforted by coloring or drawing their feelings and experiences.

4. Be professional.

After encouraging the student to take a moment, proceed with your responsibilities to get the class engaged in learning. Do not hover over the angry student.

The effective teacher will proceed with the class without showing anger or dismay toward the angry student. Allowing the student a few moments will

- give the student time to calm down, and
- give the teacher time to analyze the situation.

Your best defense will be your professionalism.

5. Talk to the student.

While students are completing their opening assignment, approach the angry student calmly. Ask if he or she would like to talk now or after class, or even after school. Again, give the angry student options. With options, the student is less likely to feel cornered.

If the student wishes to talk, invite the student to the hallway or to a quiet corner. Never deal with the issue in front of the class because a public discussion will ignite the issue, instead of solving the problem.

Speak slowly and gently. Do not argue with the student or use sarcasm. Make occasional eye contact with the student, but do not stare. Be understanding and ask the student to explain what is causing the anger.

If the student wrote about the cause of the frustration, ask if he or she would like to share the notes. Be a good listener.

An angry student will expect a confrontation. Remain professional and caring. You are responsible for creating an atmosphere of resolve—not one of rage.

If listening to the student is going to take more time than you can afford to be away from the classroom, suggest that the student

- stay after class;
- return at the end of the school day; or
- visit the school guidance counselor to discuss the problem.

6. Communicate effectively.

An angry student is not seeking a lecture. An angry student wants to be listened to and to be heard. Use short phrases when talking with the student and let the student know you understand.

When speaking to the student, use the student's name as much as possible. Anger is not an everyday emotion, so a student who is angry is not acting as he or she would normally behave. Calling a student by name will help the student return to his or her normal behavior.

If a student has an angry outburst in reaction to something you've said, don't dwell on the issue. Call the student by name and say, "You may be correct, but please remember the procedure for contributing in class." Continue with the lesson.

Don't respond to an angry comment with unprofessional conduct. Students will be impressed by the teacher's calm handling of the situation. Move on and don't carry a grudge.

7. Make use of body language.

Be aware of body language when talking to an angry student:

- Standing too close to an angry student and invading his or her space may be interpreted by the student as aggression

- Placing hands on hips when speaking or listening can also signal aggression

- Crossing the arms on the chest displays defensiveness

- Clasping hands behind the back can be interpreted as frustration

- Pointing a finger can be taken as confrontational

Using negative body language will not open the lines of communication with your students.

Convey your sincerity to the distressed student:

- Speak to the angry student with palms open to show sincerity and openness.

- Tilt your head to indicate you are genuinely interested.

- Smile and nod your head to communicate you understand.

Using positive body language will convey to students you want to help.

8. Develop a procedure for time-outs.

An effective teacher plans ahead. If there is a student in the classroom who struggles with anger management and has frequent outbursts, there needs to be a procedure to offer this student a time-out to calm down.

A time-out card system works well. Create time-out cards—each worth five minutes—that can be issued to an angry student. When a student is angry and needs time to calm down, he or she may be given a time-out card to

- sit in the room and lay his or her head down,

- sit in another teacher's room (prearrange this with a colleague), or

- sit alone in the hallway or the counselor's office.

Allowing the student a time-out will give the student space and time to calm down and think without creating a scene in the classroom.

The Death of a Student*

Dealing with the death of a classmate can be traumatic for the entire class. Students react in unexpected ways. Being flexible and understanding will create a caring atmosphere in the classroom.

THE SOLUTION

When a tragedy occurs, you must give the students and yourself time to grieve. Adjust lesson plans, give students time to mourn, and be sensitive to the needs of students during this difficult time. Your manner will comfort and support students while they undergo the loss of their classmate.

This procedure provides these opportunities:

1. Dealing with the loss
2. Returning to the regular classroom routine

*This procedure is not taught to students with the three-step approach. It is a teacher procedure with steps shared to show you how to do it.

THE **BACKGROUND**

A popular student passes away, and the school is in mourning. Students gather in the hallways, talk in hushed whispers, cry, and hug; there are more than a few red eyes in class. It's hard to teach because the students are distraught and distracted, maybe even angry. You cannot help but be affected.

By being prepared for the unexpected, you will help the class return to the consistency they need to get them back to normalcy.

THE **PROCEDURE STEPS**

When a student passes away, some students may learn of it before coming to school, but others will only learn of it at school. The routines you expect in the classroom will be interrupted. Your actions will help the students comprehend the loss and come to terms with it over time.

1. Be flexible.
When the death of a student is announced, be flexible with the curriculum plans:

- If a test is scheduled, postpone the test.
- Allow students to read quietly.
- Lead a class discussion, so students can talk and express their feelings.
- Ask a school counselor to speak to the class.
- Allow students to go to the counselor's office as needed.

2. Let students talk.
Give students class time to share their emotions and reflect upon past events connected to the deceased student.

Some schools set up a location as an emergency crisis center, so students can gather under the guidance of school counselors. Encourage students who are openly distraught to go to the crisis center.

Take the time to go to the crisis center during your planning or lunch period. Sit with students and talk to them. Students need to know you care about their grief.

3. Give students time to grieve.
Students need time to grieve the death of a student; however, this grieving period should not be indefinite.

Don't pretend the student was never in the class. Leave the desk of the deceased student in the room. Do not move the desk or rearrange the room until after the student's funeral.

Time Alone

Some students may find it extremely difficult to return to the classroom they once shared with the deceased student.

Be an understanding teacher. Allow the student to miss class and sit in the counselor's office the first few days, but then encourage the student to come to the classroom during your planning period when no other students are in the room.

The student may need time in the room with just the teacher and the counselor, or even time alone before joining the regular class. Allow the student to sit in their deceased friend's desk if needed. With time, and with the teacher's help and support, the student should be able to readjust to the classroom.

Judy Akins ▪ Fort Smith, Arkansas
Counseling Department Head, Southside High School

The desk should not become a shrine, but students need time to recognize that the student is no longer there and will not be returning to class. Encourage students to bring a flower or write a note to the family.

Give students time to grieve, but also provide students with as much structure as possible. Routine classroom procedures must still be maintained. Not all students will be emotionally affected in the same way, so everyone's needs should be taken into consideration while moving forward. Return to the regular classroom routine as soon as possible.

4. Be observant.

As time passes and the class settles back into the regular routine, watch for students whose grades suddenly drop, become lethargic, or who begin to exhibit sudden flashes of anger. These students may need extra counseling to help them cope with the loss.

5. Be sensitive.

Although the death of a popular student often touches the entire student body, the passing of a quiet, *unknown* student should be treated as significantly as that of a well-known student.

Be aware that some students who are disconnected from the deceased may experience trauma and show signs of grief because they relate the death to a past or present illness in their own family.

Be sensitive to cultural differences. Some cultures quietly grieve the loss of a loved one, while others openly display distress. Understand and respect cultural differences and be sensitive to the family's spiritual beliefs. Don't expect all students to grieve in the same way.

6. Take care of yourself.

The loss of a student can be traumatic for you, too. Allow students to see your sadness—it will help students acknowledge their own emotions.

Time is needed to grieve and deal with the loss of a student. The school counselor and fellow teachers can help provide support through this difficult time.

7. Achieve closure.

When normalcy begins to return to the class, prepare the deceased student's file. Give the file to the counselor to include with possessions from the student's locker—for the family.

Attend the funeral if possible. This can be difficult, but students need the support of caring teachers, and parents appreciate the presence of the child's teacher.

It is more than a gesture; it is an act of caring they will never forget. Sign the guest book as the deceased student's teacher and indicate the subject taught. For instance, write "Mrs. Jones, John's Sophomore English Teacher."

The respect shown by the teacher is encouraging to the student's family and helps bring closure.

8. Return to the normal classroom routine.

The first day in class without the deceased student will be very difficult. Students will talk, cry, grieve, and seek the comfort of friends. Crucially, they will depend on the teacher to help the class return to normal.

The second day after the death of a student should consist of an appropriate level of normalcy.

Return to the regular schedule the day after the funeral. Before the students come to class, remove the deceased student's desk from the classroom and start with a new desk arrangement, if only for a short time. Create a new seating chart.

Review with students any routines that may need reinforcing.

Be sensitive to material selected for instruction, such that it doesn't contain reminders of the recent tragedy.

Crisis Signs

These are symptoms anyone could display when going through a crisis. Be aware, so you can respond accordingly.

Prolonged sadness	Panic
Sudden behavior problems	Withdrawal
	Clinging behavior
Eating problems	Stomach aches, headaches
Sleeping problems	
Scared reactions to alarms	Age regression
	Sullen
Frightened response to loud noise	Disconnection from school

In Tears the Class Proceeded

Bill Acuff, the principal of a junior high school in Texas, led his staff through the loss of a much-loved student who was working extremely hard to change his life for the better. On a Saturday evening bicycle ride, he would never make it home.

"We had an eighth-grade student who was truly turning his life around. He learned that one of his teacher's son was having a birthday party, so he walked for eight miles to arrive early to attend and help. That was the character of this boy.

He received a bicycle one Saturday morning and proceeded to ride it to our annual Rice Festival. On the way home that evening, he was hit by a car, thrown into a ditch, and died.

On Sunday evening I called the staff to alert them of the situation, and I proceeded to follow the boy's schedule on Monday.

When I saw his English teacher, she was standing at the door in tears. She had her assignment posted; the students picked up their notebooks and got to work. The class proceeded with everyone on task.

Because the school had procedures and routines, the students and teachers made it through the day.

The teacher later acknowledged, "I guess there's more to be said about routines than I thought. They helped us all make it through a very difficult day."

The Death of a Parent*

The death of a student's parent affects everyone. Be there for students and other parents in the classroom, but also remember to take care of yourself.

THE **SOLUTION**

f the death of a student's parent happens, or a student's parent becomes terminally ill, it helps the grieving process if you know how to handle the loss. **Allow time to grieve while bringing normalcy back to the classroom as quickly as possible.** Ask for help and guidance from others who may have experiences to share.

This procedure provides these opportunities:

1. Lessens the trauma to students

2. Keeps students focused

3. Helps students cope with loss

*This procedure is not taught to students with the three-step approach. It is a teacher procedure with steps shared to show you how to do it.

THE **BACKGROUND**

All members of the class have to deal with the loss when a student's parent dies—especially if it's a parent who actively volunteered in the classroom and built a strong rapport with the class. Be understanding, flexible, and observant to help everyone cope with the loss.

THE **PROCEDURE STEPS**

Knowing the steps to take to help you and your students cope with the unexpected loss will give you strength and confidence in guiding your students during a difficult and emotional time.

1. Be flexible.
You will have to be flexible with the students and the curriculum in the ensuing days. Postpone planned lessons and scheduled tests. In their place, allow for reading time, discussions, drawing, or writing—all of which are helpful emotional outlets for the students.

2. Let students talk.
Allow students to share memories of the parent and their feelings for the bereaving classmate. Allow students to grieve. Invite the school counselor or administration to talk with the class.

3. Give students time to grieve.
Allow students and other parents in the classroom to grieve in their own ways and at their own pace. Encourage students to write notes or draw pictures for the bereaved student. These pieces of writing or art can help students show their support to their classmate. The process of writing or drawing can also be helpful for students going through the grieving process.

Students will need to return to the normal routines of the classroom as soon as possible. This is especially important when the bereaved student returns to school. Delaying the return to a normal classroom routine may make it harder for students to deal with this tragic event.

4. Be observant.
Observe and listen to the students. Some students may not show clear signs of grieving. Some may even be quiet about grieving but act out or do poorly in school. These students may need additional counseling. Their families may need to be contacted, so you can share your observations with them.

5. Stay emotionally strong.
Give yourself time to grieve and deal with the loss. Talk with fellow teachers and seek help counseling if needed. The grieving process is unpredictable, so be patient.

Attending the funeral may help bring closure for you. The bereaving student and family need to see your support. Sign the guest book or memory book of the parent. The sharing of some personal testimony on how the parent was involved in the classroom helps the child remember the parent in years to come.

Helping the Healing Process

When I received the news that my Room Parent passed away unexpectedly, I was devastated. It was very difficult to go into the classroom the following school day and try to be strong for my students when I was falling to pieces inside.

When you have an involved parent in the classroom, it can be hard to know what words to say to offer comfort and support—especially to the bereaving student. I found that by letting my students have the freedom to ask questions, talk, draw pictures, and write letters helped us.

My student and her family were moved by the sympathy cards received and memories shared, as well as our attendance at the funeral. I still don't feel that I am 'over' this event. The experience affected me and changed the way I look at my students and their families each day.

Sarah Jondahl ■ Brentwood, California

Substitute Teacher Handbook*

A Substitute Teacher Handbook prepares a substitute to take on the teaching responsibilities for the class in your absence, so learning continues in a business-as-usual manner for students.

THE **SOLUTION**

A Substitute Teacher Handbook equips the substitute teacher with all the necessary information to be successful. With a handbook, the substitute teacher will be less likely to struggle through the day. The day will be productive, and student learning will continue uninterrupted during your absence.

This procedure provides these opportunities:

1. Briefs the substitute teacher on how the classroom is organized and run

2. Minimizes disruption to student learning during the teacher's absence

3. Equips the substitute teacher for success

*This procedure is not taught to students with the three-step approach. It is a teacher procedure with steps shared to show you how to do it.

THE **BACKGROUND**

Your car breaks down on the highway, your child is ill, or there is a family emergency. Teachers are some of the hardest working people in the world, but there are times when you are forced to miss several hours, an entire day, or even several days at work.

The school arranges for a substitute teacher, but it is your responsibility to maintain student learning while you are away from the classroom.

Substitute teachers are usually given a schedule with the beginning and end times for each period; but if there is no lesson plan, or no indication of where the class is in the lesson plans, the substitute teacher will be at a loss. This is when some substitute teachers simply let students loose in the media center, give them extended physical education time, or show them videos in a bid to kill time.

A substitute teacher is a teacher—not merely a babysitter. If you are prepared for both planned and unplanned absences, student learning need not suffer.

The established classroom procedures, routines and rules that keep your classroom running smoothly will not fail, provided you inform the substitute teacher of the procedures, routines, and rules, and teach students what is expected of them when you are absent. With up to 150 students to manage in a day, the substitute teacher must be equipped with all the information necessary to be effective in your absence.

Let your students know classroom procedures, routines, and rules remain in effect when you are absent. Learning will take place as usual, and lesson plans will be followed. All work done in your absence is expected to be of the same caliber as if you were delivering the lesson.

THE **PROCEDURE STEPS**

A Substitute Teacher Handbook is well-organized with information that is easy to find. Keep the information in a binder to allow for updates. Put dividers in the binders for quick access to information. Include pockets in the binder to hold special slips.

1. **Welcome letter**
Write a welcome letter thanking the substitute teacher for covering the class in your absence. Emphasize that students must follow detailed procedures, daily routines, and rules, and students know they must follow the information even when no one is monitoring the classroom.

A Substitute Teacher Handbook quickly updates the substitute teacher on how the class functions in your absence.

2. Student roster and seating chart

If you use an electronic record book, you can easily print student rosters. These rosters list the names of students in each class, with options for marking students as present, absent, or tardy. If you do not use an electronic grade book, you will have to make copies of the current class roster for inclusion in the binder.

Seating charts that show where students sit in each class period are helpful for attendance-taking and class-management purposes.

Include information on what the substitute teacher is to do with the roster once attendance has been taken. For instance, if the roster is to be returned to the office, provide the name of a student in each class who is to deliver the roster to the office.

3. Information about students

List any important background information on the students.

- Students get picked up by a specific person
- Students go to speech class and at what time
- Students have ADHD or ADD
- Students have behavior issues
- Students have learning disabilities and need help in certain areas
- Students who need to be monitored a little closer than others for any reason

4. Daily schedule

Briefly list what the daily schedule is for each day. Include when the class goes to "specials," such as physical education, library, computer lab, or music. Also include recess times, lunch time, and dismissal time.

5. Lesson plans

Leave a copy of the weekly lesson plans in the handbook. The substitute teacher can refer to them if you are unable to send a copy before the start of the day.

If the lesson involves handouts, have the handouts copied and ready to be distributed. If work is to be collected, inform the substitute teacher where papers are to be kept.

A general lesson plan that describes skills to work on and activities to do is helpful in case there is any spare time during the day or if more detailed lesson plans are unavailable. For instance, a math teacher might include a set of math problems, while an English teacher might provide a set of writing prompts for students to write an essay. Include a reading assignment or learning activity for students who finish assignments early.

Tell the substitute teacher where teaching materials and manuals are located in the classroom.

6. Classroom procedures

Keep a copy of the classroom procedures in the binder. This can be the same information given to the students at the beginning of the school year. A substitute teacher can study the procedures and understand how the class is normally run. Knowing the established procedure for things like sharpening a pencil, using the bathroom, or what to do with unfinished work helps maintain consistency while you are away.

Include emergency procedures for fire drills and lock down in this section. Include the exit route maps the substitute teacher is to follow during an emergency, as well as the meeting point for students. If the school has coded emergency drills, include an explanation for these codes.

You Are *THE* Teacher

Imagine the expectation you set when you leave this message for your substitute teacher.

"Please don't allow the label of 'substitute teacher' to bother you. You have the opportunity to make a difference in the life of a child when you become the TEACHER in this classroom. Seize the day!

"I've prepared for you to make the most of each moment. Please help these students grow and learn.

"Thank you!"

7. Classroom rules

List the classroom rules, along with any consequences and rewards used with the class. Encourage the substitute to enforce the rules in your absence.

8. Referral slips

Many schools have preprinted forms for referring students to the office. Let the substitute teacher know what to do in the event a student becomes defiant, angry, or disrespectful and needs to be referred to the office. Include referral slips in the binder pocket.

Your school may have a form for sending ill students to the school nurse. Include these forms with specific instructions detailing the procedure for their use.

9. Contact information

Leave your contact information for the substitute teacher in case there are any questions. Include contact information of a colleague at the same grade level and how to reach the school secretary or front office, as well as the custodian.

10. Blank paper for notes and comments

Leave some pages of blank paper in the binder, with a memo to the substitute requesting that a note be left behind on how the day went and what you can do to make the experience a more positive one for any substitute teacher. This is where the substitute can document the material that was taught, activities conducted, and how well the class performed. This helps the regular teacher know where to continue in the curriculum.

11. Classroom review

After an absence, review the substitute teacher's notes and compliment students appropriately for their outstanding efforts during your absence. Work on areas of difficulty noted by the substitute teacher. If necessary, hold individual private meetings with students who performed poorly.

No one can replace you. However, you can help the substitute teacher alleviate fears, help your students alleviate fears, become more organized, and lead a day that is rich with learning for your students when you act upon any feedback and plan for a successful day in your absence.

 32 •))

Help your substitute teacher be prepared for any situation encountered.

What Was Missing

I began teaching in an old building in New York City with an enormous class and scarce materials. I was tossed into a disheveled, former 'shop' room, wished good luck, and told to go 'teach.' It was all so overwhelming. After two years, I took a break to attend law school. By the end of the first year, I decided that becoming a lawyer was a poor substitute for a career in education.

I resumed teaching in New Jersey at an inner city, alternative public high school. Most students had emotional and/or behavioral problems. It was clear that structure, routine, and a consistent plan were missing in these students' lives.

I immediately put into practice your classroom management techniques. Students became more academically productive, and student behavior improved dramatically. Students repeated many of my sayings . . . probably because I uttered them so often! 'Do the right thing' (the procedures). 'Control the impulse and you will control the behavior.'

Many students made drastic changes in the way they handled their responsibilities in and out of the classroom. I am proud of them for realizing that their potential far exceeds their past self-expectations.

John Faure ▪ Jamaica, New York

Effective Teachers Are Proactive

There are two kinds of teachers—PROACTIVE and REACTIVE. Proactive teachers have a classroom management plan that prevents problems from occurring, and if a problem does occur, everyone knows what to do. A proactive teacher has a classroom that is a well-oiled teaching and learning machine with engaged, happy, and respectful students. The students are given the opportunity to take responsibility and know what to do even when the teacher is away from the classroom.

Proactive teachers are effective classroom managers. They

- have planned procedures for classroom organization,
- have instructional procedures to maximize student engagement, and
- systematically teach these procedures.

Ineffective teachers are reactive. They spend much of their time putting out brush fires and doing damage control. This is because reactive teachers do not have an organized plan, so they react to every problem by threatening and coercing students into compliance. They go home angry, tired, and stressed out. The students have no idea what the teacher wants, or what they are supposed to do, and thus both students and teachers flounder in a disorganized classroom every day.

Ineffective teachers are always asking questions, seeking relief from their misery.

- What do I do with this kid?
- Why can't I get my students to follow directions?
- Why does no one participate in class discussions?
- What do I do to stop them from talking all period long?
- Why don't my students get to work when the bell rings?
- Why do my students belittle each other?
- Why don't my students bring their books to class?
- Why do my students try to skip my class?
- Why does no one want to sub for my class?

Reactive teachers blame the school, the neighborhood environment, the demographics of students, or the lack of administrative support for their suffering. It's always someone or something else that is to blame. They look for programs, believing that the right program will do the teaching for them. In reality, the chaos in their classroom is due to the lack of a classroom management plan.

Proactive teachers are ready for the challenge of teaching any student, in any school, in any neighborhood, knowing that they have a classroom management plan that works. They know that if they do not have a plan, the students will plan the class for them. Proactive teachers know how the classroom is run because they have created a plan. By being proactive, they are ready to have a rewarding and successful teaching career.

The Substitute Teacher

Student learning will continue when the classroom teacher and the substitute teacher are working as a connected unit. **Melissa Boone**, a successful art resource teacher in Texas, prepares her substitute teachers with a list of what to expect while in her classroom.

Substitute teachers love to sub for some teachers and they cringe when they have to substitute for others. **Melissa Boone** has no problem with getting people to substitute in her classroom. As part of her success strategy, she leaves a note for her substitute teacher that says, **"Here is a list of routines to help you pace each of the classes from start to finish. I have included the procedures my students are familiar with."**

Daily Class Procedures for My Substitute Teacher

1. *Wait* at door for each class of students to arrive.

2. *Remind* the students to quickly and quietly begin their bellwork.

3. *Explain* the lesson for the day.
   - Lesson may be something we've been working on, or
   - See the *Substitute Lessons for the Day* I have left for you.

4. *Call out* list of supplies needed for the project.

5. *Choose* a quiet student from each table to be "Table Leader" and instruct the student to gather the supplies needed for this class period.
   - The table leaders can help pass out the papers, prepare supplies and materials, and put them away at the end of class.
   - Use a chart to record and track who has been table leader.

6. *If* the class has already started the project, their papers will be on the designated shelf. (North side of room)

7. *Quieting* the class only requires that you say, "Give me five, please."

8. *Remind* the class to take care of the supplies—especially paints, brushes, and materials that can be used repeatedly—as they work.

9. *Clean-Up*—depending on how messy it gets, you may need to allow 5–10 minutes for clean-up before class adjourns.
   - Let the students know that you are looking for tables that are cleaned fast and well—this usually gets them moving!
   - Table leaders can help to pick up supplies and make sure they are returned where they belong or on the counter (some things may need to air dry).
   - Have the kids clean up as much as possible—this will make it a lot easier on you at the end of the day.
   - Allow time for students to clean brushes and things that require extra attention.

10. *Look* for tables at which all students are sitting quietly.
    - Call these tables to line up first, one table at a time (the numbers are hanging above each table).

11. *Have students sit* on the floor, parallel to the computer table, as they wait. This helps keep them clear of the door while they wait for their next teacher to arrive.

Now that you're familiar with this Daily Routine, have fun! The day has just begun!

A Teacher Aide*

A teacher aide enables you to have more time for lesson planning and teaching. When you plan and prepare for the teacher aide to work in the classroom, everyone benefits.

THE **SOLUTION**

Establish and maintain a good working relationship with your teacher aide to reap the benefits of the assistance the position offers. **An aide is in the classroom to assist you and your students.** Planning will maximize the aide's effectiveness in the classroom.

This procedure resolves these issues:

1. Idle time wasted while the aide is waiting for direction
2. Uncertainty about the teacher's expectations
3. Lack of communication between the aide and the teacher

*This procedure is not taught to students with the three-step approach. It is a teacher procedure with steps shared to show you how to do it.

THE **BACKGROUND**

A teacher aide—also referred to as an instructional aide, teacher assistant, or paraprofessional—is an extra pair of hands, ears, and eyes in the classroom. Time invested to ensure that you and the aide work well as a team is time well spent.

The aide can work one-on-one with struggling students, lead review in small groups, and help with administrative tasks. An aide gives you more time for lesson planning, teaching, and being a more effective teacher for the entire class.

THE **PROCEDURE STEPS**

A teacher aide's educational experience may range from a high school diploma to limited college training. Some aides are required to have at least two years of formal post-secondary education, experience in helping special education students, or the ability to speak a foreign language. These aides bring expertise and a desire to help in the classroom. Determine the expertise of your aide and make the most of it.

1. Keep a teacher aide notebook.
This notebook provides the aide with necessary information and can be revised as needed throughout the year. Include this information:

- Overall responsibilities and expectations for supervising and working with students individually or in groups
- Marks used to score papers, how to compute percentages for letter grades, and how to use a rubric
- Computation of the percentage grade to match up with the letter grade noted on papers
- Take attendance, make copies, and maintain the classroom
- Classroom schedules, procedures, and rules

In addition, this notebook can be used as a communication journal. Encourage the aide to write about curriculum taught, encounters with students, and assistance needed to help students at the end of each school day. Leave comments and suggestions for the aide to read before beginning work with students the next day.

2. Hold regular meetings.
Meet periodically with the teacher aide so that a good working relationship can be formed. Set up specific dates and times for these meetings.

3. Be considerate.
Working closely with students is rewarding, but it can also be physically tiring and emotionally draining for an aide. Be considerate of the tasks the aide is asked to perform. Vary the tasks when possible and thank the aide for the work done to help the classroom run smoothly.

Be a Team

While your aide is an individual, together you are a force for your students. Consider these pairings and the impact they have had as a team.

Andy Taylor	Barney Fife
SpongeBob	Patrick
Sherlock Holmes	Doctor Watson
Ben	Jerry
Batman	Robin
Captain Kirk	Spock
Pat Sajak	Vanna White
Fred Flintstone	Barney Rubble
Han Solo	Chewbacca
Lone Ranger	Tonto
Tarzan	Cheetah
The Captain	Gilligan
You	**Your Aide**

THE **PROCEDURE**

Parent-Volunteers*

Parent-volunteers can be assets as long as there are procedures in place to guide their contributions to the classroom.

THE **SOLUTION**

Having procedures in place will help parent-volunteers better understand their roles as volunteers in the classroom while allowing the teacher to effectively employ parents' time and expertise.

This procedure provides these opportunities:

1. Using parent-volunteers wisely
2. Helping parent-volunteers understand their important role in the classroom

*This procedure is not taught to students with the three-step approach. It is a teacher procedure with steps shared to show you how to do it.

THE **BACKGROUND**

Parents are committed to their child's education and are often willing to volunteer their time and expertise. Parental involvement in the classroom can positively impact the attitude and conduct of students in the classroom. **Research has shown that students whose parents help at school have a better attitude in the classroom and maintain higher academic achievement.** Parents who help in the classroom also feel better prepared to help their child with schoolwork at home.

Typically, parents do not volunteer at the secondary level as actively as they do at the elementary level. However, plenty of parents are eager to help out in the secondary classroom if invited and given simple guidelines for assisting. Check with your school for the policy concerning the use of parent volunteers.

THE **PROCEDURE STEPS**

Let parents know you welcome them in the classroom. Provide various opportunities for parents to volunteer. Offer multiple time slots to better fit the working parent. Invite the adults in a child's life to be a part of the education process.

1. Create a job list.
Create a list of classroom tasks with which parent-volunteers can help. At Back-to-School Night or Open House, distribute a copy of this list to each parent. Ask parents to sign up to help with any of the areas on the list. Some parents may choose to be more behind the scene with making copies, gathering supplies, or organizing the classroom library, while other parents may want to be directly involved with helping students on a project. Provide a variety of tasks.

- Providing assistance to students
- Organizing classroom work
- Aiding with labs and technology

- Helping with classroom projects
- Assisting in writing workshops
- Supervising classroom library
- Handling book orders
- Copying materials
- Making parent presentations
- Maintaining bulletin boards
- Working on data entry
- Performing as a rehearsal pianist
- Overseeing art activities
- Creating, maintaining, and updating website
- Donating needed materials
- Serving as a room parent
- Organizing files
- Tutoring students
- Being a homework helper
- Providing software expertise
- Purchasing supplies
- Accompanying class on field trips

On the list, provide an "Other" option. Parents may have areas of expertise that enable them to contribute in unexpected ways not on the list.

Post the list on the class website.

2. Survey parents.
Not all parents will attend Back-to-School Night or Open House. Create a survey for all parents to complete and return, asking about their areas of expertise and if they might be willing to serve as volunteers in the classroom. Sending this survey home with each student will increase the classroom volunteer base.

Parents who work as editors or reporters on the local newspaper might enjoy helping young writers with a writing workshop. A parent who is active in community theatre can be an asset to students studying drama. Most parents have valuable knowledge and skills that can help enhance student learning. Ask them to volunteer and share their expertise.

3. Make a schedule.

After parents have returned the survey and signed up for specific jobs, create a parent-volunteer schedule and include

- dates,
- times,
- specific tasks, and
- detailed job descriptions.

Send this schedule home with students to give their parents. Post the schedule to the class website.

Call the parents to thank them and invite them to attend the parent-volunteer orientation meeting.

4. Schedule a parent-volunteer orientation meeting.

At this meeting, discuss in detail

- parents' role as volunteers,
- classroom procedure and rules,
- school dress code, and
- when and how to praise students.

Parents need to understand their primary purpose in the classroom is to enhance learning for students and to assist with daily tasks. Teach them what they need to know to become an outstanding parent-volunteer. Let parents know their help is appreciated and they are welcome in the classroom.

5. Make a To-Do list.

Based on responses to the job list and the parent survey, make a specific To-Do list for each parent-volunteer. A To-Do list might look like this:

- Make 150 copies of the study guide for *The Tragedy of Julius Caesar*.
- Shelf class library books.
- Help Brandy in 3rd period to edit her rough draft.
- Give Jay and Mona their vocabulary make-up test in 4th period.
- Sort materials in totes for tomorrow's project.
- Laminate posters.
- Post student projects in the hallway.
- Type weekly newsletter.

Prioritize the list, so the most urgent tasks get accomplished first. Include specific times and periods for the work to be completed.

If several parent-volunteers are scheduled to come in on the same day, let them know the times when you would appreciate their help and assign tasks to specific parents accordingly.

6. Schedule an appreciation event.

If the school participates in a schoolwide parent-volunteer program, a thank you breakfast of coffee, juice, fruit, and pastries, or an afternoon tea with cookies can be scheduled in appreciation of all volunteers. Present certificates of appreciation during the event.

Ask students to write thank you letters for volunteers. A framed picture of the class holding up a thank you sign is also a nice token of appreciation for volunteers. The appreciation does not have to be costly. It truly is the thought that counts in making volunteers feel appreciated.

Procedures Help Teachers Become Better Parents

We have used the research of good teaching management practices in our classrooms and to help us be better parents.

The evidence is in our children, now 20 and 17, and seeing how they have enjoyed school, have conducted themselves with peers, and adults (social skills; lots of manners!), and what amazing young adults they are becoming.

Procedures have helped us be 'teachers for life!'

Hilton and Laurie Jay ■ **Saskatoon, Saskatchewan**

The Foundation of Effective Teaching

Lucy Quezada teaches in San Marcos, Texas. She compares her skill of throwing pottery to the skill required to create an effective classroom.

There are many steps or procedures to follow in order to make a ceramic piece functional. It starts with the foundation and consistency of the clay, while it is being thrown on the wheel. As the clay is spinning in the center of the wheel, you take control so that it doesn't wobble, and then you put it into shape. It is crucial to know how to move your hands as you shape your piece, and you have to repeat the procedure to be successful.

Just as making a piece of pottery requires procedures, managing a classroom demands them, too.

When procedures are followed, the ceramic piece turns out well and can be put to use. When procedures are in place in the classroom, the children work and learn effectively. The students pay attention and participate and can work independently without creating chaos or disruptions. **Effective teaching happens when the teacher structures a foundation with procedures.**

What happens when the structure of the fresh piece of clay, as it is being thrown, falters or is too weak? It creates a mess and it falls apart! Luckily it is only clay and not a student; but the clay is flexible and can be reshaped. Likewise, students can be taught to rehearse procedures when they get out of shape.

By following a routine with procedures, the students will have a strong support structure that becomes the backbone to their success as they learn any subject or ceramic technique.

When effective teaching occurs in the classroom, you will find happy children, and the finished product is a successful classroom! Or a pretty cool and functional ceramic piece!

Classroom Visitors*

View classroom visitors as opportunities to model good teaching and organizational skills. Be prepared for planned and unplanned visits from the school administration, parents, and outside visitors.

THE **SOLUTION**

Classroom visitors should not be viewed as a disruption to lessons. **The established classroom procedures that keep the class running smoothly will ensure that the class is ready for all visitors—announced or otherwise.** Be proud of the students and demonstrate the power of effective classroom management.

This procedure resolves these issues:

1. Teaching under pressure
2. Welcoming an unplanned visitor

*This procedure is not taught to students with the three-step approach. It is a teacher procedure with steps shared to show you how to do it.

THE **BACKGROUND**

Oftentimes, the teacher does not always know ahead of time if there will be visitors to the classroom. Regardless of whether the visit is announced or not, the lesson does not come to a halt. **Your students are your first priority, not the visitors to the classroom.**

Relax. Breathe easy. If you've planned your lesson and have procedures in place, you and your class will not miss a beat even if one hundred faces show up at the door. The beauty of procedures is they create a classroom that flows, seemingly effortlessly.

Implement the lesson as planned and demonstrate to visitors just how rewarding teaching is in a well-managed classroom.

THE **PROCEDURE STEPS**

1. Introduce and welcome the visitor.
If the visit to the classroom is planned, introduce the visitor to the students and tell the class the purpose of the visit. Decide in advance where the visitor is to sit, making room at your desk, preparing a student desk, or placing a chair to the side of the room.

If the visit to the classroom is unplanned, briefly pause the lesson to welcome the visitor and let the person know where to sit or stand to observe.

2. Follow the agenda.
Your posted agenda serves as a roadmap for students and will show the visitor how the lesson is structured. The agenda will also help you stay focused and to transition smoothly. Remember, even the experienced teacher may feel pressure when a visitor is in the classroom.

3. Reference the objective.
The purpose of the lesson will also be clear to the classroom visitor. Sometimes, visitors will wish to talk to students to see if they understand what they

are being taught. This objective will be helpful when a student is responding under pressure to a visitor's questions.

Let students demonstrate to visitors that the lesson is structured and well-planned.

4. Distribute the classroom newsletter and the classroom procedures and rules.
Keep extra copies of the classroom newsletter and the classroom procedures and rules handy for visitors.

If the visit is planned, give this information to the visitors as they enter the room.

If the visit is unplanned, take a few moments to meet with the visitors as they exit the room. Hand visitors the classroom information and thank them for observing the classroom. The visitors will be impressed with your preparation.

5. Shine.
Regardless of whether the visit is planned or unplanned, this is the time for you to shine and be at your best. Be confident. Don't be afraid to ask difficult questions of students. Implement the lesson as planned.

Don't make last-minute changes to incorporate unexpected visitors. Visitors come to see the everyday structure of the classroom—not something that has been memorized or rehearsed.

Maintain eye contact with students and smile warmly—show students that the lesson will continue as usual. **Effective teachers do what they always do; they teach.**

THE **PROCEDURE**

Parent-Teacher Conferences*

Parent-Teacher conferences are productive meetings that focus on helping students become successful in class. It is a time to work together to help the child succeed.

THE **SOLUTION**

Parent-Teacher conferences need not be stressful or confrontational. Your organization of this time will keep parents focused on learning goals and help them become partners with you for their child's success during the school year. **Create a meeting that is pleasant and productive that will foster a working relationship.**

This procedure provides these opportunities:

1. Using meeting time productively
2. Providing the structure for the conference
3. Portraying a confident and organized picture of professionalism

*This procedure is not taught to students with the three-step approach. It is a teacher procedure with steps shared to show you how to do it.

THE **BACKGROUND**

Parent-Teacher conferences are usually the second time parents meet you. At Back-to-School night, parents form an immediate impression of you and your effectiveness. Parent-Teacher conferences will confirm or reverse those first impressions. **It is important to be at the top of your game come conference time.**

Whether the student attends this conference is a choice usually left up to you. Whichever way you choose, be consistent in inviting the student to attend or not having the student attend for all the meetings you host during conference time.

Just as effective teachers prepare for class with a well-planned agenda with the lesson objective and an opening assignment, effective teachers plan and prepare for Parent-Teacher conferences.

As students do not like to come to a classroom not knowing what is going to happen, parents do not like to come to a meeting not knowing what is going to happen.

Your organization will set the tone for your time together and squelch any tirades from happening. You can avoid the possible scenario of a parent marching into the classroom, progress report in hand, saying, "My daughter says she has no idea why she got a C in your class. Could you tell me why you gave her such a low grade?" The parent is terse and upset. She sits down, arms crossed, and waits for the answer.

You are caught off guard and brace yourself for a battle.

THE **PROCEDURE STEPS**

Your preparation will produce a successful meeting time. Your confidence, demeanor, and organization will prevent confrontations and will speak volumes to your command of the classroom and how well you know your students.

1. Plan and prepare.

The first conference is usually held after the first six- or nine-week grading period. At this meeting, prepare to share with the parents

- the course content that has been taught;
- what tests, projects, or activities went into making the average grade for the grading period;
- what will be taught in the next nine weeks of school; and
- upcoming projects and activities the students will need to complete.

Prior to the Parent-Teacher conference, email parents or send a letter home sharing the agenda for your meeting time. Also, let parents know the length of the meeting and thank them for being on time and for being courteous to parents while waiting for their meeting. Letting the parents know beforehand what your agenda is for the meeting and how long you anticipate it will last keeps everyone on task.

Prior to conference time, share with your students what will be covered during the meeting. The Parent-Teacher conference is not about secret meetings. They help ensure student success. Let students know ahead of time what their parents will be hearing from you.

Some students may require a one-on-one meeting with you, so you can share areas of possible parental concerns. This gives students a chance to explain themselves at home before the parents arrive for a professional explanation from you.

Should a parent enter the conference wishing to immediately discuss a child's grade, smile and say, "I'm really glad you came to see me about your child's grade. Let's look at what we have been studying in class first and what went into making that grade before we discuss your child's grade."

Responding in this manner can be helpful in relieving tension and diverting the parent's anger. It gives an angry parent a chance to calm down before discussing the grade and puts you back on track with your agenda.

2. Greet parents with a smile and a firm handshake.
When a parent or parents walk into the room, greet them with a friendly smile and a firm handshake. Welcome them with confidence and warmth.

3. Prepare a sign-in card.
Ask parents to write their names and their child's name on a sign-in card. Ask for contact information—phone, email, and home address—and the best method and time for contacting them. Have these cards ready for completing as the parents wait for their conference time. Ask for the card at the start of your conference and confirm the accuracy of the contact information.

If the parent has difficulty completing the card, ask the questions and write in the responses for the parent.

Student's Name			
Your Name(s)			
Relationship to Student			
Phone Number			
Email			
Address			
Best Method for Contact	Phone	Email	Home Visit
Best Time for Contact			

4. Keep a notepad.
Be prepared to take notes. Parents may share information they think is important—record this information. By taking notes, the parent knows the information has been heard.

Keep the notes in a secure place for future reference. Treat all conference notes as confidential.

5. Print grades.
Most school districts use an electronic grade book. This allows the user to generate an assignment report for each student with this information:

- Every assignment made
- Date the assignment was made
- Date the assignment was due
- Average class grade for the assignment
- Student's grade on the assignment

The assignment report provides the explanation for a student's grade. If a parent is concerned about a low grade, a glance at this report shows the probable reasons:

- Zeros for incomplete work
- Missed tests
- Incomplete make-up work
- Lack of study and application
- Excessive absences

Having an assignment report printed in advance is a *must* for an efficient conference.

If a parent is upset about a grade, respond by saying, "I do not *give* grades, but let's look at the grade your child has *earned*." The assignment report will need little explanation—it will present clear and unbiased results.

When class resumes, distribute assignment reports to students whose parents did not attend conference time, and ask them to take it home to share.

6. Set a timer.
Setting a timer keeps conferences on schedule. At conferences, most parents only wish to know what they can do to help their child improve. Be prepared to offer suggestions for any problem areas. During the conference, give the parent the tools to help their child succeed in the classroom.

When the timer beeps, stand and continue talking, but slowly begin walking the parent to the door even if the conference is not finished. The parent will follow.

Thank the parent for coming to talk about their child's progress, but let them know that other parents are waiting. Offer to schedule an additional conference to further discuss their child's work if needed.

Set the timer for one minute shorter than the scheduled conference. This gives you time to

- conclude the conference,
- thank the parent,
- walk the parent to the door, and
- greet the next waiting parent.

7. Invite suggestions.
After reviewing the assignment report, ask the parents if there is anything they can suggest that might help the student be successful. Record this information in your notes.

8. Follow up.
Review your notes from conference time. Schedule any follow-up meetings, place phone calls of thanks, or meet with students to plan for ongoing success. Organize yourself to execute the plans discussed.

Impressions of the Classroom and You

Conferences are a time to put your best foot forward. Parents are invited into the classroom.

Take a few minutes to organize your piles, straighten the books, and create an environment that welcomes parents into their child's classroom.

Your attitude and your dress will send a message of welcome, as well. Put a smile on your face, no matter how stressed you may be, and dress professionally.

This is a meeting to talk about their child's future. Your attire should match the importance of this meeting.

Back-to-School Night*

Erase the fears and "butterflies" of meeting parents for the first time by being prepared in thought, actions, and setting. Be organized and outline what needs to be said ahead of time.

THE **SOLUTION**

Back-to-School night determines the relationship you will have with your students' parents. Smile, relax, be confident, and speak positively. If necessary, rehearse. Show you enjoy teaching and know how to teach by doing exactly that—*teach*.

This procedure answers these important questions:

1. What to wear?
2. How to prepare?
3. What do parents want to hear?

*This procedure is not taught to students with the three-step approach. It is a teacher procedure with steps shared to show you how to do it.

THE **BACKGROUND**

Your every move, thought, and action will be scrutinized. This is one of the most important evenings of your year. On this night, parents form an impression of you and often make the decision about how competent you are to instruct their child—and it all happens in ten to fifteen minutes. Parents' impressions of you begin to form even before you begin to speak.

THE **PROCEDURE STEPS**

Back-to-School night sets the pace for the rest of the year with parents. If you are new to the school or a novice teacher, ask the teachers with longevity how this night has gone in the past and what you can expect. The more you are prepared, the easier the night will be for you.

1. Dress for success.
First impressions are based on outward appearances. A teacher who does not dress professionally gives the impression of incompetence. Dress professionally to receive respect and to project credibility and professionalism.

This is appropriate attire for men:

- A crisp, pressed collared shirt with a tie
- Slacks with a belt
- Dress shoes

This is professional dress for women:

- A suit or pant-suit in a subdued print or color
- A tailored dress
- Dress shoes

Avoid loud colors, bold patterns, rumpled clothing, faddish attire, oversized jewelry, and anything that is flashy or distracting.

2. Greet parents at the door.
Greet parents at the door with a warm smile and a friendly handshake. Thank parents for coming and invite them to put their signatures on the sign-in sheets distributed throughout the classroom.

Prepare several sign-in sheets requesting their name, their email address, and their child's name. Scatter the sign-in sheets to avoid lines of parents and long waits.

Prepare a trifold brochure and hand it to parents as you greet them. The brochure contains such information as this:

- Classroom procedures and rules
- Course overview
- Contact information

Parents can read this information while waiting for the session to begin.

3. Be prepared.
Think about questions that parents may ask and include the answers in your presentation to parents.

- What is the homework policy?
- What projects are planned for the year?
- How much time are students given to complete assignments?
- Will technology be used in the classroom?
- What kind of software will students use?
- What are the required readings?
- Will students go on field trips?
- What is the school's tardy policy?
- What is the school's absentee policy?
- What is the school's grading scale?
- How can I help my child at home?

4. Create a list of talking points.
Back-to-School night involves the teacher, but it is not about the teacher. Start with a personal introduction, but keep it brief. Parents need to know something about you. Give your qualifications for teaching—where you went to school, how long you've been teaching, and what grade levels you have taught.

What you say and the way you say it reveals your dedication and how much you care about the students. Assure parents that you

- genuinely care,
- are fair,
- will treat students with respect,
- value students' education, and
- will keep students' best interests in mind.

Parents want assurance. Tell parents you are prepared to teach well and give your best every day. In return, students are expected to complete homework and to give their best every day. This is what parents want to hear at Back-to-School night.

5. Provide contact information.
Explain how parents can contact you. If parents were given a brochure at the door, refer them to the contact information in it. Share with them the following:

- Your planning period
- The school's website and email address
- The class web address
- Your email address and phone number

Create a takeaway item with your contact information. Make a magnet with a mail label and flat magnet. Invite parents to put the magnet on their refrigerator door, so it is always handy.

 33 •))

Read the surprise students left for parents at Back-to-School night in Cindy Wong's classroom.

6. Share important information.
If you have a class website, demonstrate to parents how to access it and navigate the site. Show parents how to

- use the website to access homework assignments;
- access important links; and
- find sample student projects.

Explain the homework and make-up work policy.

Display textbooks and samples of student work.

7. Ask for questions.
Give parents the opportunity to ask general questions. Remind parents that personal questions about their child should be addressed in private and invite them to email or call you to discuss their child or to schedule a meeting.

If the session has been well planned, parents will not have a lot of questions to ask. However, giving parents the opportunity to ask questions is important—it demonstrates that students will also be given the opportunity to ask questions in class.

8. Thank parents.
Thank parents for taking time out from their busy schedules to attend.

Tell parents that you enjoyed meeting them and like tonight was for them, every day in the classroom, their child can expect a productive and informative day worthy of their time.

Job Sharing—The Best of Both Worlds

Job sharing allows two teachers to come together and collaborate with each other for the benefit of their students—while still giving teachers time away from the classroom. Job sharing can offer the best of both worlds for parents as well.

Job sharing allows you to work with students in the classroom and to keep that passion for teaching alive, but it also provides time away from the classroom to raise a family. The days away from the classroom give you time to volunteer in your own child's classroom, be present at more of your child's school functions or daily activities, or do research and study to improve yourself.

Job sharing teachers teach part-time but give full time on the days they are with their students.

Job-sharing teachers must plan together before the start of school and work together in the classroom for at least the first two days of school. These first days of school are essential for building a strong classroom environment, building rapport with students, and setting the tone for the classroom management plan.

Both teachers must plan on being in the classroom for Back-to-School night, Open House, Parent-Teacher conferences, and any class musicals or performances.

The most successful job-sharing arrangements occur when two teachers plan together for the success of their students. Setting common procedures and expectations provides consistency for the students and will allow them to easily transition between teachers. Parental fears and concerns are alleviated when planning and structure is visible. They soon will come to realize their child has the best of both worlds!

Home and School Connection*

By providing different ways for parents to keep abreast of classroom assignments, activities, and information about their child, a teacher encourages parents to communicate and offer support.

THE **SOLUTION**

Create lines of open communication to inform and involve the home in the happenings of the classroom and the school. **The more the home is connected to the classroom, the more positive the relationship becomes, the greater the chances are for your success and every students' success.**

This procedure provides these opportunities:

1. Building a strong home and school connection with a variety of communication tools
2. Encouraging parents to be in touch with classroom activities

*This procedure is not taught to students with the three-step approach. It is a teacher procedure with steps shared to show you how to do it.

THE **BACKGROUND**

Time is a guarded commodity to be used wisely. In many households both parents work full-time. You need to offer different forms of communication, so it is convenient and efficient for parents to stay involved in their child's school life. The more ways you can communicate with parents about school assignments, activities, issues, and events, the more likely all parents will stay connected with the classroom.

THE **PROCEDURE STEPS**

There are many different tools for building a strong home and school connection. Before the start of school, decide which communication tools will be most appropriate for the class and parents.

In the first welcoming letter you send to students and parents, include information about these forms of communication. Parents will feel more confident and comfortable about the school year ahead knowing you have tools in place for keeping them informed about their child's school life.

1. Weekly Classroom Newsletter

A weekly newsletter is sent home with students at the end of the week. The newsletter is a one-page, easy-to-read synopsis of the week that includes

- material that will be covered the following week in each subject area;
- important upcoming dates; and
- quick reminders of things parents need to know.

The newsletter can be a hard copy that is hand-delivered to the home or an electronic copy emailed directly to parents. The parents know to look for this newsletter at the end of every week.

2. Class Website

Create a simple class website where students and parents can find updated information at any time that includes any of this information:

- Homework assignments
- Upcoming events
- Test dates
- Useful links related to material the class is studying
- Weekly spelling words

Parents can easily check the website and get updates from any location at any time.

Update the website at the end of each week with new information. The class website address should be posted on each student's weekly assignment sheet, in all parent letters, and at the bottom of emails as part of your electronic signature.

A class website is an excellent communication tool, so parents can see, at a glance, what is happening in the classroom.

There is no need for extra bells and whistles on a classroom website. Make your website simple for you to set up and maintain throughout the year and easy for parents to access and read.

3. Email

Most parents have email access at home, work, or on some personal electronic device. Use this option to communicate with parents quickly. Give parents your email address as early as possible and invite them to email you at any time with a question, concern, or comment. As with all written correspondence between parents, be sure to save all emails sent to and from parents until the end of the school year by setting up a folder.

4. Voicemail

Encourage parents to leave a voicemail for you without disrupting teaching time. Parents who do not have access to email, or who feel more comfortable speaking to you, will find this communication option useful.

Check your voicemail at the end of each day and return calls promptly.

5. Weekly Reports

At the end of the week, a weekly report is emailed to parents or sent home for students with missing homework or classwork assignments, or who have had other issues during the week. A parent must acknowledge receipt of the email or sign the hard copy of the report and return it on Monday morning. This report should have space allocated for you to write comments and for parents to respond. These weekly reports keep parents up to date with their child's progress, as well as any missing assignments the child needs to complete.

34 •))

See some sample letters teachers use to connect with the home.

Writing a Parent Connection Letter

Most parents want to be involved in the education of their student. **Research shows that parent involvement increases student achievement.**

The parent connection letter will establish communications with the parent and outline what the parent can expect from you. **This sheet of paper can be the single most important document you send home all year.** Follow these seven steps to write an effective parent connection letter:

I. Create a personal profile.

A personal profile lets parents know your teaching experience level and training background. Share

- colleges attended and degrees attained;
- certificates and special skills, such as foreign languages; and
- any other training relevant to teaching.

2. Establish classroom expectations.

What can students expect from you? In turn, what do you expect from students? Parents need to know your expectations, so they can work with you to help their child succeed. Set positive expectations and make a mutual commitment to these positive expectations by putting them in writing.

This is what students can expect from you:

- Quality instruction each day
- Extra help
- A well-organized, positive learning environment
- Credit for practice and grades for evaluation of learning
- Respect for all students and acknowledgment of their abilities
- Fairness
- Giving your best to students each day

This is what you expect from students:

- Come to class ready to work and learn.
- Bring necessary books and supplies.
- Have assignments neatly done and fully completed.
- Follow the posted procedures and rules.

- Keep a positive attitude.
- Always try your best.
- Listen and stay focused.

3. Develop clear overall objectives for the year.

Most schools have mission statements. A key objective for the year is completion of your mission statement.

- What is the purpose of students attending your class each day?
- What will students have learned and accomplished by the end of the year?

These are questions to consider when formulating a yearly objective. The yearly objective tells parents that the teacher is a professional with clearly defined instructional goals and expectations.

4. Develop an overview of learning for the year.

An overview for the year provides a roadmap to reaching the objectives. Most secondary schools divide instruction into quarters, with learning for each quarter determined by state guidelines.

You need to meet state learning expectations by teaching specific content. List the general content that will be taught each quarter, so parents have a picture of the learning that will take place. The overview for an English classroom might look like this:

Ist nine weeks: selected short stories; autobiography, and narrative writing

2nd nine weeks: drama and expository writing

3rd nine weeks: poetry and persuasive writing

4th nine weeks: novels and a research paper

If desired, this overview can be provided in greater detail by listing the specific short stories, drama, poetry, and novels to be taught.

5. Provide contact information.

Parents need to know how to contact you. Including this information gives the parent a reason for keeping the parent connection letter. Share with parents how and when to contact you.

- Email address
- Planning period
- Class website
- School phone number
- School fax number

Just knowing there is line of communication can prevent apprehension and frustration on the parent's part.

6. Discuss attendance and make-up work procedures.

Tell parents that a direct correlation exists between a student's attendance and grades. When a student is absent, he or she misses valuable classroom instruction.

When students are absent, parents need to know the procedure for making up missed work. Share the policies regarding

- absences,
- missed work, and
- late work—be sure to specify if late work is accepted.

These procedures establish fair standards for all students and prevent misunderstandings.

7. Choose an appropriate format.

Keep in mind secondary students are likely to bring home up to seven parent connection letters on the first day of school. Make your letter easy to read in a format that is not overwhelming. Present the information in a precise, uncluttered format.

Invite the parents to read your information by

- bulleting the text,
- keeping sentences and paragraphs short, and
- opting to send home a tri-fold brochure instead of a letter.

It does take extra time and effort to create this piece of information. Keep it as a template that will need only modifications in the years ahead.

 35 •))

See how Oretha Ferguson presents this information to parents on the first day of school.

50   THE **PROCEDURE**

Technology in the Classroom*

Helping students understand their responsibilities when using technology will ensure students stay safe while navigating the unlimited information available online.

THE **SOLUTION**

Technology opens new doors to learning for students and teachers. **However, using technology in the classroom comes with responsibilities.** It is your job to ensure learning takes place and students are kept safe.

This procedure resolves these issues:

1. Questionable browsing
2. Student safety

*This procedure is not taught to students with the three-step approach. It is a teacher procedure with steps shared to show you how to do it.

THE **BACKGROUND**

Most teachers have computers in the classroom or have access to a computer lab or a mobile lab for student use. The World Wide Web provides unlimited information, and students have numerous opportunities to use an ever-changing array of technology to support learning.

It is your responsibility to put procedures in place for using technology in the classroom and surfing the Internet.

THE **PROCEDURE STEPS**

These steps are general in nature to cover the multitude of devices available for classroom use. Adapt the steps to suit the type of technology used in your classroom and how you want the technology to be used for learning.

1. Develop an Online Safety Pledge.

Students need to be instructed in what you and the school consider safe in connection with the use of computers and other technology in the classroom. What a student considers safe and what you consider safe may not be the same thing! Assume nothing and plan for everything when allowing students to browse the Internet.

Prepare an Online Safety Pledge that you, the student, and a parent must sign before the student is allowed to use technology in the classroom. Keep the pledge on file and remind students of the pledge before starting projects that require online research.

MY ONLINE SAFETY PLEDGE

I will not use or reveal my

- full name,
- address,
- telephone number,

- school, or
- private information like passwords.

I will not send a picture of myself or others over the Internet without my teacher's and parent's consent.

I will not fill out any form or request online that asks for my personal information.

I will not use bad language.

I will not participate in any activity that hurts others, is against the law, or violates my school's policy.

Require a parent and student signature on the pledge before the student goes online.

2. Prepare a Parent Waiver.

Prepare a Parent Waiver that outlines the technology students will be using in the classroom. These are some of the items to include:

- Email
- Message boards
- Chat rooms
- Blogs
- Wikis
- Internet browsing

Be sure to state that you, the school, and the district do not any accept responsibility for harm caused either directly or indirectly to users of the Internet.

Require a parent signature before the student goes online.

3. Help students understand their responsibilities.

Talk to students about the privilege of using technology in the classroom. Remind students that privilege comes with responsibility.

Let students know they are trusted, but also tell them that their usage will be monitored. The more trust you place in students, the less likely students are to disappoint you.

36 •))

View and download the Online Safety Pledge Oretha Ferguson uses with her students.

If your trust in them is violated, let them know there is a possible loss of this privilege or something greater, depending on the extent of the abuse. Students should understand that abuse of this privilege will not be tolerated.

Remind students of their responsibilities each time they use technology in the classroom.

Display a poster listing the cost of replacement of all equipment used in the classroom. Let students know they are responsible for replacing any equipment that is damaged due to their abuse.

4. Monitor student use of technology.

Most schools that have technology for student use have filters in place to block questionable websites. No filter, however, can replace your watchful eye. **Walk around and closely monitor student browsing activity.**

Clearly define what constitutes appropriate browsing, language, and content. Be very specific and ask for questions. Tell students that if they have to ask if something is appropriate or not, it probably isn't. Randomly check computers' browsing histories.

Assign students to the same computer throughout the year. Any problems can be traced back to the user.

Frequently remind students of their responsibilities and reinforce the consequences. Do not tolerate inappropriate use of technology in the classroom.

Students Will Rise to the Occasion

My students enjoy having a predictable environment. They feel 'safe' because they know exactly what to expect each day. They like consistency in a world that can be very inconsistent. If you expect your students to do well, they will rise to the occasion. Procedures are simple, but their impact is enormous.

Chelonnda Seroyer ■ Atlanta, Georgia

Going Green in the Classroom

Your students look up to you. They observe the way you interact with the environment and model themselves on how you speak, act, and think. When you run a green classroom, students are likely to take your message of reducing, reusing, and recycling beyond the classroom walls.

Show you care about the environment and raise the consciousness of your students by using some of these green ideas in your classroom.

I. Create PowerPoint presentations.

Instead of preparing lessons on paper, create PowerPoint presentations that can be easily updated and reused repeatedly over the years.

2. Start a class website.

Instead of sending out paper memos, use this website to communicate with students and parents about classroom policies, homework assignments, grading rubrics, upcoming events, and contact information.

3. Use email.

When communicating with parents, colleagues, and administration, use emails to cut down on or eliminate the use of paper. This includes requests for substitute teachers, field trip proposals, meeting agendas, meeting requests with parents, or positive calls about students.

4. Use online resources as educational tools.

Send students to the Internet to do research on topics related to their learning objectives. Teach them how to bookmark information for easy retrieval to share with the class or study later.

5. Encourage double-sided printing.

For items that must be printed, use the double-sided print option to save paper. Check your printer for options that reduce the amount of ink used and energy saving modes and use these settings to economize your printing.

PLANS
For the First Days of School

My Personal First Day of School Script

Jessica McLean is a bilingual elementary teacher in Minnesota. This is the plan she uses to prepare BEFORE the students enter her classroom and during their time together on the first day of school.

Before Class

- Hang a sign on or near the door with illustrated instructions for what to do upon arrival:
    1. Go eat breakfast
    2. Hang up backpack
    3. Get right to work
- Place name cards on the tables, so students can find their seats
- Place boxes of school supplies on each table
- Write and post Consequence chart next to yellow Rules chart:
    1. Yellow = warning
    2. Orange = time out
    3. Red = lose recess
    4. Double Red = time out in another classroom, note written to parents
    5. After that = sent to behavior office
- Make Classroom Rules poster:
    1. Be safe
    2. Be kind
    3. Be responsible
    4. Raise your hand to speak
    5. Listen and follow directions
- Label each number with a student's name, so each student has their own set of colored cards
- Place morning work at each student's desk
- Place a sign indicating today's specialist on the wall outside the door
- Set up a Turn-In/All-Done basket on the shelf, so students know where to put their papers when they are finished

- Make an illustrated "I'm done!" poster, and hang it in the classroom:
    1. Work on unfinished assignments in your red folder
    2. Read books from your Book Box while quietly at your seat
- Hang the Bathroom poster on the wall under the word wall
- Make illustrated Active Listening poster, and hang it on the lower part of word wall:
    1. Look at the speaker
    2. Listen to what they are saying
    3. Think about what they are saying
    4. Respond (by raising your hand to speak)
- Make a Seating Chart and put on clip board
- Write the date on the board
- Put nametags on each student's desk
- Make Popsicle sticks with each student's name; have them put one in the cup as a way to take attendance
- Make cards for a Job Chart with everyone's name and cards for jobs:
    1. Attendance folder
    2. Line leader
    3. Door holder
    4. Hand sanitizer
    5. Clean up the library
    6. Clean up the bathroom
- Make a small poster with the Daily Schedule on it; put on the easel to share with students during the Morning Meeting

- Make sticky nametags for each student (white labels)
- Get Book Boxes for students who don't have them yet
- Make a paper that says, *'Yo puedo compartir'* (I can share) and make copies for the class book

7:50: Greet Each Student at the Door

- Say, *Good morning!* to everyone
- Ask the names of students who are new to teacher and/or the school (give them a sticky nametag)
- Send to breakfast (with backpacks, jackets, etc.)
- Upon return, have them put their name Popsicle stick in the cup
- Ask them if they know their bus number
- Tell them to choose a hook, hang up their backpack, and find their seat
- Tell them seatwork is on the table; pencils are in the pencil box (on top of the stack)
- When all students have arrived (8:10), take attendance (use attendance sheet, not computer)
- Send student to the office with the attendance sheet (refer to Job Chart)

8:15: Transition to the Morning Meeting

- Introduce the bell signal
- Practice responding to the bell signal:
  1. STOP
  2. Eyes watching
  3. Ears listening
  4. Hands empty and on your head
  5. Body still
  6. Mouth closed
- Model the correct way (one student), wrong way (two students), correct way (same students)
- Once students understand the bell signal, explain transition and expectations for transition
- Have one student demonstrate how to clean up quietly, walk to the carpet, and sit (outside the circle part)

- Have tables (note table number on boxes, one at a time) clean up, walk, and sit
- Practice transition if not carried out correctly:
  1. Quietly clean up
  2. Walk to the carpet
  3. Quietly sit down
  4. Wait

8:20: The Morning Meeting

- Explain why we have Morning Meetings
- Explain rules for Morning Meeting:
  1. Empty hands
  2. Crisscross applesauce
  3. Raise your hand to speak
  4. Be an active listener
  5. Greet everyone
- Have everyone say their own name; have everyone else greet them
- Say, *No sharing this week, we are learning how to follow rules and procedures. We will share next week.*
- Share the Classroom Rules and the Consequences if rules are not followed
- Tell students the importance of learning: *Learning is why we are here. We have rules so that everyone can learn in a safe and happy environment.*
- Go over the rules; make sure they're understood; and give short examples
- Parents will get a copy of the rules
- Show and explain the Consequences chart
- Explain Time Out:
  - *Where is the chair?* (on the landing)
  - *How do we walk to time out?* (directly and quietly)
  - *How do we behave in time out?* (sit quietly, do work if incident occurs during work time)
  - *How do we get out of time out?* (quietly raise a hand; talking, yelling out teacher's name, or playing will extend your time out)

8:40: Break and Game Time

- Introduce game rules:
    1. Hands to yourself
    2. Body in your own space
    3. No talking
- Introduce one morning meeting game (beach ball greeting)
- Show how to roll the ball (don't throw it)
- "Hands up" if you haven't had a turn
- If you break the rules, you don't play
- If three or more students break rules, the game stops

8:45: Daily Schedule

- Talk about the schedule for the day and the week
- Talk about what we will learn while together
- Talk about Science tomorrow (short morning meeting, walk outside to the tent, actively listen)
- Tell students, *We will be active listeners whenever a teacher is talking.*
- Explain active listening, model (listening, retaining, responding), then practice with class

9:00: Reading/*Lectura*

- Tell students:
    - *We will read in Spanish.*
    - *I will wear my bufanda (scarf), you will turn around and say, "es-pa-ñol."*
    - *You will stand up and sit down quietly.* (this is a transition)
    - *You will be active listeners during the lesson.*

9:05: *Leccion* I–I can share!

- Tell students:
    - *When an author writes something, they want to tell us something. They always have a message.*
    - *The author tells us what the characters do to show us what we should do in our own lives.*

- *While we read, let's think: What does the author want to tell us?*
- Read the story, ask for predictions; briefly discuss the characters' feelings:
    - *What do you think the author wants to tell us?*
    - *Now, we're going to make our own book to remind ourselves and each other of the importance of sharing.*
    - *What kinds of things can we share?* (make a list together on the board)
    - *Here's what you're going to do.* (model a page from the book):
        1. Name
        2. Date
        3. Write: I can share … (finish the sentence)
        4. Draw and color a picture
        5. Turn in your page, and if there is time, make another one

9:20: Independent Work

- Work on I can share …
- Give students procedure for transition:
    1. Walk to your seat
    2. Quietly sit down
    3. Get started right away
    4. Share the materials
    5. Use the hand signal if you need to use the bathroom (don't yell or get up)
- *I will call students table by table to choose books for their book boxes.* (at their level, this item is one of high interest)

9:45: Break and Practice How to Line Up

- Share procedure for lining up:
    1. Hands at your sides; be calm
    2. Eyes forward
    3. Shoulders forward
    4. Mouth closed
    5. Stay closest to the friend in front of you

6. Straight lines like a stick, not wiggly like a snake
7. Quiet feet

- How to walk to line:
    1. Wait for teacher's instructions
    2. Stand up, walk quietly to the door
    3. Go to the END of the line (not the middle)
    4. Stay in one spot the whole time
- Model, practice
- *When it's time to go to art class, we'll do it again.*
- *You walk, and I'll watch.*

10:00: Lesson 2

Good friends know it's important to share.

- *Let's remember what it means to be an active listener.*
    - *What does your body do?*
    - *Your eyes?*
    - *Your ears?*
    - *Your hands?*
    - *Your brain?*
- *We'll read "The Pigeon Finds a Hot Dog!"*
- *To help us understand the story, we'll retell it after we read. Listen for these parts of the story:*
    1. *The characters*
    2. *The setting*
    3. *The beginning*
    4. *The middle*
    5. *The end*
- Read the story and stop at the duck's entrance
    - *Who are the characters?*
    - *Where are they?*
    - *Who has a problem?*
    - *What problem does he have?*
- Keep reading and hold discussions, including the solution and ending
- Reflect with class How Did We Listen?

10:15: Break and Practice How to Get Ready for the Bus

- Tell students the procedure:
    - *Stay quiet*
    - *Go to your seats, table by table*
    - *The quietest table will go first*
    - *Stay quiet while you wait:*
        1. *Sit with your mouth closed, head on the table*
        2. *When you hear your table number, walk to get your backpack*
        3. *Walk back to your chair with your backpack on and sit quietly*
        4. *Wait quietly until it's time to line up*
        5. *When I call your table, stack your chair*
        6. *Walk to the door; make two quiet lines*
        7. *The quietest line goes first, the second line follows behind*
    - *Remember how we walk in line*
- Practice (until they follow the procedure)
- *Put things away, go back to the carpet*
- *At the end of the day, we'll do this again.*

10:25: Procedures for Lunch and Recess

- Tell students the procedure for lunch:
    1. *Walk into the lunchroom*
    2. *Follow your lunch teachers' directions*
    3. *Stay seated and quiet until you are sent to get food*
    4. *Clean up your trash*
    5. *When I come back, make two straight, quiet lines in front of me*
    6. *Remember to walk, not run*
- Tell students the procedure for recess:
    1. *Play safely*
    2. *Play kindly*
    3. *When you hear my whistle, come to me*
    4. *When recess is done, stop playing*

- *Don't run until I say it's okay*
- *Walk in one of the two lines when we leave and return from recess*
- *If someone is alone, invite them to play with you*
- *If you are in time out, do not bother friends who are playing*
- *If a friend is in time out, do not bother that person*
- *If you don't hear my whistle but you see friends coming toward me, go with them*
- *When we are in line, do not continue to play*
- If there is time, introduce Daily 5

10:40: Art class

- *We'll have Art all week*
- *Remember how to line up*
- *Same procedures apply in Art as in our classroom*

11:40: *El Almuerzo*

- Go to lunch; remember lunch procedures
- Refer to Job Chart for hand sanitizer person

12:15: Recess

- Go to classroom first and review expectations
- Go outside and play

12:30: Come Inside

12:35: Math

- Share Math expectations:
  1. Only talk about Math
  2. Be an active listener
  3. Raise your hand to speak
  4. Take care of the tools
  5. Do your best thinking
- Review bathroom rules
- Math routine 1: Pocket day (10 min.)
- Introduce Math game 1 (15 min.)
- Play Math game 1 (15 min.)

- Reflect on how well the class followed procedures
- Introduce Workshop time
- Introduce Work Board for Workshop time
- Share expectations for Workshop time:
  1. Focus
  2. Share
  3. Take care of the tools
  4. If you finish, play again
- Do one rotation

1:30: Clean Up and Sit Down

- Review procedure for going home

1:35: Pack Up for Home

- Remember to stack chairs

1:45: Going Home

- Quiet line goes first
- *Goodbye!*
- *Tomorrow will be another exciting day.*

PE Expectations

On my wall in the gym, I have PE ExPEctations.

ExPEct to listen. ExPEct to follow directions. ExPEct to move. ExPEct to learn. ExPEct to have fun!

After sixteen years here, my students have come to ExPEct certain procedures in the gym. It provides comfort to those students who have no boundaries at home. It's a place where there are only good surprises and they are comfortable. It gives students ownership in my class and makes them feel responsible for their own learning.

Andrea Gehweiler ■ Marietta, Georgia

A Partial Script for the First Day of School

Teri Norris developed this script after twenty-five years of teaching
and experiencing one of the worst classes of her career.
She threatened to quit and go talk to the plants at Home Depot!
Instead, she developed a plan and used it for five years with great success.

On Each Student's Desk

- Numbered Math Book
- Numbered OCR Book
- Journal
- Pencil/eraser sharpened

Materials on My Desk

- Overhead of first Journal page
- Overhead Morning Routine
- Overhead and poster for "Give Me 5"
- Overhead Village Form
- Poster Adopted Procedures
- Sentence Stub chart
- "Simon's Hook"
- Adopted Rules copies for students
- Bio Glyph sheets (3)
- Print Binder tabs (in print folder by subject)

Must Do's at the Start

- Journal "Simon's Hook"
- Bio Glyph
- *Welcome to another school year! My name is Mrs. Norris. There it is, on the board.*

On your desk you'll find many books and supplies for this school year. Please leave them on your desk until I give you directions about what you are to do with them.

Each one of your books has the exact same number. That is your number for the entire school year. Please put your books in your desk and leave your journal, the pencil, and eraser on top of your desk.

I am looking forward to being your teacher this year. Relax. I have over twenty-five years' experience as a teacher. I am an experienced, veteran teacher. In addition, I go to workshops, conferences, in-service meetings, college classes, and seminars. I also read everything I can get my hands on. I am a competent, knowledgeable, experienced, and professional teacher.

Let me tell you a bit about myself and my family. I have a wonderful husband and four sons. One has graduated from Tennessee State and the other three are still in college.

I have many things that I enjoy doing. I love computers and the Internet. I love to read, listen to music, and go to concerts. I spend most weekends in my garden growing vegetables, and I'm what you call a TV addict. I love TV.

As much as I love TV and computers, my real passion, the thing that gives me the most joy, is teaching. I love to teach. I am proud that I am a teacher and I am happy to be your teacher this year. So relax. You are in good hands this year with me, Mrs. Norris.

You are going to have the greatest educational experience of your life. We will not only study everything I can think of, but I will also share with you some life skills traits that will help you be successful citizens.

I can assure you that if you run into me at the mall twenty-five years from now, you will say, "You were right, Mrs. Norris. That was the most memorable, exciting, and fascinating year I ever had!"

So, Welcome to Room 33 and fourth grade!

***Before we begin to go over our procedures and routines**, we're going to start with a story, "Simon's Hook." Please take out your journal. Write your name as neatly as you can on the front. Please use cursive.*

- On the first page, write your first and last name *(repeat) and today's date. (Repeat and demonstrate using overhead.)*
- Review Sentence Stubs (chart)

Morning Routine

- *Now, it's time to get down to business. Mrs. Norris does not start the class. The bell does not start the class. YOU start the class.*

  This is what will happen when you come to class each day. There is a Morning Routine you are to follow. You immediately go to your seat, unpack your things, get out your Handbook and Planner, and your homework. (use overhead)

  *Your homework will be checked, and you are to begin working on your **Must Do's**. The Must Do's are located here. (point)*

  The morning Must Do's are meant for you to do alone! It is a quiet time.

  *During the Morning Routine, it is a **quiet time**. That means there is absolutely no talking. It also means that you **may not** talk to me. It is very busy in the morning. There are many tasks I must do, and I can get them done quickly if everyone comes in and follows the routine.*

  The Morning Routine will always appear on the overhead. (show)

  Let's start today's routine together. What do we do first after you come into the classroom? (unpack) Please do it.

  After you have unpacked, place your backpack in the closet. When you unpack, you must make

sure you have everything you need. You will not be allowed to go into the closet until the end of the day.

After you unpack your backpacks what do you do? (take out homework and agendas)

This is a good time for me to pass out your temporary Planner. (pass out and explain)

Let's review. What is the first thing you do in the morning? (come in quietly and unpack)

What is the second thing you do in the morning? (take out homework and agendas)

What is the third thing you do in the morning? (begin Must Do's)

- Pass out the Bio Glyph and explain
- *Now, you are going to have some Must Do time. Are there any questions about the Morning Routine? Well, it looks like we are ready to begin.*
- Begin Must Do's and allow 15 minutes
- *Please put your Rules and Inventory aside. Does anyone have questions about what to do during the Morning Routine?*

  You did a terrific job following the steps of the Morning Routine—thank you! It's time to move on.

Procedures Script

- *As you can see, you are all seated in groups of four. You are sitting in your 'village.' Please take a moment to read the name of your village and what the name of your village means.*

  Each week a different village member is the Village Captain. (show form on overhead) It is the Village Captain's job to keep track of the points. (point to the overhead) You can gain points for the following:

  - □ *Paying attention*
  - □ *Following directions*
  - □ *Being on task and on time*
  - □ *Exercising self-control*
  - □ *Turning in your assignments*
  - □ *Keeping your desk clean*
  - □ *Turning in good work*

Coincidentally, these are also the classroom **Adopted Procedures that must happen in order for us to learn**.

We are here to learn, and these procedures will help everyone accomplish that goal.

We are here for **YOU**, so you can succeed and enjoy the class. Because I care for each of you, I am here to help you. I will not allow you to do anything that will interfere with your success in fourth grade.

We will be working together this year. We need to have a class where you can come and feel safe. Because I care for all of you, I will not allow you to do anything that will interfere with someone else who is trying to learn.

I am the teacher, and I set the procedures. I am looking forward to being your teacher this year. I have an exciting year of learning planned for you, and I will not allow you to do anything to interfere with my desire to teach you. Nor will I allow you to do anything that will interfere with all of us having an enjoyable year.

So that **YOU** can learn, so that **WE** can all learn, so that **I** can teach, I have a set of general procedures to ensure that we will have an orderly classroom. (distribute Adopted Classroom Procedures)

The first procedure is **Pay Attention**. Can someone tell me what that means? (elicit responses from several students)

Let me give some examples:

1. When I am teaching, your eyes should be on me.
2. When your classmates are participating in class discussions, your eyes should be on them.
3. You shouldn't be reading a book, getting supplies, passing notes, or making eye contact with friends.
4. When we are in assemblies you give the presenter your attention.
5. When morning announcements are made, you stop what you are doing and pay attention.

All of these examples are what I mean when I say 'pay attention.'

The second procedure is **Follow Directions**. Can someone give some examples of what I mean? (elicit responses)

This means if I don't call on you right away, you still must raise your hand and not yell out my name. I will try to get to you as fast as I can, but yelling out slows me down and is a violation of a classroom procedure.

The next procedure is **Follow All Directions the First Time Given**. Who knows what I mean by this? (elicit responses)

Everyone had good points to add about this procedure. Let me give you some examples:

1. When I say to get out your Math book, it means to get it out without having to ask you a second time.
2. When I say to put something away, it means to stop what you are doing and put it away, without having to ask you a second time.
3. One direction that is always followed in Room 33 is for you to raise your hand and wait for me to call on you.
4. It also means that all Math should be done in pencil, and all Finals assignments are to be done in ink.

Now, who can repeat exactly what I mean when I say, 'Follow directions?'

Excellent. Let's move on to procedure three, which is **Be On Task and On Time**. On time is easy. What do I mean by be On Time? (elicit responses)

Yes, I mean you are to be at school each day before the morning bell rings at 8:00.

What do I mean by being On Task? (elicit responses)

Good examples. Now here are mine. Being On Task means that you do these things:

1. Work during work times
2. Listen during lessons
3. Talk during discussions

Being On Task means that you don't use class time to take care of playground issues.

What do I mean by being On Task and On Time? (elicit responses) Great job!

Our next procedure is to **Control Yourself**; *do not play around in class. By this I mean that you may NOT wander around the room and do whatever you please. You must remain in your seat. If you want to sharpen a pencil, hold it in the air like this until I see you.* **I will give you permission to sharpen it.**

Control yourself means that you will not yell out or have playground conversations in this room.

Who can give me examples of playing in class? (elicit responses)

The next procedure is to **Turn Assignments in On Time**. *This is critical. We are here to learn, and you must complete your end of the bargain, which means you MUST turn assignments in on time.*

If you choose not to turn in assignments, you will have no privileges or fun activities at school. You will be miserable—trust me. Use your class time, do your homework, and turn your assignments in ON TIME.

Why do you think you need to turn your assignments in on time? (wait for responses) *Wow, good ideas.*

The next procedure helps keep our learning village a pleasant place. It says that you must **Keep Your Desk, Personal Floor, Notebook, and Box Clean and Empty of Clutter**. *This one seems simple, but it is hard for fourth graders. You are not to stuff papers in your desk or your box. Everything has a place, and I expect you to keep your things and assignments in it!*

What does that mean? What is clutter? (wait for responses) *Good, good examples.*

And our last procedure is that you must **Turn in Quality Work**. *Why would it be important for you to turn in quality work?* (wait for responses) *That is right, you always want to show your best first . . . so do your best and turn in your best work.*

Now, let me move on to some ways I will **Call the Class to Order** *when I need your attention. The first one is called* **Give Me 5**. (show on board)

1. *Stop moving, talking, working*
2. *Put down pencils, crayons, and pens, or close books*
3. *Quiet*
4. *Eyes on Mrs. Norris*
5. *Listen*

Or, if you can hear me clap twice; please do this:

1. *Eyes front*
2. *Chime*
3. *Clap pattern*

Does anyone have any questions? Since no one has questions, we have all adopted the procedures that must happen for us to learn.

It's time to move on.

Binders

■ *Now, we are going to organize our binders. Please take out the binder you brought to school.*

I am giving each of you five dividers. We will put our binders together as a team.

Everything you use and do in class will go in this binder.

    □ *Papers don't belong stuffed in desks; they belong in your binder.*

    □ *Papers don't belong balled up in backpacks; they belong in your binder.*

    □ *Papers don't belong shoved in books; they belong in your binders.*

    □ *Papers must be in your binder, under your box, or turned in; there are* **no exceptions** *to the procedure.*

I told you earlier that it is your job to be a student. This binder is one of your business tools. Since binders are for your business, you may not write on them, glue things on them, or place stickers on them. Your job is to keep them clean and neat.

■ Pass out tabs and have students place in binder.

■ *You have five sections of your notebook. These are the tabs:*

1. *Miscellaneous*
2. *Reading*
3. *Math*
4. *Social Studies*
5. *Science*

■ *. . . And so starts her first day of school.*

A Middle School First-Day Script

Kara Moore, a middle school social studies teacher in Coal Grove, Ohio, uses a plan to help her remember all of the important things she needs to share with her students on the first day of school.

Overview Reminders

- Get to school early and make sure everything is in place (room decorated and desks arranged to create a warm, positive, and welcoming environment)
- Greet students at the door
  1. Distribute yellow index cards with locker combinations
  2. Have a colored Post-It note ready with a number on it
  3. Tell students to match their colored Post-It note with the matching Post-It note on their desks
  4. Tell students to quickly find their seats (be firm)
- Pass out school handbook and school folders
- Pass out syllabus, guidelines, and student/parent contract (go over each item with them)

Welcome Speech

Welcome, Class! My name is Ms. Moore, and I will be your Social Studies teacher this year! I hope everyone had a wonderful summer and is ready for an exciting, new school year. This is going to be a challenging, yet rewarding, journey together. I know without a doubt, if you work hard and do your best in this class, you will be successful.

Classroom Procedures

- Entering the Classroom
  - Please enter quietly
  - Have a seat
  - Take out your materials
  - Review the agenda board
  - Begin on bell ringers
- When You Are Tardy
  - Enter quietly
  - Excused: Place "excuse" on my desk
- Getting Your Attention: I will . . .
  - Stand in front of the class
  - Raise my hand
  - Wait for everyone to be quiet
- Student Responsibility Card "Pink-Slip"

  If you are not prepared for class, you must fill out this slip, sign it, and date it. Place it in the homework basket. This slip will be shared with the principal and your parent or guardian. REMEMBER—they will see this documentation.

- What to Do If You Finish Your Work Early or What Do I Do Next?
  - Work on unfinished assignments
  - Review your notes or vocabulary
  - Read a history book from the shelf

- "EXCUSED" Absences
  - ☐ Check the notebook board
  - ☐ Write down everything that you do not have in your notebook
  - ☐ Go to the handout folders and get the work that you have missed
  - ☐ Unexcused absences will not be allowed make up work
- Turning in Papers
  - ☐ At the beginning of each class, place your homework in the center of the table
  - ☐ One student will collect everyone's homework
- Classroom Discussions
  - ☐ Please participate
  - ☐ I want to hear what you have to say
  - ☐ Make all questions and comments relevant to the current discussion
  - ☐ If your question is off topic, write it down and ask later
- Moving Around the Classroom
  - ☐ Ask permission
- Be Organized
  - ☐ Staying organized is key for success
  - ☐ Keep your binder organized
- No Cell Phones!
  - ☐ Cell phones not allowed in classroom
  - ☐ Phones confiscated and sent to the principal's office for pick up
- Class Dismissal
  - ☐ The teacher dismisses, not the bell
  - ☐ Do not start packing up prior to the bell
  - ☐ Wait until the teacher finishes and officially dismisses with, "Have a nice day!"

Parent's Task

- Remind students to take home packet with contract
- Remind students to sign contact

- Remind students to have parent or guardian sign contract and return
- Read signature parts to students:

  For Parents—I understand that my child has received the packet for 8th Grade Social Studies. I understand that the packet contains information listing the materials needed, classroom procedures, classroom guidelines, and student behavior expectations.

  I have read and reviewed this information with my son/daughter. (get signature)

  For Students—I have received and shared the packet for 8th Grade Social Studies with my parent or guardian. I understand that the packet contains information listing the materials needed, classroom procedures, classroom guidelines, and student behavior expectations.

  It is my responsibility to review this information with my parent or guardian. (get signature)

Classroom Orientation

- Show students their lockers
- Have students take the yellow index card given to them when they entered the classroom, find their locker, and use the given combination to get into their locker
- Tour around the room
  - ☐ The basket—each class period has its own colored basket. This is where your name cards will be placed and where you will turn in papers.
  - ☐ The cards—they allow me to take attendance in a quick and simple way.
  - ☐ The board—every day when you walk in the classroom, look at the board and begin on the board work.
  - ☐ The bell—you need to be in your seat before the bell rings, working on your bell work.
  - ☐ The Student Station—this is an area where students can get pencils, use the stapler, hole punch, and other supplies. There are also two marker boards:

1. One board will always have the day's agenda and objective, so look at the board every day.

2. The second marker board will always have a list of what should be in your notebook. If you ever miss class, do not ask me what you missed. Look at the board, see if there is something you do not have, and then get that paper or assignment out of the black tray. All papers, assignments, and other handouts will always be put in the black trays.

☐ The Green Board is something special for the class. This is OUR classroom. Bring in pictures, poems, magazines articles, anything you want to share, to put on the board.

Introductions

■ Introduce myself (more personal)

My name is Kara Moore. I will be your 8th grade social studies teacher this year. I graduated from Ohio University with my teaching degree, and I am also a graduate of this high school. I actually had 8th grade social studies in this very same classroom.

Even though it is my first year teaching here at Coal Grove, it is not my first year teaching. I taught 8th grade social studies at South Point Middle School last year. I am the assistant high school cheerleading coach and the middle school yearbook advisor. I have 3 sisters and a beautiful baby niece.

This is going to be a fun year, if you let it be. I have tons of interactive lesson plans and group activities. I have lesson plans where we will be building events that took place during the Civil War, using clay and other craft materials.

There is so much I have planned for you, but you have to be willing to be mature enough to handle these activities and follow directions. There is not a doubt in my mind that you can do that.

■ Get to know the students

OK class, I want to get to know you. When I point to you, please stand up and tell me your name, something about yourself, and if you could have a super-hero power, what would it be and why?

■ Right before the bell rings, remind them that the bell does not dismiss them. I do.

■ Tell them, *Remember . . . I truly believe in your potential. I want you to believe in it, too!*

Organization Leads to Success

I feel very strongly in setting up a highly-organized and effective learning environment for students. With a well-thought-through classroom, I can foster students' independence and responsibility in their own learning.

I have taught kindergarten, first, and fifth grades and structure my first day of school differently for each grade level. Regardless, one thing always remains the same—set clear expectations for the students. Tell them your goals and objectives. If nothing is a surprise, they will always know what to do, what you expect from them, and what they can expect from their day.

I believe in taking time 'up front' to set and maintain good expectations and routines for students. This 'up front' time will pay back as the year progresses. The students are soon able to successfully use the time in our school day for academic and social growth; no wasted time.

Eryka Rogers ■ Oak Brook, Illinois

A High School First-Week Plan

Karen Rogers, a high school science teacher in Kansas,
shows how she manages teaching and reinforcing procedures
while at the same time teaching the instructional content.

Day One

Classroom Management

1. **Introduce Bell Work Procedure**
   - Check bell work table and get handout
   - Sit in assigned seats
   - Start bell work assignment

2. **Teach Three Important Procedures**
   - Entering the class (bell work procedure)
   - Quieting the class
   - Dismissing the class

Instructional Program

1. **Bell Work**
   - Make a name tent
   - Read over course information sheet

2. **Welcome and Introductions**
   - Teacher introduction
   - Student introductions

3. **Course Information, Part 1 (brief overview)**
4. **Closure/Dismissal**

All School Advisory Time (30 minutes)

1. Hand out student schedules, maps, planners, and IDs
2. Using planners guidelines
3. School Value = Organization

Day Two

Classroom Management

1. Reinforce Bell Work Procedure
2. Reinforce Quieting the Class Procedure
3. Reinforce All School Procedures Using Planners
4. Teach Turning in Papers Procedure
5. Reinforce Dismissal Procedure

Instructional Program

1. **Bell Work**
   - Put up name tent
   - Fill out "Getting Organized" worksheet

2. **Recite student names**

3. **Getting Organized Lesson**
   (taught in all school classes today)
   - How to stay organized and use planners
   - How to get around (navigate) the school

4. **Closure/Dismissal**

All School Advisory Time

1. Activity on showing respect
2. Icebreaker activity
3. School Value = Respect

Day Three

Classroom Management

1. Reinforce Bell Work Procedure
2. Reinforce Quieting the Class Procedure
3. Reinforce Using Planners Procedure
4. Teach General Class Procedures
   - Tardy and absent
   - Getting materials
   - Leaving seats
   - Getting help
   - When work is complete
   - Emergency procedures
5. Rehearse Turning in Papers Procedure
6. Reinforce Dismissal Procedure

Instructional Program

1. Bell Work
   - Write daily objective in planner (class procedures)
   - Fill out "Getting to Know You" form
2. **Course Information, Part 2 (course details)**
   - Materials
   - Grading
   - Rules
   - List of topics (indicators)
3. **Classroom Procedures (take notes and turn in)**
4. **Closure/Dismissal**

All School Advisory Time

1. Discuss social skills
2. Social skill activity
3. School Value = Social Harmony

Day Four

Classroom Management

1. Reinforce Bell Work Procedure
2. Teach Test-Taking Procedure
3. Rehearse Turning in Papers Procedure
4. Rehearse When Work Is Complete Procedure
5. Reinforce Dismissal Procedure

Instructional Program

1. Bell Work
   - Objective in planner (comprehensive pretest)
   - Write name and hour on answer sheet
2. **Take Comprehensive Pretest**
   - Explain purpose of pretest
   - Explain how to take it
   - Students take pretest
3. **Closure/Dismissal**
   - Thank students for a great start
   - Motivational science demonstration

All School Advisory Time

1. Discuss the importance of getting involved in school
2. Extracurricular activities and opportunities
3. School Value = School Spirit

Day Five

Classroom Management

1. Reinforce Bell Work Procedure
2. Reinforce Quieting the Class Procedure
3. Reinforce Using Planners Procedure
4. Rehearse Returning Papers Procedure
5. Teach Lab Safety Procedures
6. Rehearse Turning in Papers Procedure
7. Rehearse Getting Materials Procedure
8. Reinforce Dismissal Procedure

Instructional Program

1. Bell Work
   - Objective in planners (lab equipment and safety)
   - Complete lab equipment review sheet
   - Take lab safety quiz
2. Lab Equipment Review
3. Lab Safety
   - Correct and grade quiz
   - Discuss lab safety
4. Room Orientation
5. Closure/Dismissal

Students Love to Come to This School

At Samsel Upper Elementary School, our schedule on the first two days is altered so that teachers have extra time in class to teach and rehearse the procedures the students will need to learn to be successful.

In the afternoon the vice principal and I call for dismissal a half hour early. We teach the proper procedure for dismissal from the school, correct bus line, walking out to the bus, and quickly finding their seats on the bus.

We have created schoolwide procedures and have a culture of consistency.

The teachers and students love to come to this school. It is a happy place filled with 900 fourth- and fifth-grade students.

Come see us in action!

Ed Aguiles ▪ Parlin, New Jersey

An Elementary First-Ten-Days Plan

Sarah Jondahl has a set of procedures in place from day one
and teaching the students about these procedures makes
the education experience in her third grade classroom extremely effective.

Day One

Classroom Management

- **PowerPoint of Procedures**
  - Lining up
  - Backpacks
  - Cubbies
  - Attendance
  - Bellwork and Workshop
  - Bathroom Passes
  - My Time/Your Time
  - Class Jobs
  - Math Timed Tests
  - Weekly Assignment Sheet
  - Home-Learning

Instructional Program

- **Sticker sharing** (favorite things)
- **Timed test** (math)
- **Name art**
- **Introduce daily spiral review** (math)
- **Fill in BINGO cards**
- **Introduce goal boards**
- **Beginning writing assignment**
- **Go over first day packet**
- **Daily Closing Message**
- **Teacher trivia**

Day Two

Classroom Management

- **Review Procedures**
  - Weekly Assignment Sheet
  - Bellwork and Workshop
- **Teach New Procedures**
  - Heading Paper
  - Turning in Notes from Home
  - Silent Reading (RAP Time)

Instructional Program

- **Daily spiral review in math** (bellwork)
- **Timed test** (math)
- **Math, Lesson 1**
- **Sweet sharing** (favorite things)
- **Name art**
- **Goal boards**
- **Read The Little Engine that Could**
- **RAP Time**
- **Play BINGO**
- **Daily Closing Message**

Day Three

Classroom Management

- **Review Procedure**
  - ☐ Weekly Assignment Sheet
- **Teach New Procedures**
  - ☐ Morning Meeting
  - ☐ Marble Jar
  - ☐ Unfinished Work
  - ☐ Adjusted Day Lunch and Dismissal

Instructional Program

- Daily spiral review (math)
- Timed test (math)
- Math, Lesson 2
- RAP Time
- Goal boards
- Daily Closing Message

Day Four

Classroom Management

- **Review Procedure**
  - ☐ Unfinished Work
- **Teach New Procedures**
  - ☐ Computer Lab
  - ☐ Class Library Sticker Levels

Instructional Program

- Daily spiral review (math)
- Timed test (math)
- Math, Lesson 3
- Unit 1, Opener (literature)
- Goal boards
- Daily Closing Message

Day Five

Classroom Management

- **Review Procedure**
  - ☐ Morning Meeting
- **Teach New Procedures**
  - ☐ Test Taking (cardboard dividers)
  - ☐ Cursive Writing
  - ☐ Art
  - ☐ Catch Up/Relish
- **3rd Grade Getting to Know You Mingle**

Instructional Program

- Choose a Star Student for next week
- Beginning of the year test (literature)
- Cursive Aa and Bb
- All About Me body cut outs
- Daily spiral review (math)
- Timed test (math)
- Math, Lesson 4
- Goal boards
- Daily Closing Message

Day Six

Classroom Management

- **Review Procedures**
  - ☐ Morning Meeting
  - ☐ Weekly Assignment Sheet
- **Teach New Procedures**
  - ☐ P.E.
  - ☐ Workshop
  - ☐ Home-Learning

Instructional Program

- Morning Meeting
- Daily spiral review (math)
- Timed test (math)
- Math, Lesson 5
- Unit 1, Lesson 1 (literature)
- Work on home-learning
- P.E.
- Daily Closing Message

Day Seven

Classroom Management

- **Review Procedures**
  - ☐ Workshop
  - ☐ Home-Learning
- **Teach New Procedure**
  - ☐ Library

Instructional Program

- Morning Meeting
- Daily spiral review (math)
- Timed test (math)
- Math, Lesson 6
- Unit 1, Lesson 1 (literature)
- Work on home-learning
- Library
- Daily Closing Message

Day Eight

Classroom Management

- **Review Procedures**
  - ☐ Adjusted Day Schedule
  - ☐ Unfinished Work
- **Teach New Procedures**
  - ☐ Class Read Aloud
  - ☐ Writer's Workshop

Instructional Program

- Morning Meeting
- Daily spiral review (math)
- Timed test (math)
- Math, Lesson 7
- Unit 1, Lesson 1 (literature)
- Writing (brainstorming)
- Work on home-learning
- Class read aloud (<u>Charlotte's Web</u>)
- Daily Closing Message

Day Nine

Classroom Management

- **Review Procedure**
  - ☐ Computer Lab

Instructional Program

- Daily spiral review (math)
- Timed test (math)
- Computer lab
- Math, Lesson 8
- Unit 1, Lesson 1 (literature)
- Writing (prewriting and first draft)
- Work on home-learning
- Class read aloud (Charlotte's Web)
- Daily Closing Message

Day Ten

Classroom Management

- **Review Procedures**
  - ☐ Cursive Writing
  - ☐ Catch Up/Relish
- **Teach New Procedures**
  - ☐ Checking Reading WEBS
  - ☐ Buddies
  - ☐ Spelling Test
  - ☐ Literature Test

Instructional Program

- Morning Meeting
- Daily spiral review (math)
- Timed test (math)
- Math, Lesson 9
- Unit 1, Lesson 1 test (literature)
- Spelling test
- Writing (editing)
- Cursive Cc
- Buddies (getting to know you)
- Catch Up/Relish

37 •)))

Access more ideas to see how other effective teachers plan for student success.

■ A Principal's Guide for a Teacher's First-Day Script ■

Sisseton Middle School is on the Lake Traverse Indian Reservation in South Dakota. Karen Whitney views the historically high dropout rate and low achievement scores of Native Americans as a professional challenge—and she succeeded—with a plan.

A Culture of Consistency

Karen Whitney was a teacher for fourteen years before becoming principal of Sisseton Middle School (SMS). She says, "I loved being a classroom teacher, and my favorite duty as a principal is still being a teacher. I am now a 'teacher of teachers.'"

Karen did not implement programs, change the structure of the school, or install any fads or buzzwords. Instead, she taught her teachers the value of procedures and how to teach a procedure.

She harnessed the most valuable resource in a school—The Classroom Teacher. Karen created a first-day script or plan, and she teaches her teachers how to start the first day of school. She had the teachers collectively implement a set of schoolwide procedures beginning on the first day of school to create a school with a **Culture of Consistency**.

Teacher Preparation

- Prepare seating assignments.
- Have a task for students to do immediately as they enter the classroom.
- Create a presentation about yourself and classroom (possible PowerPoint, displays, room arrangement, cubbies, and storage area for backpacks, etc.).
- Know the first procedures you will teach.
- Practice explaining all the exciting things students will be learning.
- Create a sign with your three to five classroom rules to post.

Suggested Classroom Procedures to Teach on the First Day

- Entering the Classroom
- Bellwork/Fast Start
- Assignment Headings: Name, Date, Period, Title
- What to Bring to Class Each Day
- Procedure for Leaving the Class—Bell does not dismiss class, the teacher dismisses the class

Suggested Classroom Rules

- Follow directions the first time they are given and any time thereafter.
- Raise your hand and wait for permission to speak.
- Stay in your seat unless you have permission to do otherwise.
- Keep hands, feet, and objects to yourself.
- No cursing or teasing is allowed.

Teacher Procedures to Do on the First Day

1. Stand at your door and greet each student as they enter.
2. Tell each student how to find their assigned seat, where to find their first assignment, and to begin working on the assignment.
3. Answer the seven questions all students want to know on the first day of school. (See *THE First Days of School*.) This will allow you to enthusiastically

welcome your students and share about yourself. Talk about all the work they will be doing in your class, how much they will learn, and how successful they are going to be in your class.

4. Introduce the word **PROCEDURES**.

5. Explain and demonstrate that you will be standing at the door every day (perhaps with a student, too). Explain how they will be greeted, and how you want them to respond when they enter the classroom every day.

6. Teach the procedure of the morning routine (teach, rehearse, implement).

7. Teach the procedure of using the agenda, schedule, and bellwork to start each day. Show students where they will find their first assignment.

8. Point out the sign that shows how to head a paper (e.g., Name, Date, Period, Title). For your first-day activity, have the students do this activity on the assignment, and teach the procedure that goes with the completion of this activity. Check each paper for understanding.

9. Present your classroom rules and show where they are posted. Review and check for understanding.

10. Teach the procedure of what to bring to class each day.

11. Teach the procedure for exiting the classroom.

12. Stand at the door as students leave class. Create positive interactions with students as they exit.

Classroom Procedure Observation Rubric

Karen created a rubric, so her teachers can do a self-assessment of their first-day script. She also uses the same rubric as an assessment tool (for formative review to guide improvement) to help her teachers make progress in implementing these procedures.

Karen's success began in the summer between her first and second year when she purchased a copy of **THE First Days of School** for every member of her staff, including paraprofessionals.

The teachers viewed the video series, **The Effective Teacher**, at every faculty meeting and began to install procedures. They installed suggested procedures the first year. This is now an expectation for every teacher.

At the end of the school year, Karen shared that what made Sisseton Middle School great was the successful implementation of procedures, **how the common procedures bonded the staff to work as a team, and how good those procedures had been for the academic achievement and success of the students**.

Everyone was on the same page at the school, and the school's improved tests confirmed Karen's belief in creating a firm foundation of consistency beginning on the very first day of school.

The **Culture of Consistency** created at the school allowed teachers the time to teach, and it gave students the assurance that all of the love and care demonstrated by the teachers was for one reason only—their success.

 38 •))

Use the Observation Rubric to create a schoolwide Culture of Consistency.

A classroom should be a pleasant, relaxed place for children to learn and develop, while remaining <u>work</u>-centered. Students should be expected to accomplish specific tasks. A system of clearly communicated procedures is the basis of an effective, accountable system.

Carolyn Evertson ■ Vanderbilt University

Classroom Procedures Observation Rubric

Teacher	Date	Class

EXPECTATION	SCORE	COMMENTS
Teacher is at the door greeting students as they enter the classroom.		
Bellwork is posted.		
Students enter the classroom and immediately begin working.		
Agenda for the day is posted.		
A beginning of class or morning routine is utilized.		
Objective(s) for the day is posted.		
Transitions are smooth with minimal loss of teaching/learning time.		
Teacher can quiet the room quickly.		
Individual classroom procedures are evident.		
Students know how to correctly set up an assignment.		
Students know how to ask for help.		
Teacher dismisses the class.		
Teacher is at the door as students exit the classroom.		

1	Exceeds Minimum Expectations	3	Does Not Meet Minimum Expectations
2	Meets Minimum Expectations	N/A	Not Observed

Common Procedures Create a Team

At the end of the first week, our middle school staff looked at each other in wonder. Things were going better than we expected. A lot of that is a direct reflection on our commitment to create procedures and routines to make our new school run smoothly.

The teachers decided what procedures they wanted to introduce and how and when they would introduce them. We mulled over many and started with a few common procedures to start the year. Each classroom teacher implemented the procedures, so students would know the routine throughout the school.

1. *We taught the procedure of entering the room quietly and getting to work on the 'bell ringer' work posted on the board.*

2. *We showed how to pass papers, moving from side-to-side instead of back-to-front.*

3. *We set up a common place and procedure for missed class work. Students' names are printed on any handout sheets and put into a basket. If the assignment is in the book or of a different sort, the assignment is written down by another student or the teacher and placed in the basket. In this way, students do not miss work when they have missed school.*

4. *We all agreed that teaching procedures allowed us to calmly handle routines and reduce disciplinary action. This is a difficult, but important, concept for all teachers, because it reinforces their role as a provider of information and not an enforcer of compliance.*

5. *Our teachers discussed the best way to present ourselves professionally. We agreed upon a common, general dress code.*

Probably the best result of all this is that we created a culture within our new school that might have taken much longer to establish if it had not been through this common work. *I believe that teachers who work together, end up caring for and supporting each other. In working with common procedures, we are making a statement to each other, the students, and parents that we are a team.*

Mary Lacombe ■ Plattsburgh, New York

EPILOGUE
A Call to Action

I Can't Wait to Start School Every Year

Candi Kempton of Pikeville, Tennessee, is an effective principal today because of her effectiveness as a teacher. She knows the power of having a classroom management plan.

My first year of teaching was horrible. I had thirty-two kids in my class and thought I knew what I was doing because I managed to keep them quiet. However, by the end of the year, I was exhausted.

As I evaluated the year, I realized, I hadn't really taught them. So, that summer, I read and studied *THE First Days of School*. When school started in the fall, I was ready. I had all my procedures in place, and the kids responded

to that quickly. I couldn't believe what a difference! Every year since then, my classroom has been great!

Today, I am a principal. I know I wouldn't have become the teacher I was without implementing classroom management techniques and setting up the classroom procedures. I love my job and can't wait to start school each and every year.

Execute and Follow Through

> "Hard work" is what gets the job done.
>
> Carol Dweck ∎ Stanford University

Successful People Execute

The difference between teams that win, companies that make profits, and schools and classrooms where students succeed is the ability to execute. **There is a direct relationship between execution and results.** This book has been created to help you structure a classroom with procedures so that students can execute the task or assignment and be successful.

Hall-of-Famer **Jerry Rice** is considered by many as the greatest receiver to have ever played football. If he caught a pass during practice, Rice would run it the length of the field just to rehearse another touchdown. That was the goal of every pass, not to catch it and stop, but to run it for a touchdown.

He was ready to execute what he practiced over and over again whenever he got his hands on the ball.

ex' • e • cute

Definition: carry out or put into effect
(a plan, order, or course of action)
to perform; do

People get things done when they execute. They follow through. Louis Gerstner, the CEO credited with turning around a struggling IBM, said to his headhunters upon his retirement, "Find me a guy who can execute!" In the business world, all employees are expected to perform to get their work done.

Work Ethic

In football they are called "reps," which is short for repetition. Players run plays over and over again to make sure they are executed correctly.

In music, it's called "practice." Musicians practice over and over again to be sure that the music is executed correctly.

In theatre, it's called "rehearsal." Actors rehearse over and over again to be sure that the production is executed correctly.

In math class, it is called "drill." Students drill math facts over and over again until they are executed as automatic responses.

Students and teachers who are successful will attribute it to hard work. They do not eschew memorizations and repetition. They are focused on a goal and value the sweat and perseverance in getting the work done.

People who succeed in life do not complain about the hours they have to put in. Instead, they often lament the hours that are wasted.

In a football game, everyone is focused on the goal line. Coaches shout at their players, "Execute, execute!" This means to run the play, follow through, and finish strong. In a game, that play may be called only once, but that one time could be the game-winning play or a formation to prevent an opponent's score. Either way, the play must be executed correctly.

In many schools, there is no goal line, no game plan, and no focus—just the constant flux of programs, fads, technology, initiatives, and ideologies. **This hodgepodge of tactics is not execution. People execute. People get things done.**

Effective schools recognize that the teacher is the single most important factor affecting student achievement—at least it is the single most important factor we can do much about!

Effective teachers execute. Teachers who execute

- make things happen.
- get things done.
- follow through.

When students know what to do and how to do it, you have created the optimum learning environment. **Teaching a student how to execute a procedure and follow through creates the routines of successful classroom.**

Follow Through and Finish the Job

In business, employees are given a plan or project to complete. Their job is to execute the plan or project.

> **You are paid for successfully executing and generating productivity.**

The world respects and rewards people who can execute well and do it correctly with a degree of courtesy and graciousness. This is what you expect of the service you receive when you are a customer in a bank, office, or store.

39 🔊

Read, print, or post these reminders of your potential as an effective teacher.

Crystal Moore, a teacher at the Elite Academy in Georgia, has a sign posted in her classroom that says, "Tell me I cannot, and then watch me do it."

Melissa Dunbar of Kerrville, Texas, on her first day of school PowerPoint presentation, says: "I 'can't' is the acronym for 'I Completely Admit I'm Not Trying.'"

My expectations of each and everyone of you!

- ✱ I know you are ALL smart and never want to hear different.
- ✱ "I can't" is the acronym for **"I Completely Admit I'm Not Trying."**
- ✱ You can do anything you try.
- ✱ Why? Because I believe in you!

The structure you create with procedures in your classroom will help your students to

- work hard.
- get it done.
- get it done right.

The Perseverance to Follow Through

The setting was the 1968 Summer Olympics in Mexico City. The scene was the track in the Olympic Stadium for the final lap of the grueling 26-mile, 385-yard Marathon.

More than an hour earlier, Mamo Wolde of Ethiopia crossed the finish line winning the coveted race for his homeland and fellow countryman, two time Olympic medalist, Abebe Bikila, who was forced to drop out during the race due to a broken bone in his leg.

The final spectators were clearing the stadium when they heard sirens and police whistles. Looking toward the stadium gates, they saw a lone figure hobbling onto the track. Wearing the colors of Tanzania, it was **John Stephen Akhwari**. His leg was bloody and bandaged, and he grimaced with each step. He had severely injured his knee and dislocated the joint in a fall.

The small crowd stopped and applauded the courage of this man as if they were cheering the winner. Akhwari painfully finished the run—the last to cross the finish line. Then he slowly walked off the field without turning to the hailing crowd.

Later when asked why he didn't quit, since his task was so painful and he had no chance of winning a medal, he said, "My country did not send me 5,000 miles to Mexico City to start the race. They sent me 5,000 miles to finish the race."

If you are a results-oriented, focused, visionary person, this book has taught you exceptional classroom management skills to help you make a significant impact in your classroom, in your school, in education, and the world.

The Greatest Asset of a School

The <u>single greatest effect</u> on student achievement is the effectiveness of the teacher. It's not rocket science—the better the teacher teaches, the better the opportunity for the students learn. **Teachers are the greatest asset of a school and of humanity.**

You have an awesome responsibility. A child has only one childhood. Your charge is to give every child the skill and hope for a brighter tomorrow, to help children realize their potential and worth.

The greatest contribution you can offer a child is your belief in him or her as a person with potential. The organization of your classroom will provide the

Execute Your Dream

Vision without execution is hallucination.

Thomas A. Edison ■ Inventor

foundation for that belief to flourish and grow, so every child can execute and be the person he or she was meant to be.

You entered teaching to impact lives; to make a difference in students' lives. A qualification—You don't make a difference as much as you **ARE** the difference. Thank you for your dedication to being the difference for every child in your classroom.

**That's why you are called a Teacher—
The noblest of all professions.**

A Last-Day Letter

Shirley Bert Lee is retired. She tirelessly modeled what she wanted for her students in herself each day she taught. She was the consummate professional and brought great honor to the noblest of all professions. Her legacy will live on in her students.

Dear Class,

Since I know I won't be able to say all of the following without shedding a lot of tears, I hope you don't mind letting my computer speak for me.

This year with all of you has been an incredible year for me and one that has the fondest of memories of one of my favorite classes in all of my twenty-six years of teaching. You have been the kind of class that all teachers dream of having each year—a class who works together, a class who cares about one another, a class who works hard, a class who likes to have fun, a class whom everyone tells their teacher how great they are, and a class who is huggable and loveable.

You must understand the uniqueness of our class this year because I'm sure all of you have been in classes which were the direct opposite of the one I just described. Our procedures have made us truly a family, and all your actions throughout this year have proven that fact to me time and time again. It makes me love you even more.

When I wake up every day, I look forward to seeing all of you with your bright faces and your positive attitudes. You have made it a joy for me to go to work each day knowing the terrific group of kids who were waiting for me at the door of Room 17.

I have hopes for all of you for your future:

- *I want each one of you to be the very best you can be and to make a positive contribution to our society.*
- *I want you to believe in yourself that you can achieve any goal you set your mind to accomplish.*
- *I want you to be happy with yourself and the positive choices you have made in your life.*
- *I want to be there when you graduate from high school, and you tell me how proud you are of yourself and the decisions you have made.*

I see so much potential for each one of you because of all of the talents with which you have been blessed. Don't settle for second best when you know you can be a winner because there is someone in Room 17 who believes in success in each one of you. Weigh your choices carefully as you embark in this new phase of your life.

Saying good-bye is not easy for me to do because I want all of you around for another year and another year and another year and another year. It has been a special pleasure to be your teacher this school year. Please stay in contact with me.

I love all of you very much.

Love,
Mrs. Lee

QR Code Summary

There are forty unique QR Codes in *THE Classroom Management Book.*

Page in Book	QR Code #		Text in Book
viii			**There are forty QR (Quick Response) Codes** scattered on pages that lead you to additional information, PowerPoint presentations, rubrics, and ideas to help you develop a classroom management plan.
PROLOGUE 3			**Explanation of QR Codes**
3	1		Read how effectiveness relates to **The Four Stages of Teaching.**
5	2		Read how to implement **Kounin's six behaviors of good classroom managers.**
9	3		Access **Nile Wilson's Orchestra Handbook** and learn how she plans for student success.
PREPARATION 19	4		See what **Karen Rogers** uses to remind herself what it takes to start the school year successfully.
21	5		Access more examples of first-day scripts and put together one before your first day of school.
28	6		View all of the PowerPoint slides in **Diana Greenhouse's** presentation to beginning teachers.
35	7		Rap along with **Alex Kajitani's** "The Routine Rhyme" and find the procedures in the song.

PREPARATION (continued) 36	8		Sarah's blurbs are an excellent compilation of the basic procedures taught in many classrooms.
43	9		View another example of a PowerPoint presentation that has been shared with us.
45	10		See how Karen Rogers checks for understanding after she introduces her classroom management plan.
51	11		Read this simple dialog to understand the words to use when teaching a procedure.
56	12		Students want to know who you are and the answers to these seven questions.
PROCEDURES 75	13		Richard shares some of his favorite quotes he has used as part of his **Bellringer** activity.
99	14		Learn how to create a free, class web page, so your students can access their work.
103	15		This is a **Homework Checklist** to help students establish a consistent routine.
115	16		Check your emergency preparedness information against what others do.
119	17		"Give Me Five," made famous by Cindy Wong, is a classic technique used across grade levels.
136	18		Learn more about how praising a deed is more effective than complimenting the student.

PROCEDURES			
(continued) 144	19		Learn the methods and benefits of assigning each student in your class a unique number.
149	20		Learn how to keep materials organized to ease the confusion experienced during many transition times.
159	21		Watch Chelonnda Seroyer tell how the Pink Slip saved her life and a grandmother's life.
161	22		Read Thomas Guskey's article, "O Alternative" for other scoring options.
168	23		Listen to Chelonnda Seroyer share how she uses the Guideline Infraction Notice.
176	24		Learn a card trick from a college professor and how she calls on students in her classroom.
178	25		Learn the value of wait-time and how it improves students' responses.
182	26		Learn some ways to quickly form groups without using any cards, marbles, candy, or other objects.
182	27		Browse these free countdown timers to alert students to get ready for transitions.
191	28		Jeff Gulle shares his SQ4R template with you to use with your students.
212	29		Access some templates for Happy Grams to send throughout the year.

PROCEDURES (continued) 213	30		Learn to identify autistic and **ADHD** children and how to help them be successful.
217	31		Listen to Robin Barlak's class sing the Snack Song.
245	32		Help your substitute teacher be prepared for any situation encountered.
262	33		Read the surprise students left for parents at Back-to-School night in Cindy Wong's classroom.
266	34		See some sample letters teachers use to connect with the home.
267	35		See how Oretha Ferguson presents this information to parents on the first day of school.
269	36		View and download the **Online Safety Pledge** Oretha Ferguson uses with her students.
PLANS 290	37		Access more ideas to see how other effective teachers plan for student success.
292	38		Use the Observation Rubric to create a schoolwide Culture of Consistency.
EPILOGUE 297	39		Read, print, or post these reminders of your potential as an effective teacher.
FRONT COVER			Listen to a special message from Harry and Rosemary.

To access this information without a QR Code scanner, go to **www.EffectiveTeaching.com**, click on *THE Classroom Management Book*, and open the QR Code tab for the links to each piece of information.

Index

www.HarryWong.com

Visit our website for additional materials to help you become a very effective educator.

THE First Days of School

This is the companion book to **THE Classroom Management Book** and considered the "bible" for new and experienced teachers. It helps you know and practice the three characteristics of an effective teacher.

- Free, 54-minute DVD, *You Have Changed My Life*
- Free, downloadable, comprehensive *Implementation Guide*
- 336-page book with 53 "Going Beyond" folders of resources

Using THE FIRST DAYS OF SCHOOL

Chelonnda Seroyer shares how she puts **THE First Days of School** into practice in her classroom. She tells story after story filled with insights, humor, and practical techniques.

- 60-minute video
- Digital access only

Classroom Management with Harry and Rosemary Wong

This eLearning course brings to life how to create an effective classroom environment. The final product is a binder with your own classroom management plan.

- 20 hours of course work
- 6 lessons that correlate to **THE First Days of School**

Coming in 2019—**THE Classroom Management Course**. This will update our current course and correlate to **THE Classroom Management Book**. The outcome of the course will still be the same—the creation of a personal classroom management plan.

The Effective Teacher

This DVD series has prepared thousands of teachers. Harry Wong shares the best practices used by effective teachers and motivates you to become the teacher you were meant to be.

Available as a set or as instant access over the Internet.

- 8 DVDs, 5 hours total time
- Book, *THE First Days of School*
- *Facilitator's Handbook* on all DVDs

Coming in 2019—**THE Classroom Management Video.**

An Invitation

THE Classroom Management Book is a compilation of the many stories, emails, school visits, conference handouts, journal readings, and personal encounters that have been shared with us through the years. We invite you to share your story, your techniques, your classroom, your journey as you help children grow, learn, and succeed.

Our email is **RWong@HarryWong.com**. We'd love to hear from you and, in turn, share with the profession.

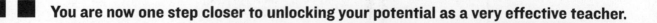

You are now one step closer to unlocking your potential as a very effective teacher.